MASTER BUILDERS ASSOCIATION
OF
KING AND SNOHOMISH COUNTIES

One Hundred Years of Building Community

by L. Beth Yockey Jones

Published by

abecedary press

5219 16th Avenue SW
Seattle, WA 98106

www.theabecedarypress.com

Museum of History and Industry (MOHAI) photos are available for viewing online at www.seattlehistory.org
University of Washington Special Collections photos are available for viewing online at http://content.lib.washington.edu/index.html

Library of Congress Control Number:2009910517

ISBN: 978-0-9764839-5-3

Back jacket photos: (clockwise from top left) Bennett Homes Built Green Idea Home; "Old Timers" dinner, 1959; Jackson Remodeling REX Award winner; home at Issaquah Highlands; First Seattle Home Show, 1939; General Membership Dinner, 2007.
Front photo courtesy of Burnstead Construction Company. Community: Waterton at Harbour Pointe.

Factual content is solely the responsibility of the author. Any questions concerning possible omissions or errors should be addressed to the author, care of Abecedary Press. All inquiries concerning reproduction and permissions should be addressed to the Master Builders Association of King and Snohomish Counties, Bellevue, Washington.

First printing 2009. Printed in South Korea by Amica International, Kent, Washington.

This book is dedicated to the tens of thousands of men and women who have made the Master Builders Association of King and Snohomish Counties an engaging, vibrant and successful organization. From the founders whose names have been lost to history to the newest members, a sincere thank you for all you've done.

TABLE OF CONTENTS

CHAPTER 1

Building the Foundation

1909–1918

When a group of Seattle builders got together in 1909 to respond to a growing concern about the quality of construction in the young city, their solution was clear: form the Seattle Master Builders Association. Then, Seattle was a very different place from what it would become, with fires, fights and festivals each vying for the public's attention. The first written Association records dealt with the 1914 election of the first recorded Association President, John Frantz, who constructed homes in Capitol Hill. In 1916, the Master Builders Hall was opened in the Arcade Building, on Second Avenue between University and Union. Many of the houses built in this era are still standing, largely unchanged a hundred years later, as testament to the effects of the Master Builders' commitment to quality. The economic boom of Seattle continued through World War I, when an unprecedented flood of immigrant labor resulted in a corresponding construction boom. Builders couldn't keep up, and in 1918, the Seattle Master Builders created the More Homes Bureau. By the Armistice of November 1919, more than 2,000 new homes had been built by member companies.

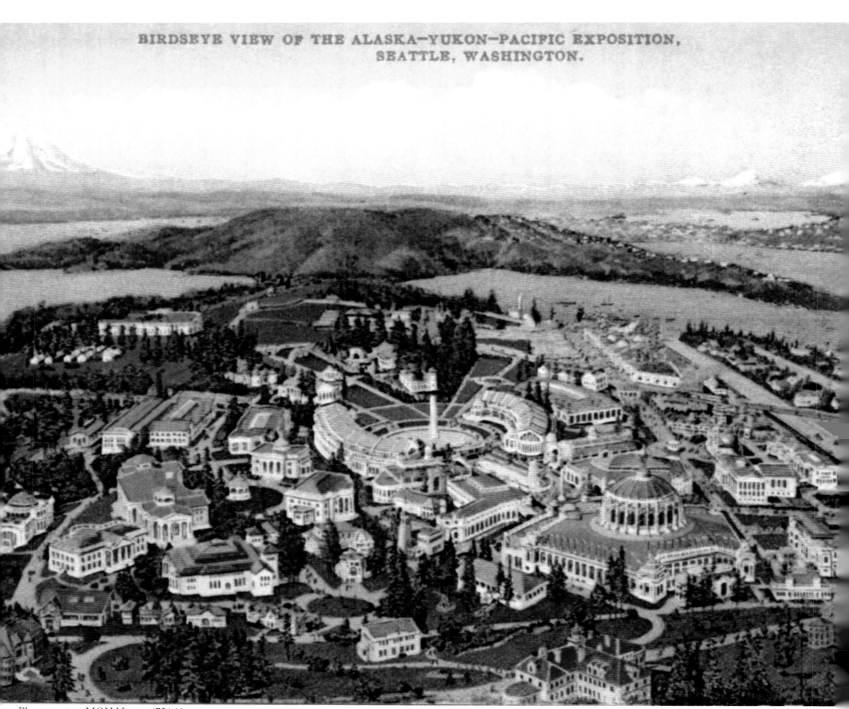

BIRDSEYE VIEW OF THE ALASKA-YUKON-PACIFIC EXPOSITION, SEATTLE, WASHINGTON.

Photo courtesy MOHAI, neg. 4756.11

Seattle was proud to invite the world to its "coming out party" - the Alaska-Yukon Pacific Exposition. Between its opening on June 1 a
its closing five months later, on October 16, more than 3,700,000 visitors marveled at the Exhibition. Highlights included a scale mo
of a Newcastle-area coal mine, the Japan pavilion, and a building devoted to the role of women in pioneering the American W

Seattle, 1909

"It was a 'sea of fire.' ...We are all in sorrow now... The business portion of Seattle is in ruins. Seattle which the day before yesterday was a beautiful city today is in ashes."[1]

So wrote fifteen-year-old Helen Mae Anthony to her uncle in a letter dated June 8, 1889. It was just two days after the Great Seattle Fire and the still-glowing coals were a smoldering reminder of what used to be a bustling boomtown. If this was a moralistic tale, that would be the dismal end. In actual fact, it was not the end at all. The very next day after the fire, the merchants set up tents on Second Avenue and the bustling resumed. Seattle was destined to expand, and the fire was the catalyst for a change.

On June 7, 1889, city leaders started reviewing what went wrong, how it could be fixed, and how they could capitalize on this opportunity to start from scratch. They decided to create a building code in an effort to standardize the reconstruction of the city.

Before the Great Fire, Seattle was a frontier town. Like most frontier towns, the design, construction and arrangement of buildings were a chaotic hodgepodge with few rules or regulations governing how they were built. Plans were typically left to the discretion of the builder. The new uniform code was adopted in June of 1893. In addition to mandating brick and stone construction, it zoned a larger portion of the downtown area as commercial property. The new zoning effectively pushed private-home construction out of the center of the city into the Denny Regrade (now Belltown) and up onto First Hill. It didn't stop there. The population of the city was rapidly outgrowing its developed areas.

The arrival of the railroad in 1893 brought a new wave of workers, merchants, and entrepreneurs. They all needed places to live. Yet another tsunami of people arrived in 1897 when the steamship *Portland* arrived with gold onboard. The Alaska Gold Rush had begun! With its deep port and railroad line, Seattle was the ideal location for people arriving from the East Coast. Here they would stock up on provisions and make sail for the Yukon. At the mouth of the Klondike River, the miners would say, "there's gold in them there hills." In Seattle, shopkeeps cried, "there's gold in them there prospectors!"

With the rush of people and money that resulted, expansion pushed ever further into the clear cuts and forests that were east and north of the city. Queen Anne, Capitol Hill and the fringes of downtown Seattle started to sprout residential tracts. It was a glorious time for architects, builders, land developers and real estate agents. Unfortunately, there were plenty of folks out there looking for an easy buck, and quality construction wasn't part of their business plan. These less reputable builders were giving the whole industry a bad name. There wasn't a method for the discriminating buyer to differentiate between builders of good repute and those of lesser character.

At the turn of the century, there was a tipping point in the demographics of the city. Before the shift, Seattle was an outpost made up mainly of pioneers, adventurers, speculators and scoundrels. As the city matured it started to attract more refined residents, and more professional tradespeople. Although it is impossible to pinpoint an exact time or circumstance of the shift, it seems likely that the change occurred sometime during the year 1900. Consider this case: In 1899, the Seattle Public Library was moved into the Yesler Mansion. Over the course of that year, City Librarian Charles Wesley Smith petitioned the library philanthropist Andrew Carnegie to donate funds for a dedicated structure. Carnegie refused, saying that Seattle was just a "hot air boom town."[2] By January 1901, things had already changed enough that when the Yesler Mansion was destroyed by fire,

Carnegie reconsidered and gave $220,000 toward the construction and outfitting of a new library.

The number of wealthy, refined citizens grew in number, increasing the demand for a different kind of development. The cultured classes required a higher level of craftsmanship, better design, more amenities and a higher class of neighbors. For the first time, there were tracts specifically dedicated to upscale residences. Now, it was no longer just "the nicest home on the block," but blocks of the nicest homes. The best known, perhaps, are the James Moore estates on "Millionaire's Row," Fourteenth Avenue East's mansions, near Volunteer Park in Capitol Hill. Equally grand estates were also being developed in Madrona, First Hill and the western slope of Queen Anne Hill.

By 1906, Seattleites were ready to show the world the beauty and elegance of their burgeoning city. They organized the Alaska-Yukon-Pacific Exposition (AYPE) to serve as their city's coming-out party. It was modeled after a World's Fair. They chose the new grounds of the recently relocated University of Washington for their location, and hired John C. Olmsted of the Olmsted Brothers firm (designers of New York's Central Park) as the architect.

As civilized as Seattle thought it'd become, there were still the remnants of the old frontier

*The view from Capitol Hill's Volunteer Park water tower was very popular to visitors and photographers alike.
Here, looking south, the stately mansions in the foreground give way to more modest houses in the background.
Master Builders member John Frantz was responsible for a lot of construction on Capitol Hill.*

The Seattle Master Builders Association was formed, in part, to prevent shoddy construction. Houses like the one seen to the left, which was between Sixth and Seventh Avenues near James Street, were all too common in the time before building codes and materials standardization.

opportunitism. During the groundbreaking ceremony in June 1907, after the officials had their photo opportunities while holding a gilded pick and shovel, a man came out of the crowd, grabbed the gold-painted pick, broke ground, and then darted back into the crowd with his souvenir. As officials tried to get it back, someone else swiped the gilded shovel.[3] Despite the inauspicious beginning, and the fact that no alcohol was (ostensibly) allowed at the Exposition, the AYPE was a tremendous success. Having had three years to prepare, and with a national economy that was on an upswing, the 1909 Exposition entertained and impressed more than three million visitors during its 138-day run.

Another momentous event happened in 1909. Perhaps buoyed by the success of the AYPE, or maybe to combat the negative perception of the industry by the public, or possibly to more effectively lobby for zoning and regulation changes, five unidentified members of the builders' community met in the recently constructed Central Building and agreed to the formation of the Seattle Master Builders Association. However, there are no written records from the meeting. We have to rely on the oral history of the members who would hear the tale later, and can only guess at the motives and conversations of those five men. Suffice it to say that it was the beginning of the first 100 years of Master Builders Association history.

Housing Styles

As Seattle's residents became more domesticated and refined, there came a need for a more domesticated and refined style of housing. If someone purchased a home between 1909 and 1919, they had but five styles to choose from: Victorian, Foursquare, Colonial Revival, Tudor Revival or Craftsman Bungalow.

The Victorian style by this time had pretty much run its course. It featured high-peaked gable roofs, varying textures of shingles, turrets, towers, and large quantities of finely detailed decorative elements, called "gingerbread." Because of all the ornamentation and detail it was a very time-consuming and expensive process to build such a home; most of the Victorian homes were sold to wealthy clients who wanted to show off their fortunes.

Foursquare visually opposed the Victorian style. Rather than prominent displays of decoration and elaborate floor plans, a Foursquare-style house was essentially a big box. It had a square floor plan with one room in each corner. Many were two-story homes with a staircase taking up the space of one of the corners. The exteriors usually had very sparse detail, and the interiors would be mostly left to the taste of the owners.

A variation on the theme was the Seattle Box. Where most houses have a porch that projects out from the face of the home, the Seattle Box had a porch that was inset, taking away from the interior space, but providing a covered patio area for enjoying the damp outdoors.

The absence of complicated angles, the flat façades, and the simple layout of the floor plan coupled with the use of cheaper lap siding made them an excellent choice for families. One could afford a much larger house with the cost savings that resulted from its simplicity and thrift of construction.

Colonial Revival was similar to the Foursquare in that the floor plan had been simplified to just a rectangle. The departure in style came mostly in the design of the façade. In a Foursquare, the entrance was almost always off to one side of the front façade. This was necessary because, when you split a square into four rooms, a wall runs down the center of the house. On the other hand, Colonial Revival homes were symmetrical. The entrance door would almost invariably be in the center. If it had two windows to the right of the door, it would have two windows to the left of the door. If it had a porch, the door would be in the center. This style of home often had shutters, though by the 1900s, they were purely decorative and not functional. Another hallmark of a Colonial Revival home was the use of neo-classical elements: Greco-Roman columns, porticos, friezes and semi-circular Palladian windows. As with the Foursquare, these homes could be scaled to any size. With the extra detailing, though, Colonial Revival homes were made for a more affluent family.

The next two styles popular in the early years of the Seattle Master Builders Association came out of the Craftsman tradition of the early twentieth century. The Craftsman style was descended from the Arts-and-Crafts Movement of nineteenth-century Britain. That movement began as a rejection of so-named "soulless" items created with the use of machines in a mass-production factory. The ideology was that a well-designed product, built by a master craftsman, was a far superior object to a poorly designed item duplicated slavishly by unskilled workers at machines.

Gustav Stickley brought the movement to America. However, he decided that the ideology wasn't quite as important as the bottom line, and chose to use machines to create his line of "Craftsman" furniture. His emphasis was on the simplicity of form, and the beauty of the material.

He expanded out from his core business of furniture construction and started designing homes using the Craftsman design aesthetic. He even started his own magazine, *The Craftsman*, to spread the gospel of this new style, and in every issue there was a plan for a Craftsman home.

Tudor Revival homes took aspects of the Craftsman style and married them with medieval elements. These homes were well built. They featured asymmetrical façades, steep pitched roofs with curves to echo the look of thatched roofs, rounded top doors, decorative half timbering and accentuated chimneys. The interiors highlighted the beauty of the material by using different woods in their natural colors to create different shades, and keeping the paint color to a minimum. The style was so evocative and they were so well built, that even 100 years later, the majority of these homes still exist. Even more impressive is the fact that most of them, in the Seattle-area anyway, still feature the same interior wood detailing.

Craftsman Bungalows were also based on the design aesthetic of Stickley's Craftsman style. As with the Tudor Revival homes, the end design of the structure was not as critical as remaining true to its promised purpose. The Bungalow form was derived from a design popular in India, in fact, the very word means "house in

Laurence and Ida Colman built this home in West Seattle's Fauntleroy neighborhood in 1911. This hand-colored photograph shows off the Craftsman bungalow style popular at the time. The home was described in a local architecture magazine as being "within the forest yet by the sea." The architect was Daniel R. Huntington.

This home, built in about 1910, exemplifies the Colonial Revival architectural style. It has one room on each corner in the lower story, with a porch in the center in the front. Though there is some ornamentation on its columns and second floor shutters, the house is generally without artifice.

the Bengali style."[4] Craftsman Bungalow homes were usually one to one-and-a-half stories, and featured low sloping roofs with exposed framing details and wide overhanging eaves. The eaves often projected out far enough to cover porches, supported by prominent, highly emphasized piers. The interiors, like the Tudor Revival homes, relied heavily on the warmth and natural beauty of the wood. Bungalow homes took it one step further; as the colors of the furniture, the rugs, the artwork and even the bric-a-brac were all expected to fall into the same color palette as the natural woods.

Official Business

The years between the 1909 inception of the Master Builders Association and its incorporation in 1914 are not formally documented. If there were meetings, they were most likely infrequent and informal affairs involving a fair amount of alcohol, cigar smoke and boisterous voices. Who could blame them for not keeping records when everything was coming up roses? They were in an incredible period of growth, and probably had enough to do just tending to the process of creating a city. Consider this: from the beginning

Construction in the streetcar suburbs of Seattle was booming, as this photo of homes being built in Queen Anne in 1910 shows.

of 1912 through the end of 1914, Seattle issued roughly 29,000 building permits. Assuming ten percent of those were for commercial development, 8,700 residential permits were issued per year. That constituted a tremendous amount of homebuilding and development that needed to be done. The real estate stock of the city grew by $30,000,000 in those three years alone.

It was in this atmosphere, in August of 1914, that John J. Frantz of Booker, Kiehl & Whipple Construction Company was elected as the first (recorded) President of the Master Builders Association. In that first official meeting they settled on several things. They agreed to meet each Friday afternoon at 3:30 p.m. in their temporary headquarters located in the Boston Block at the corner of Second Avenue and Columbia Street. They decided to address thorny issues such as trade contracts and disputes, the competitive bidding process, self-regulation of the industry and a commitment to promoting a more positive image to the public. They also ratified a set of principles that are still in use today. Those principles are:

- To associate home builders for the purpose of mutual advantage and cooperation.
- To develop and maintain within the homebuilding industry a high appreciation of the objectives and responsibilities of home builders in fully serving the public.
- To advocate and encourage the constant improvement of homebuilding techniques and practices.
- To promote and protect home ownership among all the people.
- To cooperate with other trade associations in all matters related to advancing the homebuilding industry.
- To advance the standardization of building codes throughout the nation.
- To collaborate with distributors and manufacturers of building materials and equipment to the end that maximum quality at minimum cost to the customer may be achieved.
- To issue such publications as may be necessary to disseminate information of value to its members and the public.
- To serve, advance and protect the welfare of the homebuilding industry in such a manner that adequate housing will be made available by private enterprise to all Americans.
- To operate without profit and no part of the income of this organization shall inure to the benefit of any individual member.

No. 195.

By the beginning of 1915, the bloom was off the rose, as there was a downturn in the home building industry. The "War to End All Wars" had begun in Europe, and a sense of foreboding caused a wave of uncertainty in the American economy. The ripple effect was felt in Seattle as evidenced by a thirty percent drop in the number of building permits issued. Alarmingly, a large number of the homes that were being built were being constructed by day laborers who were not affiliated with the Master Builders Association. To make matters worse, when Canada entered the war in 1914, the homebuilding industry in Vancouver, British Columbia, came to a virtual halt. The tradesmen who didn't join the war effort made an exodus to nearby Seattle. With an over-abundance of labor and an under-abundance of jobs, the friction started to create heat, and soon the pot was boiling. Flare-ups started to occur between association members and accusations were hurled back and forth. The fledgling organization was on the verge of a meltdown.

Keeping his cool, Association President John Frantz fought the fire head on. In a move most likely aimed at creating camaraderie and congenial fellowship, the weekly meetings were moved from Friday afternoons to Tuesday evenings at 8:00 (after the day's work). Frantz organized additional social events – up to three or four each month – to encourage more personal relationships between members of the Association. He also encouraged having joint meetings with groups that weren't part of the Master Builders Association yet were vitally linked. There were events that brought Association members together with the local chapters of the American Institute of Architects, the Master Plumbers Association and the Structural Building Trades Alliance. The relationships formed through these gatherings served well in healing the animosity, and led to the amicable resolution of some contentious issues such as wage-rate disputes, subcontracting regulations and an agreement to discourage "sympathy strikes." The members of the Master Builders Association

(right) Construction workers on a home site Woodland Park take a lunch break

were pleased enough with the efforts of John Frantz that they re-elected him to a second term in 1915. By the end of his term the following year, as testament to his success, even in light of a downturn, the membership roster had nearly tripled to seventy members.

In June of 1916, Charles C. Cawsey was elected the new President of the Master Builders Association. Cawsey was a twenty-nine-year veteran of the Seattle building trade. Starting out as a brick-mason, he arrived in Seattle just in time to capitalize on the building boom caused by the Great Seattle Fire. He made an early name for himself by finishing the first building project constructed over the ashes of the fire; the Wah Chung Building at 410 Second Avenue Extension. Concurrent with his election, the Association

members voted to adopt a new constitution and a new set of bylaws. In the new bylaws, the officers made the decision to hold elections in January. Although Cawsey's tenure as president was a short five months, he presided over the inauguration of their new, permanent quarters: The Master Builders' Hall in the Arcade Building on the corner of Second Avenue and Union Street in Seattle.

For reasons that are unclear, Vice President Neil M. McDonald replaced Charles Cawsey in November 1916. Perhaps Cawsey was pursuing too much commercial building to the chagrin of the home builders. McDonald only served for two months until Edgar S. Booker was elected the fourth President in January 1917. Booker was a partner in the Booker, Kiehl and Whipple

Photo courtesy MOHAI, neg. 11.815

Construction Co., the very firm that had employed the first recorded President, John J. Frantz. The first few months of Booker's tenure could best be described as uneventful. The economy in Seattle was stagnant, there were not many homes being built and there was a surplus of unpurchased homes. The problem resulted from uncertainty about whether or not the United States was going to enter or be drawn into the war. Debate raged in the "other Washington" about such an act, and the citizens of Seattle had no other choice but to just wait and see.

The First Great War

In April 1917, the United States declared war against Germany and its allies. In the three intervening years between the start of the war and the United States' entry, the U.S. government had been providing limited assistance to Great Britain and France in the form of weapons, ammunition, vehicles, ships, food, raw materials and medical supplies. Those supplies and manufactured items were being made in America, and that kept the Seattle economy from declining during those years. Seattle, though experiencing no growth, was kept alive by the industries of mining, lumber, shipping, and shipbuilding. Now, with the declaration of war, the brakes were off. The full focus of the United States government was now on winning the war, and winning it as quickly as possible. The strategy was to overwhelm the opposing forces with sheer numbers: more men, more tanks, more guns, more ammunition, more rations, more planes and more ships. The United States was a land blessed with a seemingly endless bounty of raw materials and now was the time to exploit them.

Seattle was – as they say – more blessed than others, and the boost to the economy was felt immediately. The city was suddenly a boomtown again. Tens of thousands of workers were streaming in from all parts of the country to fill the jobs necessary to support the war effort. Unfortunately, this did not translate into a boom time for the Master Builders. There was a universal apprehension about developing new housing stock for a transient population that would almost certainly move on after the war ended. Additionally, due to the resources being dedicated to the war effort, the cost of materials had spiked substantially, making profit unlikely. That created a huge shortfall of housing for the influx of workers.

In late 1917, Association President Edgar Booker met with representatives of the Chamber of Commerce, the Commercial Club and government officials to address the issue of housing shortages in Seattle. By February 1918, in an attempt to ease the situation, Booker rallied the resources of the Association to create a housing bureau, which served as a free rental agency, compiling a list of all the vacant rooms, apartments and houses in Seattle and matching them with folks who needed a place to live. As a stopgap measure, it performed admirably and quickly found housing for 14,000 people. There are two results of note regarding the housing bureau: not a single house was constructed as a result of the effort and finding housing for 14,000 people didn't meet the demand.

By July 1918, U.S. participation in the war had ramped up to an unprecedented level. Four million men had been drafted, and were shipping out at a rate of 10,000 troops per day. The sheer logistical nightmare of organizing such an effort led the government to create a public/private entity to manage part of the operation. The Emergency Fleet Corporation was chartered to streamline the process of building and outfitting a marine force capable of supplying troops and materials to the overall war effort, and Congress granted it authority over

Posters like these were common sights around Seattle, as the Emergency Fleet Corporation worked to motivate steelworkers at home to work hard for victory abroad. One Seattle shipbuilding company set the national record for time from keel-laying to delivery - the West Mahomet, *built by Skinner and Eddy Shipbuilding, was launched in only 46 days.*

all shipbuilding in the United States. The Director General Charles M. Schwab and the General Manager Charles Piez were given the mandate to get things done by any means possible, and they had the budget to back that up.

Following up on their "success" with the housing bureau, the Association actively lobbied the government for financial assistance in creating a federal housing program for Seattle. The plea was not only denied, but the stakes were raised when the Emergency Fleet Corporation placed a condition on $200 million worth of contracts for the Seattle area: If there was not adequate housing provided for the work force, then the contracts would be lowered to a level more in line with the available housing. Again under pressure, President Edgar Booker worked alongside the Chamber of Commerce, the Commercial Club, local leaders and other professional groups to establish the More Homes Bureau.

Created in July 1918, the More Homes Bureau was not an entity that actually built homes; it was set up as an organization to persuade and facilitate others to build homes. It was a one-stop shop for plans, permits, architectural advice, contractor referrals, labor, materials and loans. As an incentive to spur private citizens to build new homes on land they already owned, the Bureau provided secondary mortgages. Another innovative approach the Bureau took to encourage new construction was to frame the issue as one of civic responsibility. Based on population projections for January 1919, the Bureau determined that they needed to build 5,000 new homes. In a survey taken at the August Association meeting, members decided they had the ability to immediately produce over 2,000 homes. The Bureau created a list of prospects (private citizens and landowners) that should be capable of constructing the remaining 3,000 homes. Each prospect was then given a rating: a rating of one indicated that prospect was capable of producing one home; a rating of ten would indicate the ability to produce ten homes. In September 1918, an army of 450 Seattle business-people canvassed the intended prospects, and within five days they had collected pledges toward the construction of 3,650 houses or their equivalent in apartments. The effort was a success, and by November 11, Armistice Day, more than 2,000 dwelling units had already been constructed. Even after the war was over, most of the remaining 3,000 units were completed. ♣

CHAPTER 2

Keeping the Momentum

1919 – 1929

The year 1919 began with one of the most contentious periods of labor relations ever recorded– the February General Strike shut down everything. Tensions remained, and in the wake of the strike, the Northwest Master Builders held their second annual convention; labor was the main topic. Discussions were contentious affairs, and there was a lot of unease between the Seattle Master Builders and the Associated General Contractors, which culminated with the 1923 absorption of the Master Builders Association into the AGC. Builders quickly realized that their interests were better served when they controlled their own association, and reformed the Seattle Master Builders Association in 1924. However, in 1927, they changed the name to Seattle Master Craftsmen to reflect their commitment to quality construction. Growth in the Seattle region did not meet expectations, but the Association forged through. Though the Depression was only weeks away, in 1928, the Seattle Master Builders Association opened the "Metropolitan Builders' Exhibit" at Eighth Avenue and Virginia Street. Homebuilding was slowing down, and the Association ended its second decade worried about the future.

*By the dawn of the 1920s, shops and hotels were filling the area at First Avenue
and Spring Street. The city grew around the home of Amos Brown.*

Strikes & Unions

The immediate postwar period should have been a celebratory time in Seattle. The United States with its allies won the war, and did it decisively. Seattle, for its part, had ramped up its shipbuilding capacity to such a level that during the course of the war, it had produced 36.5 percent of all the ships for the Emergency Fleet Corporation (EFC).[1] It was an amazing feat, but the good times did not last long in Seattle. Within ninety days of the Armistice, the decisions made in an effort to perform such a feat would manifest themselves into the first general strike ever in the United States.[2]

The first twenty years of the 1900s were marked by a rapid succession of industries that organized into unions. Many felt the Industrial Revolution had minimized the humanity of the common worker and had turned them into little more than cogs in a machine. At the same time, the socialist theories touted by philosophers such as Karl Marx and Frederick Engels were starting to really take hold. Added to this was the individualistic spirit that was the hallmark of the citizens of the Great Northwest. These elements all combined to create the perfect environment for union organizers. It seemed like every occupation, no matter how large or small, fought for its collective rights. There were unions for: apple pickers; auto mechanics; barbers; beer drivers; billposters; brewers; brewery workers; butchers; candy makers; carpenters; cigar makers; coal miners; coal packers; cooks; halibut fishermen; forest and lumber workers; horse harness makers; icemen; iron workers; joiners; lathers; laundry workers; longshoremen; machinists; meat packers; milk company workers; newsboys; retail clerks; sheet metal workers; shingle bolt cutters; shingle weavers; ship workers; street car employees; tanners; taxicab drivers; telephone operators; waiters; waitresses; wireless operators and scores of others.

It was a common occurrence to open the daily paper and read about the latest strike. Most strikes in those days were small affairs that basically fought for an eight-hour workday and the right to organize. Most were short-lived, and since the demands were fairly reasonable, most were successful. Over time though, the smaller unions began to combine into larger unions to increase their collective power. The two major affiliations during the general strike of 1919 were the Industrial Workers of the World (IWW) and the

Workers take to the street during Seattle General Strike,in February 1919.
The photo was taken looking west down Pike Street from Ninth Avenue.

American Federation of Labor (AFL). In addition to some cross-pollination of members, these two affiliations were linked by the organization of the Seattle Central Labor Council (CLC).

During the course of the war, the Federal Government, through the office of the Emergency Fleet Corporation, had invested hundreds of millions of dollars to build, bolster, expand, equip, supply and staff the shipbuilding industry in Seattle. Under broad powers given to them by the White House and Congress, the Emergency Fleet Corporation (EFC) had the authority to set the wages at the shipyards. Woodrow Wilson,

who had been elected as the first "Progressive" Democrat, and who was known for his support of union labor, had insisted that the contracts be based on an eight-hour workday, and prohibited the employers from discriminating against union shipyard workers. The new jobs at the shipyards were enough to attract tens of thousands of workers to Seattle and down to the dry docks. Guaranteed work and wages were a hard thing to pass up.

There were dozens of shipyards by this time, and that created a situation where each ship-building company was trying to entice the best workers to come work for them. Better workers meant better quality and more capacity. More capacity meant more ships completed and more profit for the shipbuilder. Consequently, some of the larger shipyards were offering wages that were even higher than those mandated by the EFC. These higher wages certainly brought short-term prosperity to the shipyard workers but apparently prosperity, like familiarity, breeds contempt.

Although the Armistice was signed on November 11, 1918, the wartime ship production was still going strong. The shipyard workers union saw this as an ideal time to make their stand. They sought to have their wartime salaries bumped up and locked in, and demanded higher wages for all employees (not just the skilled craftsmen). The shipyard owners recognized that the gravy train of wartime production was coming to an end, and dug in their heels. They appealed to the EFC for help, and general manager Charles Piez fired off a telegram warning them that if they gave in to the unions, they would lose their contracts. In a strange twist of fate, the telegram that was meant to go to the employers, the Metal Trades Association, was instead delivered (presumably by mistake) to the union, the Metal Trades Council. Needless to say, the

union workers were quite incensed, and voted unanimously to strike.

On January 21, 1919, a resolute force of 35,000 shipyard workers walked off the job. It could have ended up as just one more of a multitude of strikes, but there were larger issues at play and Seattle unknowingly became a test case for future dealings between organized labor and the federal government. The union felt the pinch immediately as local grocers cut off credit to the striking workers. The Cooperative Food Producers, a union-affiliated business, stepped up to fill in the credit gap, but the police summarily raided their offices. Given these circumstances, the other unions involved in the Central Labor Council began to get the impression that there was an all-out battle raging against the rights of the unions. With the apprehension that they might be targeted next, most of the unions voted to join in and participate in a general strike.

The general strike began on Thursday, February 6, 1919. 65,000 union workers were now refusing to work. With no one to operate the streetcars, no one to drive the taxicabs, and no one to conduct the trains, it prevented an additional 40,000 non-union workers from getting to their jobs. The Secretary of War, Newton D. Baker, immediately ordered the National Guard to mobilize and assemble in Seattle. By Friday, February 7, Mayor Ole Hanson had declared the strike a "Bolshevik action," and threatened to institute martial law. In a particularly dastardly move, the American Federation of Labor declared the strike an unauthorized action. They withheld support funds from the strikers, and threatened to revoke the charters of any striking union. In the face of these obstacles, and without a clear set of goals mapped out, the strike foundered. By Monday, February 10, the strike was over and everyone was back to work. On February 11 the CLC officially ended the strike action.

Although it was over in only five days, the strike was to have a long-lasting effect on the city and on the organized labor movement in America. Perhaps, just as importantly, it had a significant effect in regards to the relationship between the Master Builders Association and the Structural Trades Alliance, who chose to break their agreement with the Master Builders and participate in the strike.

On February 21, 1919 (ten days after the strike ended), the Master Builders all met at the second annual convention of the Northwest Master Builders Association. Newly elected President Charles W. Carkeek, in a probable effort to establish a conciliatory tone, issued a declaration stating "that labor and capital are partners, not enemies; that their interests are common interests, not opposed, and that neither can attain the fullest measure of prosperity at the expense of the other, but only in association with the other."

Over the course of the next eight weeks, representatives of the Master Builders Association and the Structural Trades Alliance sat at the bargaining table and attempted to come to a mutually-acceptable trade agreement before the existing one expired on May 1. There were several points of contention. On the union side, they wanted an increase on the wages they made during the war and a commitment to a "closed shop." A closed shop would mean that Master Builders members could only hire union-affiliated contractors. On the Master Builders side, there was a push to hold the line on costs. Because of the massive spending during the war, there had been a great deal of inflation and the Association wanted to bring the prices back down again to create a better environment for housing developers. The demand was there; most of the workers who had flocked to Seattle for the war boom decided to stay on and this created a huge unmet need for housing. The Association felt, however, that the supply was being strangled by the inflated costs of labor and materials in a market that was in a post-war

GARDNER GWINN

Gardner J. Gwinn, Seattle Master Builders Association president in 1927 and 1928, arrived in Seattle the same year as the Alaska-Yukon-Pacific Exposition, and he hit the ground running. Over the next fifteen years, Gwinn designed and built more than 600 homes, later branching out into apartment buildings and commercial projects. Many of his structures survive today, testaments to his reputation for quality construction and timeless design. His company played a significant role in meeting Seattle's housing needs during the construction boom of the 1920s.

Gwinn's family tree was studded with builders for several generations back. Born in Nova Scotia, Canada, on July 29, 1888, he began working construction there with his father at an early age. His family moved to Seattle in 1909. The AYPE was underway and the city was booming; housing was in demand, and local contractors had just launched the Master Builders Association to bring some order and discipline to the industry. Seattle offered ample opportunity for one as talented and ambitious as Gwinn. In 1913, he started his own firm, Gardner J. Gwinn, Incorporated.

Gwinn began as a hands-on builder, and in the early days he listed his occupation as both a plumber and a painter. But a talent for business emerged early, and he was soon putting up houses in such profusion that he had to leave the labor to others and concentrate on running his rapidly growing enterprise. By 1924, when Gwinn was only 36, his company had become the largest homebuilding business in the Northwest and employed more than 150 people. His was a one-stop shop, offering homebuyers everything from labor and material, to building plans and financing. Prices for his homes ranged from $5,000 to $25,000.

Gwinn's houses were known for their livability and sturdy construction. He focused on single-family homes, and for several years published popular plan books titled with the company motto, "Homes of Individuality." As his success increased, he started to purchase large tracts of land, then designed, built, and financed all the homes on them. Many of the first houses in the Cowen Park, Ravenna Park and Bothell Way areas were his. Always an innovator, Gwinn

ACHIEVEMENTS:
President, Master Builders, *1927-1928*

was tapped by Seattle's Electric Club in 1922 and 1923 to design and build the city's first all-electric demonstration homes, which were used to educate the public on the many labor-saving advantages of electrical appliances.

By 1925, Gwinn turned his attention to the development of apartment buildings, putting up more than fifty of them before 1930, including the venerable Marlborough House, which still stands on Seattle's Boren Avenue. Another larger project was the Benjamin Franklin Hotel at Fifth Avenue and Virginia Street in downtown Seattle. Boasting thirteen stories and 350 rooms with private baths, it was the city's second largest, and Gwinn kept an ownership interest in it for several years. In 1969, the hotel was linked to a new forty-story tower wing and renamed the Washington Plaza; in 1980 it was demolished to make way for a second tower, now known as the Westin Hotel.

Gwinn was a longtime member of the Chamber of Commerce and the Exchange Club and devoted many hours to community work. Eventually pulling back from active engagement in the construction business, he was occupied with private investments. One, a large tract of land in Seattle's Laurelhurst neighborhood, was purchased from Gwinn in 1946 for $150,000 and became the site of today's Children's Hospital and Regional Medical Center. Fifty years after settling in Seattle, Gardner Gwinn, active to the last, died suddenly while bowling at Seattle's University Lanes on October 30, 1959. Even now, another fifty years on, many of his sturdy, well-designed homes and apartments still grace the city he did so much to build.

Photo courtesy MOHAI, neg. 2002.3.485

The early part of the 1920s were a period of massive public undertakings to create a more hospitable environment. This hand-tinted photo shows the regrading of Beacon Hill - looking west towards the Duwamish, and present-day SODO.

depression. There was also an inestimable lack of trust that permeated the proceedings. Not only were there feelings of resentment on both sides as a direct result of the General Strike; there was also the notion on the Master Builders' side that the union had brazenly broken their previous commitment, and there was little confidence that the union could be relied on to uphold any future commitment.

The May 1 deadline came and went without a signed agreement. The negotiations continued on through the summer of 1919. A committee was formed that included the Association, the unions, and a public contingent that was presumably involved as a neutral party. They sought to create a building trades adjustment board: an entity to arbitrate labor disputes, and insure uninterrupted building operations. By August, they had come up with a proposal, and the Master Builders membership immediately ratified it. The Structural Trades Alliance was less keen on the proposal, and took the rest of August to deliberate on what their response would be. In the end, they decided to take the hard line approach, and refused to consider arbitration until their wage demands were met. The union went on strike on September 2, 1919. In a sympathy move, the unions for the tailors, the dyers, the cleaners and the pile drivers quickly joined in. The city was once again abuzz with the talk of massive sympathy walkouts. This time, though, nothing came of it... life and business continued on.

On October 14, after six weeks of strike, and six weeks of unproductive negotiations, President Charles Carkeek had enough. He was convinced that the differences between the two camps were never going to be bridged, and it was time for some action. He declared that the building industry was now going to be an "open shop." The unions had once again overestimated the will of the public to support their cause. They also underestimated the effort that the daily papers could have on swaying public opinion. E. R. Singleton wrote a piece for the *Seattle Times* in which he stated: "They call it the 'American Plan of Employment' which means that every man shall be protected in his inalienable right to work, regardless of political, religious, or labor affiliations; that every employer shall be protected in his right to run his own business and to hire employees without having to gain the permission of an autocrat of labor." Without the benefit of public support, the strike couldn't gain any traction. By October 31, the

V. W. VOORHEES, ARCHITECT, SEATTLE, WASH.

First Floor   Second Floor

DESIGN NO. 38 A.

Width of this seven-room house is 26 feet; length 40 feet; height of first story 9 feet; height of second story 8½ feet.
Exterior is finished with siding and shingles. Interior is finished with fir.

Approximate cost of construction, $1,600.00.
Cost of one set of plans, specifications and details, $13.00.
Cost of two sets of plans, specifications and details, $15.00.

(Any plan can be reversed to suit location.)

Dutch Colonial homes remained a popular style for construction even into the 1930s. This plan book was published by architect V. W. Voorhees in 1910. Notice that the three-bedroom home does not call for a bathroom on the first floor.

Building Trades Council was forced to call off the strike. The striking workers returned to their jobs without an increase in pay. Worse yet, they now were working in an "open shop" environment, and had lost the leverage they once had in affecting wages.

Trouble with the Unions

After all the drama of the previous three years, 1920 rang in with a muted bell. The war was over, the unions were tamed and there was an opportunity to continue growth in a less manic, more measured fashion. Charles W. Carkeek was voted in as President for a second term, and (by lack of any evidence to the contrary) seems to have coasted through the year as pretty much a "victory lap." In the meeting notes from July 5, 1920, a motion was passed that the members would go to the scenic hot springs for an outing in honor of Jud Yoho, leaving July 8.

The funds of the treasury were to be used to defray expenses.

It would seem that there was only one contentious item that occurred in the whole of 1920 as far as the Seattle Master Builders Association was concerned. During the third annual convention of the Northwest Master Builders Association, there were some overtures made by the Association of General Contractors (AGC) to lure the Seattle Association into joining their national association of builders. The AGC, which had formed in Chicago in 1918, had been aggressively lobbying all the builders' associations in the United States to merge together. It was felt that the combined clout of all the organizations would allow them to influence building-industry policy at a national level.

This was actually the second year that a merger was proposed. The first year, 1919, was in the middle of the labor dispute, and nobody in Seattle had the time to even listen to, let alone consider the idea. By 1920, however, the Association was sitting in the catbird seat. They had just survived feast, famine, fire and fallow—and were all the stronger for it. Carkeek's response to the AGC's proposal was, basically, that the Seattle Master Builders Association was doing quite all right, thank you. He couldn't see any local benefit to joining a national organization.

In January 1921, J. E. Shoemaker was elected President of the Master Builders Association. The pace of building was really starting to slow down, and there was a substantial drop in the attendance of the meetings. Without a list of obstacles to overcome, and without a booming economy to keep everyone hopping, going to meetings may have become a tedious affair. Another possible reason for the decline in attendance might have something to do with the Seattle Police Department, which had started cracking down on scofflaws who were failing to comply with Volstead Act, which prohibited the sale of liquor. Although Seattle had gone "dry" in 1916, there was little enforcement of the prohibition, until it became a federal law in late 1919. The meeting notes no longer had a disclaimer that hinted "and after the close of business a good time was had by all!"

In January 1922, J. B. Warrack became the President of the Association. His first order of business was to make it clear to the members, and to the public, the reasons why they should not throw in their lot with the AGC. He put out a statement to the press in early February explaining: "The Seattle Group is a good organization. It is doing good work, and we do not propose to lose our identity, our self-government, or accept dictation from without from some centralized authority which is not in touch with local conditions." As a follow-up to his statement, there was an editorial later that month in the *Pacific Builder & Engineer*. It made a more detailed and impassioned case for keeping their organization independent:

> Each community has problems peculiar to itself and the value of a local organization that is in close touch with every phase of these problems is of the utmost value. Its service to the community... is as a rule much more effective than if a national body should step in and undertake to settle some thing purely local in character. The Seattle Master Builders Association... affords an illustration of what consequence local organization can be in the cases of this nature... this body of men put an end to exorbitant (union) demands and did it more effectively and expeditiously than could have been done by the ponderous machinery of an organization representing a section of the country or the nation... Up to the present time the necessary initiative, vigor and leadership have been found within its own ranks. Its fame has spread to the far corners of the country, and it has vindicated its right to exist as an agency for the good of the community...

Portland and Spokane had already joined the AGC, and there was a lot of arm-twisting being done to the Seattle Master Builders to get them to do the same. The recruiting members of the AGC seemed to be using a "divide and conquer" strategy. Rather than addressing the group as a whole, they would target individual members and extol the virtues of joining a national alliance. The main selling points were increased name recognition and expanded access to public officials. It was probably stated as getting "more bang for your buck" (i.e. dues). After all, the AGC was established in 1918 at the request of President Woodrow Wilson. Wilson recognized the construction industry's national importance and desired a partner with which the government could discuss and plan for the advancement of the nation.[3] It would be hard to find a better sales technique than to have a recruiter say: "The President wants us all to collaborate to make the country stronger!" The country had just emerged from a war, and the buzz of patriotism was still at a feverish pitch.

While the actual methods used to influence the final vote are shrouded in a cloak of uncertainty, the facts remain: February's press releases indicated a united front for independence and local autonomy. The notes from the February Association meeting show a continued promotion of community activities, and the identification of goals for the future. Despite these signs of solidarity and the appearance of business

as usual, when the vote was held (not thirty days later) in March 1922, the members of the Master Builders chose to merge with the Associated General Contractors. The Master Builders Association name was abandoned, and the new organization was dubbed the *Builders Section of the Seattle Office of the Pacific Northwest Chapter of the Associated General Contractors of America*. It is unclear whether the new chapter members used the full title of the group in conversation, or just lovingly referred to themselves as proud members of the BSSOPNCAGC.

The Seattle Master Builders, unfortunately, had become victims of their own success. They had an inclusive membership policy, which meant that they had members from the residential, commercial, and industrial sectors as well as members from the building trades, the architectural trade and the real estate trade. All of this had given them great power at a local level. It allowed them to keep on top of local issues and to affect prices and regulations in a preemptive, collaborative way. Most important, though not often mentioned in their list of accomplishments, was the Master Builders' ability to raise money. Membership dues and fund-raisers had allowed the Association to accumulate a sizeable endowment, which they utilized to further their goals. It is quite likely that the endowment and membership dues were considered the real prize for the AGC, and not so much the local organizational ability.

Reaffirming Identity

After the merger it became immediately apparent that the home builders were on the losing end of the equation. Although they had created the Master Builders Association and had been the core of the organization, in this new model they were left without a voice. The Seattle Chapter of the AGC was divided into several contracting divisions. They had divisions for Public Works, Railroads, Bridges, Highways, Commercial Building and Pile Driving. Conspicuous in its absence is the Residential Building division. No reason was given for the omission, but it left the home builders in a position akin to taxation without representation. After two years of this intolerable situation a core group of Seattle home builders got together and decided to reorganize.

On April 17, 1924, a select group of men including Edward Merritt, a prominent architect and owner of the Craftsman Bungalow Company;

Gardner J. Gwinn, a successful developer of houses and apartment buildings; and Stanley Long, a well-known builder and early member of the Seattle Rotary Club met at Dartnall's Cafeteria to create a new association. This new organization would carry on the ideal of the old Master Builders Association, namely, unity of action toward a common purpose.

Edward Merritt was elected the first President of the new Seattle Home Builders Association. He was the perfect man for the job. He was widely respected around town as a veteran of the Seattle building boom, an active community member, a licensed architect and the owner of a real estate company. In addition, he had the cachet of being a college graduate at a time in the building trade when that was quite a rare thing. He could act as an ambassador to the capital side of the business, a diplomat with the bureaucratic side of the business and a representative of the construction side of the business.

Merritt gave the Seattle Home Builders Association an instant boost of credibility as they started their rebuilding and recruiting process. During their first meeting, in an attempt to avoid a repeat of the AGC debacle, the group decided to extend eligibility only to applicants who devoted more than sixty percent of their

EDWARD MERRITT

ACHIEVEMENTS:
President, Master Builders, *1924-1925*

Nothing in Edward Lovering Merritt's background marked him as a rebel. A trained architect and successful builder, he had by the 1920s gained wide respect in Seattle's business community. Yet Merritt refused to go along when most of his brethren in the Seattle Master Builders Association agreed to be absorbed by the Associated General Contractors of America. Unwilling to bow to any national group, he and a few like-minded locals started a new association to represent the interests of Seattle's community of builders. The first meeting of the Seattle Builders was held at Dartnall's Cafeteria, at noon, April 17, 1924, nominated Edward Merritt as chairman. He served two consecutive terms, in 1924 and 1925. Then in 1926, he turned the reins over to fellow developer Stanley Long.

Merritt, the son of a successful building contractor, was born in Northfield, Minnesota, on October 31, 1881. After graduating in 1900 with an architecture degree from the University of Minnesota, he moved to Seattle with his parents and sister. Merritt became a Knight Templar Mason, a Noble of Nile Temple, Mystic Shrine, and a member of the Elks Club. He was active as an architect in Seattle until his death on August 10, 1950.

In Seattle, Merritt, his father and brother-in-law formed the Merritt-Hall Investment Company, also doing business under the name Merritt, Hall & Merritt Architects. A 1910 article in the *Pacific Builder and Engineer* magazine, entitled "Bungalow Construction in the Northwest," featured a six-room, Merritt-designed home in the Leschi neighborhood, and had high praise for its interior and amenities.

Among the Merritts' competitors was Jud Yoho, a Texas transplant of formidable promotional skills. Yoho had arrived in Seattle in 1897, began building houses in 1909, and founded the Craftsman Bungalow Company in 1911. Yoho took over the California-based *Bungalow Magazine,* a publication of national circulation to promote his enterprise. Like many Seattle builders during the period, Yoho sometimes played the role of developer, designer, builder and resale agent, but he was not a trained architect. Edward Merritt would provide that cachet. There is an indication from a contemporary news account that Merritt and his brother-in-law, Virgil Hall, had worked with Yoho as early as 1912.

The Merritt family partnership dissolved in 1914, and Edward Merritt struck out on his own. Soon he became associated with Yoho, and together they designed and sold Craftsman-style bungalows that were built in Wallingford, Green Lake, the University District, and the Northgate area. By 1917, Merritt had taken over the Craftsman Bungalow Company, retaining Yoho as an associate, and they continued to publish the magazine and a series of plan books, all of which had "Craftsman Bungalows" in their titles. But tastes were changing. The magazine ceased publication in 1918, and the last plan book of bungalow designs was issued in 1920. The 1921 Merritt/Yoho plan book still carried the title "Craftsman Bungalows," but it featured Colonial-style designs that mirrored a shift in the public's taste. In the 1920s, Merritt published another plan book, entitled *Craftsman Bungalows, Sixteenth Edition*, under his name alone. It featured designs for English cottages and Colonial-revival homes, and not the traditional bungalows upon which he had built his early career.

A significant housing shortage during the 1920s led many builders, Merritt among them, to shift their attention from single-family homes to apartment buildings. In the middle part of the decade, Merritt started the Merritt Realty Company and developed several apartment buildings on Capitol Hill. One of these, the Buckley Apartments at 201 Seventeenth Avenue, was built in 1928 and is listed as a historical site by Seattle's Department of Neighborhoods.

time to the building business. Their second order of business was to establish a committee to lobby the Seattle City Council. They wanted a bill enacted that would require any plans submitted to the building department to be drawn by a licensed architect or engineer.

At their next meeting, one week later, they approved the membership of eighteen additional members. The Association was already starting to grow. Better still, one must assume that they were recruiting these new members back from the AGC. The group then agreed to meet twice a month, still at Dartnall's Cafeteria. Two weeks later, at their next meeting, they continued to show how serious an organization they had become, a mandate was given to all members: create a list of unreliable subcontractors. The list would become a "blacklist" and no members of the Association should hire them for any project. This would benefit the group in a number of ways: one, it would ensure that an unreliable workforce could not knock the building process off course. Two, by hiring only dependable, professional contractors it would be easier to maintain a higher quality standard. Three, by weeding out the less reliable contractors they could use the references of the existing members to recruit new, reputable applicants to join their association.

Although the new organization was leaner and meaner than the Master Builders Association of old, there was still some time allowed to engage in the finer points of gentlemanly competition. Edward Merritt and Gardner Gwinn would energetically debate the topic of who had the better plan book. Stanley Long laid claim to being the best golfer of the group and, apparently on a roll, Edward Merritt convinced those gathered that he was without a doubt the best hunter of them all.

Merritt served two successful terms as President. Under his leadership, the Seattle Home Builders Association grew its membership, formed a good relationship with the policy-makers of the city and helped shape the public perception that membership in the Seattle Home Builders Association was the gold standard for quality builders in Seattle.

Stanley Long, the second of the re-founding fathers, took over the Presidency in 1926. A man of regal bearing, he already had three decades of homebuilding experience behind him. He shared the philosophy of unity in action and was also a great proponent of maintaining his (and the Association's) reputation by consistently offering high-quality products. Although his tenure as President lasted for only one year, he was involved in the various iterations of the home builders association well into the 1950s.

The third of the re-founding fathers to ascend to the Presidency was Gardner J. Gwinn, in 1927. Yet another veteran of the Seattle building scene, Gwinn began his career constructing private homes. By 1925, he had graduated to large apartment buildings, and by the end of his career had built more than fifty of them. His building company was highly successful, and the reflection of his success shone brightly on the Seattle Home Builders Association as well. During Gwinn's tenure, in a move to upscale their image, the group changed their name to Seattle Master Craftsmen. Also, in June 1927, Gwinn instituted a Code of Ethics, which was distributed to all members of the organization.

With their sense of purpose, their drive for quality and their business savvy, these three local men had created an independent organization that was well on its way to matching the prestige of any nationally-affiliated commercial builders' group.

In 1928, J. L. Grandey was elected President of the Seattle Master Craftsmen. During his tenure there was a successful push to form stronger working agreements with the real estate and building trades. A resolution was passed that January, stating that "...the interests and success of the [Master Builders] and the Realtors of Seattle [were] mutual." There were also discussions with the Bricklayers, Masons and Plasterers International Union, and with the Building Trade Council.

Also worthy of note in 1928 was the decision to return to the name Seattle Master Builders Association. Over the next several months, Master Builders Association members moved forward with two initiatives. The first had to do with advertising, funded by a one-time fee of $10, and the second was the unanimous decision to create a "Metropolitan Builders' Exhibit," which would be located at Eighth Avenue and Virginia. Unfortunately, no record remains of what the Builders' Exhibit looked like.

Real Estate Market

The decade between 1920 and 1930 was a relatively slow one for builders in Seattle. The population of the city had increased by 50,000 people. In comparison, the previous ten years had shown an increase of 78,000 and the decade

The Times-Stetson Model House was constructed in a partnership between the Seattle Times *and the Seattle Master Builders Association in 1925 to show potential buyers examples of the best materials and home features of the day. It featured hardwood floors and a modern kitchen.*

before that Seattle grew by 157,000 people. It helped to professionalize the industry. Without the frenzy of the past building climate there was less incentive for fly-by-night developers. Also, more attention could be spent on policing the standards and driving out less reputable builders.

The rest of the country bounced back from the post-war recession rather quickly and experienced a growth that was unprecedented. The United States was enjoying the "Roaring Twenties" but here in Seattle, the roar was more of a low growl. There was no longer the fire in the belly to innovate and speculate. The area fell back on its old standbys: lumber, fishing and mining. The manufacturing sector in Seattle began a long, slow decline, and that meant fewer jobs to lure folks to the great Northwest.

However, there were two elements of growth that did occur during those years, and both of them had a profound influence on the builders of Seattle. The first was the ever-increasing use of electricity for lighting, and to power electrical appliances. The majority of new homes were now being wired by electricians, a trade that barely even existed ten years earlier. Though fireplaces were still the primary way of heating a home, electric ranges were taking over as the preferred method for cooking. More and more, electricity was also becoming the preferred way to heat water for the home. New standards had to be decided on regarding placement of lights, switches and outlets. In addition, home designers and builders needed to integrate more closet space into their 'modern' homes in order to store the dizzying array of new electrical conveniences.

The second innovation that gained wide acceptance in this period was the automobile. It was no longer just an oddity or a status symbol for the rich. The introduction of the assembly line for mass production made cars affordable to the masses, and that created a new issue for home builders: where does one park the car? Carports and garages started to become a standard feature in new construction. Some were detached, some were attached to the side of the house, and many were built right in as an integral part of the home.

The automobile also fundamentally changed the way that real estate was developed. Before the advent of the automobile, neighborhoods were built as close as possible to the center of the city, around a retail corridor or next to a rail line. Due to the mobility of the car, neighborhoods could now be developed much further from the city and established retail areas. Over the coming decades, people started to migrate out of the center of downtown Seattle, and the suburbs would house most of the population. ♣

CHAPTER 3

Hanging on Through Dark Days

1929 – 1939

For the first time in their twenty-year history, the Seattle Master Builders Association suffered a decline in membership. President Sam Andersen kept the Association active and alive during the dark days of the Great Depression. In 1932, there were 237,000 foreclosures in the Seattle metro area. Builders were vilified, as there was a surplus of empty, bank-owned houses, even while Hoovervilles were packed. The Association was reduced to a few members, but by 1936, the remaining men were ready to restart recruiting new builder-members. The Master Builders Association moved to Fourth Avenue, where it remained for a decade. In 1933, in an effort to spur lending and homeownership, FDR created the Home Owners' Loan Corporation (HOLC), and for the first time, Seattle Builders were eligible for federal financing. Early adopters included members E. J. Groseclose and Bernard Dahl. The incentives created by the Federal Housing Administration (FHA) had financing options that let developers take out loans on entire subdivisions rather than having to obtain one loan per lot. Tension between the unions and the Association heated up, but the organization remained strong, and was hailed as an example for builders over the rest of the country to follow. By 1939, membership was back up to sixty, and dues were set at 75¢ per month, with an initiation fee of $100.

Photo from PEMCO Webster & Stevens Collection, MOHAI, neg. 1983.10.1538.10

*The Great Depression hit the housing industry hard. By 1933, residential construction had fallen 95 percent nationwide.
However, the advent of federal subsidy programs - such as the Federal Housing Authority – made homebuilding possible again.
The majority of new homes built in Seattle during the 1930s cost less than $2,000, including the lot. Through sheer tenacity
and pride in their profession, the Master Builders Association remained intact during the Depression years. The HOLC
allowed builders to construct entire subdivisions "on spec" as member Al Balch did in View Ridge, pictured here.*

The End of an Era

When Roy Lipscomb was elected President of the Master Builders Association in January of 1929, it looked like the tide of prosperity was about to roll in. The rest of the country had been riding the wave for quite some time, and the new money that was being created in the boom was just starting to hit the Seattle shore. Optimism was high, and the songs of the day showed it in their titles; *When You're Smiling*, *Makin' Whoopee*, *Great Day* and *Happy Days are Here Again.* They were heard emanating from the newest home appliance, the radio. In his inaugural address newly-elected President Herbert Hoover stated: "Ours is a land rich in resources; stimulating in its glorious beauty; filled with millions of happy homes; blessed with comfort and opportunity. In no nation are the institutions of progress more advanced. In no nation are the fruits of accomplishment more secure. In no nation is the government more worthy of respect. No country is more loved by its people. I have no fears for the future of our country. It is bright with hope." Roy Lipscomb, buoyed by the optimism of the nation,

and seeing the wave of prosperity looming on the horizon, advised members to stay the course and make ready for full speed ahead. He was pleased to announce at the June meeting that in the first six months of 1929, members of the Association had developed 146 pieces of property. He asserted that the tipping point had been reached, everything was going to be all right and Seattle would once again be a city of industry – the homebuilding industry.

For a time, it looked as if he might be right. There was money starting to flow into Seattle and there were some significant commercial buildings being constructed downtown. Two of the more notable properties were the Frederick & Nelson building (now the Nordstrom flagship store) and two blocks away their archrival, the Bon Marché, was building their showcase store. On the residential side of things, the Queen Anne neighborhood also showed signs of resurgence. After two years of relative silence, the hills were once again alive with the sound of construction. Several apartment complexes were built during this period including the Glen Eden and the Villa Costella. Despite Lipscomb's attempts to keep the morale up and the positive signs of change, the events of the latter part of 1929 were to dash all hopes for the resuscitation of the region's homebuilding industry.

The Depression Hits

In October 1929, the stock market experienced a panic sell-off. In the course of four days now known as Black Thursday, Black Friday, Black Monday and Black Tuesday, the market lost over $25 billion in value. Eighty years after the fact, and hundreds of books and thesis papers later, the jury is still out over just what caused "The Crash." In essence, it was most likely a confluence of events.

During the years following the First World War, the Federal Reserve Bank kept interest rates low in an effort to encourage growth. The corporations and the small-business owners of the United States, being endowed with an entrepreneurial spirit, seized the opportunity and borrowed lots of money. With this money they developed businesses from Mom-and-Pop shops to department stores; from pharmacies to pharmaceutical companies; from family farms to car dealerships. As the country expanded and its population grew, the demand for more goods and services was met by the creation of these new businesses. The businesses were then able to pay back the loans and the lenders could loan out the money again. Economists considered this a perfect example of the associative relationship of supply and demand.

Unfortunately, perfect examples are often at risk of being contaminated by unknown variables. When companies wanted to grow very large, there weren't many banks that wanted to take on the risk of such large loans. In these cases the companies would go public. This would give those companies a large amount of up-front capital for expansion or innovation or infrastructure. The investors got their returns when the company made a profit at some point in the future. In a sense, it was a bet made by the individual investor that the company would use the money effectively to create a profit. In theory this split the risk amongst thousands of investors, each of whom had no more invested than they could afford, and conversely, no more than they could afford to lose. All they stood to lose (or so they thought) was their initial investment.

Here was where the low interest rate came into play: since there was a lot of excess capital to be found and the capital could be borrowed cheaply (low interest rates), hundreds of non-bank lenders (brokers) were competing against each other to attract the business of investors. In order to attract them, the brokers would offer the investor the option of buying on margin. Buying on margin was basically borrowing money to bet on the stock market. As long as the market continued to rise, and/or the company invested in made a profit, the investor could come out ahead. For a while that happened.

The roar of the Roaring Twenties was the sound of money being made by lots of people. There was a technical revolution going on and there were companies that were using the capital to grow, grow, grow. That decade saw a meteoric rise of the telephone, radio, automobile, business machines, consumer products, broadcasting industry, film industry, airline industry, petroleum industry, the petro-chemical industry, and so many others. Many of today's largest corporations owe their success to those investments; AT&T, Westinghouse, Ford, IBM, Procter & Gamble, NBC, MGM, Standard Oil (today Exxon/Mobil), DuPont and Kodak to name just a few.

Unfortunately no business, industry, country or market can continue to grow forever. In the summer of 1928, the Federal Reserve Bank reacted to a dip in the market by raising interest rates, and halting loans to banks and brokers who were lending on margin. It was felt by policy-makers that this would be enough to discourage investors from reckessly borrowing based on an assumption of never-ending growth. What they didn't seem to anticipate was the irrational behavior of the investing public. Everyone from President Hoover on down was heralding the dawn of a new age with the eradication of poverty and a better life for all. Countless investors became caught up in all the hype and continued to pour money into the market, hoping to become the next millionaire.

At this point, the brokers, who were making huge profits from the interest on margin selling, could no longer borrow money from the Federal Reserve. They then turned to private investment banks. Since the brokers were now paying a higher interest rate, they had to do something to keep their profits up and they chose to borrow on the margin. They were now borrowing more money than they had, in a gamble that their borrowers would not default. To make matters even more precarious, private banks were not required to have assets on hand equal to the loans they made. They were therefore lending more money than they had, once again gambling that their borrowers would not default.

On that fateful Thursday, October 24, 1929, something happened that caused the investors to sell. The number of trades on that day shattered the record. 12.9 million shares were traded on

IN MEMORY
SAM ANDERSEN
President, Seattle Master Builders, *1933-1935*

This picture was taken at an "Old Timers Dinner" on the night of April 2, 1959, honoring the men in the photo below. Minutes after this photo was taken, before the evening's entertainment could get under way, Sam Andersen fell unconscious and died. Apocryphally, those who knew him said, "He wouldn't have wanted it any other way."

Andersen was widely credited with keeping the Master Builders Association alive and strong even during the years of the Great Depression. He advocated for affordable housing and was a peacemaker between builders and the Associated General Contractors.

Pictured below are, top row, from left: Lew Hykes, Lyle Henton and Cecil R. Beal.
Bottom row, from left: Evro Beckett, Harry Hudson, Sam Andersen and Charles Arensberg..

that single day. When large volumes of stock are traded it tends to bring the value down, and the market value fell by 3.2 percent that day. This got the attention of the inexperienced investors. When they saw the headlines in the papers over the course of that weekend, they saw for the first time that all of their investments could disappear in the blink of an eye. On Monday morning, orders to sell came in from all corners of the country, and indeed from all corners of the world. Now people were forced to sell, just to recover any money they could to pay off their debts. By Black Tuesday, October 29, 1929 the panic had spread. Legend has it that the starting bell of the trading day could not be heard over the floor traders' shouts of "sell, sell, sell." The record volume set on Thursday was handily beaten again as 16.4 million stocks were traded on Black Tuesday. It took the stock tickers two-and-a-half hours after the closing bell to catch up. In the course of those four days, the value of the stock market had dropped forty percent, at a loss of over $20 billion.

Now the dominoes started to fall. The folks who had invested borrowed money were now on the hook. Thousands of people lost their life savings and were forced to declare bankruptcy. The brokers who had also borrowed the money on margin were unable to recoup their losses

and they had to declare bankruptcy. The private banks that were supplying the loans to the brokers didn't have sufficient capital to cover their liabilities, and they, too, were forced into bankruptcy. In 1930, over 700 banks failed as a direct result of the Crash of 1929. In the previous ten years, the average was seventy banks per year.

Builders in the Depression

The effect of the crash hit the East Coast immediately, especially in New York where the stock market was the major driver of the economy. It took a little longer for the shockwave to hit Seattle, and in 1930 there were still a fair number of construction projects being built. The funding had been secured before the crash. In 1930, A. J. Allen was elected President of the Master Builders Association and served a one-year term. Though there was some sporadic building in the first half of the year, by April it had become clear that Seattle wouldn't be immune

Photo from PEMCO Webster & Stevens Collection, MOHAI, neg. 1983.10.10788

to the national slump as the unemployment level rose to eleven percent.

As bad as the Crash of 1929 was, it was not the sole cause of the Great Depression. In 1930, the American Midwest was hit by a massive drought. The breadbasket of the United States was turned into a wasteland known as the "Dustbowl." Thousands of farmers lost all their crops and were unable to make their mortgage payments. With the double whammy of the crash and the mortgage defaults, banks started to fail at an alarming rate. In 1931 there were 2,293 bank failures, in 1932 there were 1,493, and in 1933 there were 4,000 banks that went bust.[1]

In an economic climate that severe, capital was almost impossible to come by. Nobody had any money to spend; nobody had any money to lend. Without a ready access to credit, businesses small and large were now being squeezed. They could not make their payrolls and consequently laid off tens of thousands of workers. These businesses could also no longer afford to make any repairs or improvements, causing a trickle-down effect on mechanics and manufacturers. The unemployment rate shot up to 25 percent and hovered there for three years.

With the unemployment rate so high, many homeowners used up whatever savings they had left in the bank or under the mattress. In a short time they were no longer able to pay their mortgages, and they were foreclosed upon. By the peak of the Depression in 1933, there were 1,000 homes going into foreclosure every single day.

The builders who were fortunate enough to keep their businesses and homes were vilified by the former homeowners who had been put out of theirs. While thousands of bank-owned homes stood empty, thousands of homeless were forced to live on the streets.

All across America shantytowns called Hoovervilles (after President Hoover) began appearing. Rightly or wrongly, Hoover was credited with the downfall of the United States economy, and the Hoovervilles were there as a testament to his failure and a protest to his government. Seattle was home to at least three Hoovervilles. The largest of them was located down on the reclaimed tide flats (now the home of Safeco Field and Terminal 46). This particular Hooverville was home to some 1,000 dwellers. They lived in ramshackle structures built from scavenged materials. Some were quite tidy and included amenities such as flowerboxes. Others were assembled out of found or stolen lumber, flattened tin cans, old sails, driftwood and

even rusted hulks of abandoned automobiles. The denizens of Hooverville took great pride in thumbing their noses at the federal and local governments, and had their own governing council to deal with the issues within the camp. The largest Hooverville, on First Avenue, even had its own Mayor, the Honorable Jesse Jackson.

Captain C. S. Sapp was Association President during 1931 and 1932, years when the building industry was in a total standstill. The members still went to meetings though, as evidenced by a stand taken by the Master Builders when they opposed a proposed city ordinance to license and regulate the building contractors.

During the election year of 1932, Herbert Hoover finally made an attempt to alleviate some of the suffering. He lobbied Congress, and that July they approved the Federal Home Loan Bank Act. These twelve banks were set up in various

There were three "Hoovervilles" in Seattle in the 1930s. This one, constructed on the tideflats west of First Avenue, was the largest, with "streets," a post office and a mayor. The quality and size of the residences varied widely; homes in the photo to the right seem to be relatively well-built. Opposite, a Hooverville is seen in the shadow of Seattle's downtown area.

regions of the nation. They were chartered with supplying money to the beleaguered lending institutions, banks and insurance companies in hopes that they would start to lend again. Unfortunately, the lending institutions just used the money to bolster their bottom line and didn't make any loans to the public. Hoover lost the 1932 election. Franklin Delano Roosevelt won by a landslide with his promise of a New Deal for America.

HOLC, FHA & Federal Assistance

In 1933, Sam Andersen became President of the Builders Association. Soon after, on March 4, President Roosevelt was sworn in. Andersen was elected with nothing left to preside over but the few remaining members who showed up to the meetings. Roosevelt, however, hit the ground running and by June had come up with a program to spur the lenders into lending again. The Home Owners' Loan Act sailed through Congress, and dedicated over $2 Billion to the Home Owners' Loan Corporation (HOLC). The HOLC was intended to come to the rescue of the homeowners who were still in their homes, but struggling to make their payments. It offered financing up to eighty percent of a home's value with an upper limit of $14,000. Since it was aimed as a boost to the lower middle class, the top fifty percent of the loan applicants were passed over in favor of the lower fifty percent. This ensured that the people most at risk of losing their homes were the ones who received the benefit. Another revolutionary innovation was the ability to borrow at a much lower percentage rate (five percent instead of eight percent) and to spread the payments out over 25 years as opposed to the old standard of ten years. Although this plan did slow the number of foreclosures down to a trickle, it did almost nothing to encourage the building of new homes. It did set a new precedent, though, by giving favor to single-family homes outside of major cities. This, along with the advent of better roads and automobiles, would set in motion the age of the suburbs.

In June 1934, with the explicit intent of reviving the homebuilding industry, Roosevelt unveiled the National Housing Act. It created a new governmental agency that endures to this day: the Federal Housing Administration (FHA). This agency helped to restart the market by guaranteeing insurance on home loans, creating the thirty-year, fully-amortized loan (no balloon payment at the end of the loan) and, most importantly to the Master Builders, allowed developers to borrow money for tracts of land as opposed to individual lots. Previously builders had to self finance, or take out a loan for each lot. Now they were free to purchase property and develop a coordinated new community on speculation. The FHA financing program was lauded by one Master Builder member as "the largest single improvement in the homebuilding industry."

Reviving the Organization

Although the situation in Seattle did not improve immediately, it did spur Sam Andersen into negotiating with the AGC to come to an agreement over lowering the wage scale and limiting the workweek to thirty hours. By bringing the cost structure down it was hoped that more projects could be started. Over the course of the next two years, Sam Andersen

remained the President of the Association, as the homebuilding industry started to creep slowly back into production.

By the end of 1936, the worst of the Depression was over. The economy was regaining some of its footing, the banks that were left were healthier (and federally insured) and people were starting to get back to work. This rebirth held true for the Seattle Builders as well, and in November, seven of the young guns met with Andersen at the old Gas Company Building on Fourth Avenue to plan a new future for the Master Builders Association. Those at the meeting were: (Current President) Sam Andersen, E .J. Groseclose, C. R. Beal, Harry Shaffer, Bernard Dahl, E. M. Buchholtz, James A. Acteson and Norman McKinnon. The group decided to reorganize, rewrite their charter and re-incorporate with the State of Washington as the Master Builders Association.

Within the new charter were the following articles:

> To promote and encourage integrity and honesty in all building contracts both written and verbal and to promote good will and honor in all dealings with those from whom purchases are made, to those employed and to those for whom contracts to build or sell are made.

and:

> ...to study all proposed legislation affecting the building craft, to study its

The Seattle Master Builders Association rented offices in this block beginning in 1936 and continuing through 1947. This building, at 1908 Fourth Avenue, invited visitors to learn more about how houses were constructed using small-scale model homes.

fairness and justice and in cooperation with the members of the building trades to serve the best interests of the craft and the community.

In December 1936, they filed the new articles of incorporation, and on February 23, 1937, the incorporation was finalized. In the meantime, E. J. Groseclose had been elected the new President of the Association. One of his first controversies was to settle "once and for all" whether the Master Builders would commit once again to being a union-only organization and therefore only hire union subcontractors. The committee agreed that once the vote was held, there would be "no halfway measures:" a majority vote would obligate the entire organization to follow suit with no exceptions. The vote was held, and the Master Builders Association agreed sixteen-to-one to go union only. Harry Bush, one of the union representatives who helped win the concession, went on to become a powerful organizer on behalf of the "living wage" campaign on the East Coast.

By the end of 1937, the Master Builders were back in the swing of things, and were responsible for 85 percent of all the construction in the Seattle area. The Seattle Construction League (the local affiliate of the AGC) smelled money in the air again, and sought to join forces with the newly reformed Master Builders. The effort was struck down later, though, when another union, the Building Trades Council, threatened to void its contract with the Master Builders Association if the merger went through.

In June 1938, the Association was up to about sixty members, and there was a need for a secretary to keep up with all that was going on. The builders were now too busy building to be sitting around filling out forms. J. Ray Taylor was hired on at a monthly salary of $150. He got right to work and organized an advertising campaign that ran on billboards and in the Seattle *Post-Intelligencer* promoting the new mortgages made available by the FHA.

The turnaround in the Seattle homebuilding industry was such a resounding success that the United States Secretary of the Interior, Harold L. Ickes (a surprise guest at the Seattle Builders Dinner held at the Washington Athletic Club), announced that "if cities over the nation would show the same spirit – adopt the same forward strides in building that Seattle has now set in motion – it will not only end this Depression, but all other Depressions."

Profile

STANLEY LONG

ACHIEVEMENTS:
President, Master Builders, *1926*
Director, NAHB

Stanley Long, who succeeded Edward Merritt as president of the Seattle Master Builders in 1926, started building houses in Seattle in 1906 and continued for more than fifty years. He retired just three years before his death in 1959. In 1924, Long had joined with fellow builders Merritt and Gardner J. Gwinn to revive the local Master Builders Association after its predecessor was swallowed by the Associated General Contractors of America (AGC). While not as publicly well-known as Merritt or Gwinn, Long was, if anything, even more active in the civic affairs of his adopted city.

Long was born in Rossburg, Ohio, and attended law school in Chicago before moving to Seattle in the early 1900s. There is no record of his practicing law in Seattle, and it seems that he was quick to see the growth potential of the local housing industry. After that first house in 1906, he went on develop several of the residential neighborhoods on Seattle's First Hill. By 1914 he was doing business as the "Long Building Company, Architects and Engineers."

Bungalow-style homes had been popularized by Edward Merritt, Jud Yoho, and others, and Long followed the trend. A large, lovely bungalow built by his company was prominently featured in the January 17, 1914, edition of *Pacific Builder and Engineer* magazine.

During his lengthy career, Long was active in nearly all of Seattle's leading civic organizations. He joined the Seattle Rotary Club shortly after its inception in 1909 as only the fourth such club in the nation, and became its fourth president in 1913. Under Long's leadership the Rotary raised $25,000 for Seattle Children's Orthopedic Hospital, He remained active in the organization his entire life. Decades later, Long worked with other past presidents and helped compile the history of the Seattle Rotary's first fifty years, which was published in 1959, the year of his death.

Among other accomplishments, Long also sat on the Board of Directors of the Seattle Chamber of Commerce, was active in the Municipal League, served as a trustee of Seattle General Hospital, and was a member of the Rainier Club and the Masons. In addition to his work with the Seattle Master Builders Association, he was a fifty-year member and former director of the National Association of Homebuilders, and in 1958 was honored for his long service with the award of a pair of golden cufflinks.

F. R. "Dick" McAbee, Seattle Master Builders President in 1944-1945, had fond recollections of Stanley Long: "He was a great gentleman. Stanley would walk into a room and you could feel his presence. Had a word to say to everybody. And he knew the business. By the fifties, he'd about retired. But he came to every meeting. Stanley cared about the industry, where it was going, and what he could do to help it. Yes, he was a great gentleman."

A long-time resident of Queen Anne, Stanley Long died on August 15, 1959.

Cooperation and Civic Assistance

One new concept was introduced into the reformation charter — civic assistance. For the first time, the Association had as one of its core values "To promote, encourage and develop the social, educational, charitable and community life and activities in the City of Seattle, Washington, and to encourage a more active interest in the civic welfare of the community by the building trade and professions." It was a change from the previous philosophy of doing things for the public good to a more actionable philosophy of doing good things for the public. In the future this new ideology would take the form of such programs as Rampathon, but in the early days it was seen more as a tolerance of new ideas. For example: the Wagner-Steagall Act, passed in 1937, was the last of the New Deal efforts to provide funding for the housing industry. Its mandate was "to provide financial assistance to the States and political subdivisions thereof for the elimination of unsafe and insanitary housing conditions, for the eradication of slums, for the provision of decent, safe, and sanitary dwellings for families of low income, and for the reduction of unemployment and the stimulation of business activity." The problem was, to achieve that goal, the Wagner-Steagall Act would create a new government-run building program that would be in direct competition with the Master Builders.

In Seattle, that program became the Seattle Housing Authority (SHA). In days past, that direct competition would have been fought strongly by the Association, but in their new spirit of cooperation they decided to approve the SHA program. They chose to see it as a complement to their own building activities rather than as a threat. President E. J. Groseclose commented in 1939: "The federal government bases its hopes of a business revival on the building industry. Our association of sixty-five members has built sixty-five million dollars' worth of new residences here. We are proud of the part our city is taking in the building revival." ❖

CHAPTER 4

Prosperity and Pride

1939 – 1945

In *1939, with economic recovery on the horizon, the Seattle Master Builders Association partnered with Bill McDonald and the Seattle* Post Intelligencer *newspaper to create the Seattle Home Show. In 1942, the National Association of Home Builders (NAHB) was formed, and Seattle rejected affiliation after almost a year of consideration, but no record remains why the decision was made. The Association worked closely with the National Housing Administration to construct "priority" housing for the Boeing war workforce. During the war-rationing years, a total of 10,882 homes were constructed, most by Master Builders Association members. In 1945, the Association retracted its earlier decision and joined NAHB. The Association grew to over 200 members, but there was tension in the ranks.*

(opposite) *The First Seattle Home Show in 1939 reinvigorated the public's confidence in builders.*

The "X-ray House" featured at the 1941 Seattle Home Show.

The visitors to the Seattle Home Show were permitted to inspect construction methods. In addition to the price posted on the sign in the front, the pillar next to the display lists the names of active members of Seattle Master Builders.

The Birth of the Home Show

The nation was recovering from the Great Depression. Consumer confidence was low. Franklin Delano Roosevelt was trying to get the economy moving. Businesses were encouraged to start advertising once again. The strongest avenue was the local newspapers. The New Deal was going to local papers and builder associations helping them form work shows.

In Ithaca, Ohio, a young man who was attending the University of Dayton was asked by his father to help out in the family business. The McDonald family was organizing "work shows" all across the country, and the young man, W. G. "Bill" McDonald, jumped right in. His first target was Seattle. The first Annual National Housing Exposition, as the work show came to be called, was planned as a partnership co-sponsored by the Seattle *Post-Intelligencer* and the Seattle Master Builders Association. McDonald was its managing partner. The newspaper would promote the show and the Builders Association would be a source of exhibitors. The promotion efforts agreed that although perhaps the name they had chosen was long and a "bit fancy," the National Housing Exposition of the Pacific Northwest promised displays and demonstrations that would exemplify gracious living. The front-page editorial that ran in the *Post-Intelligencer* espoused, "Seattle and its metropolitan area are definitely launched upon a building boom. This region has awakened to the fact there is a serious housing shortage and steps are being taken to remedy it."

The organizers chose Seattle's Civic Auditorium for the venue. In addition to the 75 exhibits, the first show had a full-size, fully assembled, low-cost home completely furnished by Frederick & Nelson. There was also mortgage and loan information from the Federal Housing Authority. The name was quickly shortened to the vernacular, the Seattle Home Show.

The show's primary goal was to educate consumers about housing options that were available to them, from electric appliances to mortgages. As backed by the New Deal, the national administration supported local shows. First Lady Eleanor Roosevelt arrived in Seattle to cut the ribbon on opening day. Even her husband visited, and Home Show visitors got to see FDR pound a nail into the show's model house.

SEATTLE HOME SHOW

Bill McDonald, Founder, 1939
Mike Kalian, Managing Director

To find the longest-running, largest home show in the nation, look no further than Seattle. Since its inception in 1939 as a bridge between builders, remodelers and the public, the Seattle Home Show has energized the local building industry through exciting shows, programs, and its well-earned reputation for distinction, innovation, and community service. Held each spring, the show provides an opportunity for builders to promote their products and designs to manufacturers, suppliers, professional buyers, and prospective homeowners. It is an opportunity for attendees to witness many new household technologies, and it offers a "one-stop shopping" adventure in home improvement.

The Seattle Home Show is the only show in the nation that has been family-owned and run for four generations. Mike Kalian, the current Managing Director, runs the show with the assistance of his daughter, Tara, who serves as Sales Director. Kalian remarks that a passion for the show is "in the blood." The Master Builders have always been one of the show's sponsors, and both the Association and the show's producers benefit from a mutually productive relationship. Kalian credits the longevity of this partnership for the huge credibility of the show and its continued success. Mike says, "I think the relationships that we've had with the respective executive officers and the presidents have been phenomenal. They are relationships that we value tremendously."

Recent shows reflect local and global interest in environmental preservation such as one in 2009 which used the catch phrase, "Get Your Green On." Exhibitors demontrated how they contribute to environmental stewardship, even if it was simple as recycling glass or paper, and shared how their products promote green living. On Idea Street at the show, participants built a community of model homes in a number of contrasting styles, constructed, decorated, and landscaped in just five days; several directly reflected their emphasis on living small, using water conservation features in Northwest-native plant garden areas. This Living Green design and construction philosophy is in line with the Association's Built Green program, which strives to provide housing that is environmentally friendly, cost effective over long-term use, and affordable for the homebuyer. The model homes on Idea Street not only *look* good; they *do* good.

For fifteen years, the show has donated a model home from the show to charitable organizations. Kalian explains these donated houses include foundations, permits, heating systems, and construction on a given site. In 1994, the show's producers met with then-President Bill Clinton, who awarded the Seattle Home Show organizers the Presidential Seal for their generous work.

When asked in which direction he envisions the already successful show moving, Mike Kalian emphasizes a focus on making sure the show sustains and exceeds its high standards of quality. Built on the groundwork of founder Bill McDonald's original ideas, four generations of family ownership and involvement, and a solid partnership with the Master Builders, the Seattle Home Show's tradition of excellence continues to raise the bar in the building trade show world.

The Home Show partnered with the Master Builders Association to find exhibitors for the annual show. This application for Association membership includes a Home Show exhibition space. Archie Iverson, whose application is below, joined in 1949. Archie would become Association president in 1961 and 1962, and his wife Evelyn became very active in the Women's Auxiliary.

APPLICATION FOR MEMBERSHIP
SEATTLE MASTER BUILDERS
Master Builders' Home Exhibit

1908 FOURTH AVENUE • SEATTLE, WASH. • TELEPHONE SENECA 1866

☒ BUILDER MEMBER—$25.00 Entry Fee and $2.00 a Month.　　☐ ASSOCIATE MEMBER—with Display Sign, $5.00 a Month.

☐ ASSOCIATE MEMBER—$15.00 Entry Fee and $2.00 a Month.　　☐ ASSOCIATE MEMBER—with Exhibit Space, $12.50 a Month.

Check in square type of membership desired

MEMBERSHIPS ARE SUBJECT TO PROVISIONS OF THE CONSTITUTION, BY-LAWS AND CODE OF ETHICS

ENTRY FEE MUST ACCOMPANY APPLICATION
DUES PAYABLE MONTHLY IN ADVANCE

Firm Name **Archie E. Iverson**　　Address **1919 West 85th St.**

Type of Business **Builder**　　Business Phone **HE. 5580**

Proposed by **Lars Boyd**　　Date **April 6 1949**　　Signature **Archie E. Iverson**

Check for $25 accompanied this 2nd check for $25.00 paid

The exposition ran for seven days, closing on April 2, 1939. The following day, the Seattle *Post-Intelligencer* reported a total attendance of 77,540, a turnout that "set a new record for attendance at a public event in the Pacific Northwest."

This successful event and partnership between the Master Builders and the newspaper continued the next year and the shortened name stuck: the Seattle Home Show had begun.

The region was critically aware of the housing shortage and this was one of the first steps to launching a building boom. The show was a new way to connect the building industry and the public. The building industry could showcase modernizations and advancements in methods and materials available so consumers could increase their awareness and knowledge. Likewise, Master Builders and other exhibitors could talk directly to customers and potential buyers to educate themselves about the public's needs.

In 1941, a new effort was put forth to educate the public. For the last two years, the star attraction at the show had been a model home constructed by a Seattle Master Builders Association member. This year the display went further, and the Master Builders built the "X–Ray House." With elimination of one of exterior wall, the public could inspect the interior construction,

Yesler Terrace during construction

*Demolition of existing structures would make possible
the first federally-funded housing project in Seattle.*

*The affordable housing project used wood-frame
construction. This was the first government-
subsidized project to be racially integrated.*

see how wires were run and ask an Association member questions about the hows and whys of the construction. The sign in front of the model house read, "A Master Builder will build this house on your lot for $2,750.00." The building industry and the Association had survived the Great Depression. Professional pride was high.

Yesler Terrace

Even as World War II was on the horizon, people all over the United States saw the light at the end of the Depression's dark tunnel, and proclaimed 1939 as the year that the country and Seattle got back on the move. In part to ensure that the blight of Hoovervilles never recurred, the Seattle Housing Authority was created to house residents across the city, regardless of their income or race.

The United States Housing Act of 1937 was the first federal legislation to set public housing policy, and the Seattle Housing Authority was the first agency in Washington to be created under the Act. The country wanted to support the creation of safe and affordable housing for people with low incomes. It was hoped that this would in turn help disadvantaged people reach a level of stability and self-sufficiency. Under the Department of the Interior's jurisdiction, the National Housing Act allocated funds for state agencies around the country. The funds could be used to either repair or clear slums by replacing them with new construction. $8 million was immediately available.

In 1939, Washington state passed the Housing Authorities Law and the Housing Cooperation Law. The Seattle City Council passed a resolution to establish the Seattle Housing Authority, which immediately received the first of the federal funding in the state – $3 million to develop Yesler Terrace on First Hill.

Seattle Master Builders were at first skeptical. Was the government going into competition with private builders? They shelved their mistrust and looked for answers, and once the program was better understood, they knew the federal program would help complement their activities. E. J. Groseclose, Association President, 1936-1939, promoted the partnership, "The federal government bases its hopes of a business revival on the building industry. Our Association of sixty-five members has built sixty-five million dollars' worth of new residences here. We are proud of the part our city is taking in the building revival."

For the first project, the Seattle Housing Authority would revitalize the 22-acre area known as "Profanity Hill" – so-called because lawyers cursed at having to climb the steep grade to the site of the courthouse (present-day Harborview Medical Center). To construct Yesler Terrace, the Housing Authority turned to the Master Builders Association, and members stepped up to the challenge. The project took until 1941 to complete and was not only the first housing project in the nation completed with wood-frame construction, it was also the first to be racially integrated. The government subsidy allowed the construction to be completed at market rates, even while guaranteeing the prospective residents artificially low rents.[1]

The first step was to raze the substandard housing that had been sloppily erected by loggers and transients who wanted to live on the Skid Road. Then, the Housing Authority constructed 700 units in 93 framed buildings, which cost $2,500 each. As soon as it was completed, 3,000 people moved in, and Yesler Terrace became one of the nation's and Seattle's most successful housing projects. The project served residents well, and the first major renovations that had to be done were started in 2008.

Housing for the War

President Roosevelt knew that the economy had still not fully recovered from the Great Depression when Germany invaded Poland on September 1, 1939, and he declared that the U.S. would stay neutral. That year, F. R. "Dick" McAbee, who would become President of the Association in 1944, was starting his construction company after working as a carpenter. He remembered the Salvation Army work camps of the Depression era, "It was possible for a person to forget what family life was like. The low-cost housing rebound of the late 1930s provided many people with their first permanent roof. But by late 1939, the prospect of conscription, wondering whether or not you were going to be drafted into military service, made a lot of prospective buyers think again. The market went dead."

Great Britain declared war on Germany immediately after their invasion of Poland. With the outbreak of war in the European theater, Boeing shifted into high gear supplying airplanes to the British Royal Air Force. In 1940, Boeing employed 4,000 workers. With the demand for

Boeing's B-17 bomber so high, they were forced to increase their staffing to 10,000 by July 1941. By the time the United States entered the war in December 1941, after the Japanese bombed Pearl Harbor, that number had grown again to 30,000 workers.

The rest of the Washington State manufacturing was keeping up with the Boeing pace. There was a steady need to construct mills and factories to support not only Boeing, but also other wartime needs. The constant military requirements for supplies forced the conservation of materials and labor. Consequently, the military's priorities drove industrial production. In addition, many controls were put on the economy. Price controls were imposed on most products and monitored by the government's Office of Price Control.

Unemployment was virtually ended in the United States with the beginning of World War II. Production needs were rising even as men were leaving the workforce to join combat. Women were called to factories to do "men's work" and all citizens were called on to conserve and do without. Those remaining at home grew Victory Gardens and sent tires to local military offices to be reused as rubber in the War effort. With the war jobs, government took a greater role in wage controls. By 1944, nearly every employed person was paying federal income taxes, compared to only ten percent of workers doing so in 1940.

The Second World War meant unprecedented growth to the city of Seattle. With the stringent controls on materials and rationing of everything from butter to gasoline, the government was soon to recognize that housing should be considered

a "war need." Association member Dick McAbee became actively involved with the Seattle Housing Authority to get materials allocated to home construction. He worked alongside J. Ray Taylor, who had been hired as the Association's first full-time Executive Secretary in 1939. He kept the position through 1942. Boeing's need for workers, and those workers' need for housing, ensured that Seattle received building materials that weren't used in war production.

Federal regulations placed limits on new house construction with a quota system. Only new housing that was necessary to accommodate war workers was approved. These regulations stipulated the size of new houses, as well as limiting building materials and setting the maximum selling price.

Seattle builders met these requirements by using "operative building" methods. The pre-approved materials and restrictions allowed for residential neighborhoods to be developed with speed. The result was also the look-alike homes: all 800-square-feet, with a full basement and selling for $6,000. Unlike custom-built homes, now hundreds of homes could be built at one time. The focus turned away from building a house on speculation because prices were so competitive that it was difficult to make any profit.

During the war, it was difficult to make money from selling houses, but there was an alternative method. The government war housing contract stipulated that each developer had to rent one third of the units he constructed. This forced Seattle builders into retaining ownership and taking on management of a third of their properties. Under this rule, the more established builders were able to accumulate extensive real estate holdings during the war years.

Seattle builders tackled the stipulations in three distinct ways. Some purchased large tracts of undeveloped land inside the city limits, such as large parts of Magnolia and West Seattle which already had streets and other infrastructure. Others acquired moderately priced lots usually from the King County Land Department. The lots were close enough to each other to permit operative building. Ballard, First Hill, Capitol Hill, Mt. Baker, and Rainier Valley all benefited from this practice. Also, the construction of housing projects offered builders an opportunity to design a single development within, yet differentiated from, the surrounding neighborhood. Between September 1941 and October 1945, of the 10,882 privately financed homes, more than 5,600 of them were constructed using operative building techniques.

Member Al Balch developed a million-dollar project in the Wedgwood district with homes that sold for $5,000 apiece. Balch had developed View Ridge, and his wife, Edith had always hated the name. Balch promised her that she could name his next project, and when given the opportunity, she chose, "Wedgwood, after my China pattern."[2]

Western Construction Company completed construction on Holly Park in Beacon Hill to house war workers and veterans. The Seattle Housing Authority worked with the Master Builders Association to complete the Duwamish Bend housing project in Georgetown, which became public housing for women employed at Boeing.

The Seattle area was providing jobs for many wartime industries, while other regions of the country were experiencing severe labor shortages. These jobs were also attractive to a larger part of the workforce – hiring decisions were made without discrimination to people of color or women. The region was flooded with about 250,000 people lured by the promise of high-paying jobs and steady work. By 1944, at the peak of the war, Boeing was the area's largest employer: 50,000 workers and total sales of over $600 million.

Photo courtesy MOHAI, neg. 4221

This house in Wedgwood was part of speculative residential development West of 35th Avenue NE at East 81st Street. It was developed by Albert Balch. By 1943, this neighborhood consisted of two hundred homes. Balch was concerned with coupling his designs to preserve the trees and natural growth.

Albert Balch purchased the land from the Jesuits, who decided to relocate Seattle University to another site. The sale price of the forty acres was only $22,500, barely a third of what they had paid for the land in 1929.

AXEL THORNBERG

ACHIEVEMENTS:
President, Seattle Builders & Contractors, *195*

A young Swedish painter moved to Seattle in 1919. After marrying, he and his wife began to buy lots and build on them. That was the beginning of Thornberg Construction, which continued to build quality homes for over fifty years.

Axel managed to keep the company vital through the Depression by building brick, single-family homes primarily in West Seattle. Then in 1954, after his son Harry graduated from the University of Washington, he joined his father in Thornberg Construction. The company moved into the apartment and duplex market.

When the Boeing crunch devastated the market in the 1970s, Thornberg expanded into remodeling. Harry and Axel learned that home building is a changeable business, but whether remodeling or new construction, the company motto remained "Thornberg-built means quality."

When the schism which split the Master Builders Association into two occurred, Axel Thornberg was one of the builders leading the charge out the door. Thornberg was very frustrated that some "builders" who'd never swung a hammer, who couldn't read

plans any more than they could read Japanese, were taking leadership roles in the organization. He was a so-called "Swedish builder," because, first off, he was Swedish, but also because he had a stereotypically Nordic work ethic. He was remembered by Joe Martineau as a "tremendous gentleman, he was really good at what he did."

Axel served as the President of the Seattle Builders and Contractors in 1953, and twenty years later, in 1973, his son Harry followed in his footsteps, taking the presidency of Seattle Master Builders. Harry's presidency marked the first time a second-generation builder had ascended to a leadership role in the Association.

Harry, like his father, was very active in assisting young builders. Byron Vadset recognized that Thornberg helped him many times. Harry would inquire how young Byron was doing, and ask if he was busy, then give him a couple of leads. "Harry was around for a long, long time and I used to pick Harry's brain whenever I could. We'd share stories, and have you ever seen this or this happen. It's quite nice to know you're not the only person that may have the same problems out there."

Though the end of the war wouldn't come until 1945, Master Builders President H. E. Forsman worked to get ahead of the curve with W. Thomas Conran, Chairman of the Post-War Planning Committee. Together they passed a resolution for the Association on June 23, 1943, which began: "In the waste of war, foundations should be laid for the permanency of the peace to come."

The resolution further recognized that the Federal Housing Administration had encouraged and promoted homeownership, the foundation of the nation, and aided over half a million families to be able to own their own home. Credit was given to Congress for creating the Housing Administration. The resolution pointed to the Housing Administration's ability to be self-supporting and the need for it to continue in the post-war period. "A large-scale nationwide homebuilding program will be an essential means of providing employment for, and aiding in the rehabilitation of, demobilized members of our armed forces in the post-war period, and of the re-employment of millions of men now engaged in supplying the materials of war."

The resolution assured the United States Congress that "the nation's builders, contractors, manufacturers, distributors and dealers in building materials, together with financial and

Highpoint, located in West Seattle, was the third public housing project built in the 1940s. It contributed 716 affordable housing units for ownership and rental.

mortgage institutions, are and will be ready, able and willing to undertake with private funds the tremendous nationwide, post-war homebuilding program."

The National Housing Act, while administered by the Federal Housing Administration, did not require the use of government funds. The Master Builders' resolution urged Congress to "take whatever steps are necessary to assure, not only the present, but increased operations of the Federal Housing Administration by providing for such amendments as may be needed, to the National Housing Act." They proposed more liberal financing and eliminating the maximum amount on mortgages under Title 11. The petition was for the Federal Housing Administration to be separated from the National Housing Agency, answering directly to Congress. Additionally, those agencies with authority to restrict housing during the war should be "completely eliminated."

In 1944, Dick McAbee was elected as the Seattle Master Builders Association President. He served for two terms, and saw the Association get builders back to work after the war ended in August 1945.

Yesler Terrace and other housing projects were built using wood frame construction. Here a painter mixes paint on-site using white lead; a common paint ingredient later found to be toxic.

Joining the National Association

In 1942, the National Association of Home Builders was formed when a group of builders decided that it was no longer in their best interests to be a part of the National Association of Real Estate Boards (Now the National Realtors® Association). It would take until 1945 for the Seattle Association to join with the National Association and it continued to be a very controversial decision for the local members.

The National Association recognized the need for builders to speak with one voice during the war. To guarantee that end, its Board of Directors would be elected by each local Home Builders Association, and the National Association would work through committees where every member would have an opportunity to share ideas. Its national officers would be elected each year by the Board of Directors, and include twenty Regional Vice Presidents.

The number of founding members was relatively small – about 700 men, all of whom were homebuilders. By 1949, the Association had grown to include over 14,000 members from more than 120 local chapters. The post-war housing boom proved the need for builders to have a

64

collective representation and a means to work out common problems together.

As Dick McAbee stepped down as President at the end of 1945, he was proud that the local Association had chosen to join forces with the NAHB. He was also proud of the growth in membership – in 1946, there were 200 member companies – but there was trouble on the horizon. 1946 President Cliff Mortenson had his work cut out for him in holding the Association together.

The discussion on whether or not to join the National Association centered on the need many builders saw to join in the national conversation about financing and federal housing programs. Some builders believed that there were enough local problems, so the Seattle Association should stay clear of national affairs. Others realized that it was essential to be involved nationally. Should the Seattle Master Builders Association focus their energy and resources locally or have a say in the making of law?

Dick McAbee promoted joining the National Association. "The NAHB carried quite a wallop even then. They worked with the House, the Senate, the President. It's a very big, very influential organization that has added a great deal of strength to the homebuilding industry." He diminished the fight, saying, "Some of us wanted to join. Some didn't."

One policy of the National Association drove the local Association members even further from consensus. NAHB believed that only men who worked with tools should be considered eligible for membership in their local homebuilding association. That would leave out successful businessmen who were members of the Seattle Association whose expertise came from related industries, such as those trained in mortgage banking, real estate and law. ♣

National Association of Home Builders

of the United States

Charter

Know All Men by these Presents that:

Seattle Master Builders Association

has qualified with the Board of Directors and has been accepted as an

Affiliated Local Association

In Witness Whereof, The National Association of Home Builders of the United States has caused these presents to be signed in its behalf by its President, attested by its Secretary and its corporate seal to be hereto affixed on this 28th day of September, 1944.

Attest:

_____
Corporate Secretary

_____
President

CHAPTER 5

Growing Pains

1945 – 1955

In the post-war era, there was a building boom, fueled by the G.I. Bill and the beginnings of the Baby Boom. Veterans and their families needed to be housed, and inflation was skyrocketing. Many smaller builders couldn't keep up with rising material costs. By 1949, the tension which started brewing upon joining NAHB came to a head. One faction maintained that all members should be carpenter-builders, others wanted to extend membership to associated industries, and the Seattle Builders & Contractors split off from the Seattle Master Builders Association. Suburbanization had reached a fever pitch and the automobile enabled construction ever farther from the city center. Members from both associations were instrumental in the creation of subdivisions all over the region. The Association worked closely with NAHB to revise federal housing packages. The Association co-sponsored (with the United Cerebral Palsy Spastic Childrens Clinic) the first Parade of Homes.

*The Seattle Builders & Contractors Association broke away from
the Seattle Master Builders, and they also broke land on 170 Mercer
Street. They would move into their new building in 1956.*

The Great Schism

After the end of World War II in August 1945, Boeing's Seattle employment dropped from over 40,000 to 11,000, and the company's sales dropped over $600 million. Seattle's economy had become dependent on supporting the aerospace industry and fears mounted that war workers would leave Seattle. Unexpectedly, the population increased and business boomed.

Seattle Master Builders elected Cliff Mortenson as its first post-war President. He was followed by Lew Hykes in 1947.

A memorial wall was begun in 1948 at Memorial Stadium to honor the Seattle high school youth who gave their lives in the war, though it wasn't dedicated until 1951. This was a combined effort between the Seattle Master Builders Association and the Seattle Home Show. President Harry Truman came there to give a speech in June 1948; later, the field was the site of the first-ever local television broadcast – a tied football game between West Seattle and Wenatchee high schools.[1]

The Home Show had continued to grow from its beginnings in 1939. However, with the horror of the Pearl Harbor attack and throughout World War II, the show was not held again until 1948. This time it was housed in the National Guard Armory. The Seattle Master Builders Association once again partnered with the *Post-Intelligencer* to present this event. The three-way partnership allowed for very high levels of participation by the homebuilders and members of the Association, and a degree of "free" publicity through the newspaper. They ran special sections promoting the Home Show and exhorted their readers to come out and see what builders had to offer.

With the dawn of the new decade, the Association was trying to adjust to the changing market. In the late 1940s and early 1950s, there was incredible demand for housing. The Servicemen's Readjustment Act of 1944, often called the G.I. Bill, allowed veterans to purchase homes with no money down at very low interest rates. The returning soldiers' demand for increased housing meant builders could construct on speculation, rather than on first obtaining a contract. The shift forced builders to become shrewd businessmen, rather than merely craftsmen. Homebuilding was entering a new era. Some builders were able to

Lake Forest Park was one of Seattle's first planned communities. Ole Hanson, who was mayor of Seattle during the General Strike, developed this 3.66 square-mile site in 1912. He advertised, "..the strict fiat has gone forth that all the natural beauty must be preserved; that no tree must unwittingly be cut down; that the natural wild flowers must remain; that the streams, the springs, the lake front, the nodding willows, the stately cedar, the majestic fir, the quivering cypress and the homelike maple and all the flora and fauna with which Nature has blessed this lakeshore, must not be defiled by the hand of man."
This arch, at the entrance to Lake Forest Park from Bothell Way, was erected around 1920, and taken down during the 1950s. Lake Forest Park incorporated on June 20, 1961, in order that residents could control the town's destiny without pressure from King County.

adapt to the changing environment, others could not.

Al Goodwin, who would become the Association President in 1952 and 1953, observed, "After World War II, there were hundreds and hundreds of lots throughout the Seattle area that were foreclosed by the city or county for non-payment of real estate taxes. Those people, who had vision and availability of money and who had a big enough operation to take it on, acquired the property. They built up an inventory of land that allowed very rapid expansion. The small builder did not have that opportunity because he didn't have any money; he was underfinanced. Small builders became quite frustrated."

The influx of speculative businessmen to the homebuilding industry caused some smaller builders to become quite angry. They were jealous of the more well-capitalized builders' ability to buy lots on spec, and the ongoing friction produced quite a bit of heat. Monthly meetings were filled with exploding tempers and arguments: smaller builders against larger builders; heated debates and differences of opinions over the financing programs offered by the Federal Housing Authority and the Veterans Administration; and whether or not they had made the right decision when they decided to join the National Association of Home Builders.

In 1948, in the midst of the quarreling, the Seattle Master Builders moved into the triangular building located at 1930 Sixth Avenue. Now they had the first meeting room they could call their very own. The Association also hired their first full-time manager. Vyvyan Dent became Executive Vice President supporting the current President, V. O. "Bud" Stringfellow.

Despite all the decisions being made, the two views were diametrically opposed, and the schism between the groups proved unbridgeable. The definitive break came in 1949,

when past president Bernard Dahl led a group of Master Builders to withdraw and start their own association, the Seattle Builders & Contractors Association. The Builders & Contractors group believed firmly that hands-on building experience should be a criterion of membership, and they eventually constructed their own headquarters on Mercer Street in Seattle.

V. O. "Bud" Stringfellow, who was trained in real estate, reassumed the 1949 presidency for the Seattle Master Builders Association. Bud had been very sympathetic to those builders who had come into the organization "sideways." Stringfellow made the transition from real estate brokerage into operative building. He was able to

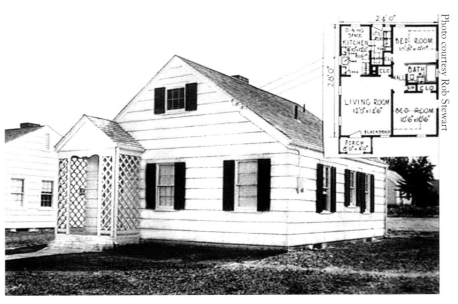

A typical 800-square-foot house that met needs of GIs returning from the war. Though it was small it served their needs, and Master Builders knew that soon the GIs and their wives would be ready for a bigger house for their expanding families.

snap up lots for sale and then hire contractors to complete the work.

This division between the Seattle Master Builders Association and the Seattle Builders & Contractors Association lasted six long years. The Builders & Contractors Association had its own presidents, and its own staff, but never did join the National Association. No record remains why they chose not to do so.

Housing in the Post War Era

The area's population continued to grow in the years following World War II. In 1947, King County was home to 54,000 manufacturing workers; a study by the University of Washington that year predicted that Seattle would need 32,000 new living units to accommodate them. The Master Builders responded, and by early 1951, more than 35,000 new units were in place. Significantly, nearly two-thirds of the new homes were outside the Seattle city limits. Entire new suburbs sprung up – Arroyo Heights, Mountlake Terrace, and Vuecrest, to name just three. Mercer Island was the fastest growing suburb and Magnolia the fastest growing Seattle neighborhood.

About fifteen major firms were responsible for nearly all of the development of the larger housing concentrations. No single house style dominated in the 1950s, and the prices varied greatly. However, builders were experiencing difficulty getting building materials. There was a shortage of materials no longer available through government programs. Smaller contractors were busy putting up scattered residences throughout the area, but they and the subcontractors were hardest hit, with some going bankrupt because of the inflated costs of materials. The profitable building of houses on speculation was now an insecure plan.

Dick McAbee remembered, "To even get supplies was difficult. When I did, I built a string of ten or fifteen houses and foolishly sold them before they were built." Foolish, because the price of materials was unpredictable. Lumber, steel, even nails and paint cost more and more each month. McAbee continued, "Every one of them cost me $1,500 more to build than what I sold them for. That's what inflation did."

The Seattle Master Builders and the United Cerebral Palsy Spastic Childrens Clinic co-sponsored the 1953 Parade of Homes to raise money and awareness about the disease. Called "The Parade with a Purpose," builders entered homes, such as the one in the background above, and were eligible for prizes.

Boeing was pivotal for the local economy. In 1947, Boeing employed about one in every five of King County's manufacturing workers; over the next ten years, this ratio had increased to being nearly one of every two. The production of the B-47 and B-52, used extensively in the Cold War, had helped to stabilize the company. Consequently, King County continued to gain population with an additional 24,000 manufacturing workers moving to the area by 1954, and the demand for housing simply increased.

Seattle-area builders were also strongly influenced by the federal government. Many local builders held the opinion that the government manipulated the national economy through the building industry, because in the 1950s homebuilding was the major employment industry in the country.

By May 1953, the government increased interest rates with the hope of attracting investors to the government-insured loan market. The effect was not an increase in building, but a decrease – suddenly buyers could not afford the Federal Housing Administration or Veterans Administration mortgages. In many cases the Federal Housing Administration's valuations were below current market levels, using out-of-date appraisals to determine the value of a home. Therefore, if the FHA appraised a house below its current market value, to qualify for the mortgage amount, the buyer would need to make a larger down payment to meet its true market value.

Both local building associations and the NAHB were exerting pressure on the Federal Housing Administration and Veterans Administration to understand the problems builders were having. Builders argued that the administration was not considering the market fluctuations that included land, overhead and profit as well as on-site improvements, to say nothing of the ever-rising cost of materials used in building the houses.

More government controls were put in place with the 1951 passage of Federal Reserve Board Regulation X, which more tightly controlled governmental money, raised the down-payments and shortened loan periods for mortgages. Then, the Veterans Adjustment Assistance Act of 1952, commonly called the Korean G.I. Bill, provided a bill of rights for veterans who had fought in Korea for more than ninety days. Those veterans were extended a builder's warranty provision to certify that the house sold under government financing not only met prescribed standards, but for ten years obligated the builder to correct any deficiencies. The Korean G.I. Bill further provided the Federal Housing Administration and the Veterans Administration the authority to impose other controls and was extended to World War II veterans, if they had not yet used home loan guarantee rights.

Another battle raged when the G.I. Loan Guaranty was extended. Texas Congressman Olin Teague, Chair of the House Veterans Affairs Committee which acted on all veterans' housing legislation, opposed the extension because "it is no longer serving its basic purpose of readjusting returning war veterans." Nevertheless, it was extended until July 25, 1957. The new insurance program, similar to the Veterans Administration program, would allow all new homebuyers to purchase homes under similar provisions as the veterans. The program would be under the direction of the Federal Housing Administration.

Prior to the 1950s, building codes were simple, and there were few land use regulations, with minimal permitting requirements. For example, the Seattle Building Code had gone through only five major revisions between its first passage in 1893 and the update affecting open-air parking bays in 1956. However, in 1955, city council members were arguing for more stringent controls, which culminated in the adoption of Building Code 85500, regulating everything from how close to a fire station a house should be built to the qualifications for masonry workers.

It was during this time when faced with increased local regulation and the continuing deep involvement of the federal government in housing issues that Seattle Master Builders began their first truly organized local lobbying efforts. They wanted a voice in the proliferation of local building codes and land-use regulations. They took up the fight for low-cost rental housing. They pushed for legislation to require the demolition of substandard structures, championing the enactment of local and state sanitation and health codes. They understood that it was their

They instituted committees to scrutinize industry concerns and form plans of actions in the interest of the Association members. At the Association's monthly meetings, members began to get regular reports on multiple topics from federal housing programs, labor relations, zoning and building. As the activism grew, also came the realization of the importance of growing their membership, and the importance of attendance, apprenticeship as well as support for each other and entertainment.

The Women's Auxiliary

A practice of a bygone era. Programs and even some new communities had beauty queens as goodwill ambassadors to the public. Fred Dally crowns Miss Parade of Homes

responsibility to maintain a high rate of housing to keep up with the needs of Seattle's growing population.

One of the first steps was taken in March 1951. The 420 members of the Seattle Master Builders, frustrated by long delays in loan approvals, filed a protest with the Veterans Administration over the agency's slow appraisal process, stating that "Further delay is intolerable."

During the war years, most of the able-bodied men who had been working in manufacturing left their jobs to serve in the military. As a result, positions and companies which had previously been closed to women found themselves having to fill employment needs with female employees. "Rosie the Riveter" became the archetype of a woman going to work in a physical capacity, and emphasized the uniqueness of this role.

While there had always been women involved with their husband's construction business, often doing the books or interior decorating, there weren't any female members of the Master Builders. One woman working with her husband was Stina Johannesen. She was fond of attending Association meetings with her husband Bill.

Bill and Stina married in 1919. Stina remembered, "In those days when we married, girls weren't allowed to continue school. Billy was 21. He was the happiest of men, a builder with a sound head on his shoulders. From the beginning he wanted me to do things." Stina got involved with interior design. During the depression she took courses through the Works Progress Administration and later from the University of Washington. Soon she was a professional designer with her own company.

In 1951, Stina submitted a report on the Women's Auxiliary to the Seattle Master Builders Association. She began,

> From the Women's Organization meeting in Chicago in 1950, I came home greatly inspired and decided to go to work immediately so that we could become women of accomplishment.
> Mr. Dent, our executive vice president, gave me his full support and at a husband and wife dinner I took the opportunity to give a report on the 1950 Auxiliary Conference. At this meeting I took a shot in the dark and announced a no-host luncheon meeting for April 18th, 1950 in one of our leading department stores, inviting all wives of builder and associate members.

There is no further record of which organizational meeting Johannesen attended in Chicago. However, it's possible that she attended the April 14, 1950, Chicago meeting called to form branches of the League of Women Voters. The hot topic of the day was that women were drawing up by-laws and organizing.[2] Whether Stina directly participated in that meeting or not, she returned to Seattle inspired.

The meeting Stina called on April 18, 1950, was a huge success. The women organized, calling themselves the Women's Auxiliary of the Seattle Master Builders, establishing dues at $2 a year, and electing officers: President, Vice President, Secretary, Treasurer, Program Chairman, Historian and Parliamentarian. After that they met regularly to work on their by-laws, publicity, monthly notices and membership cards.

On April 23, 1951, the Auxiliary celebrated its first anniversary with a birthday cake complete with one candle and all the trimmings. At that meeting the Seattle Master Builders President Ross Hebb presented the Auxiliary with their charter.

After a Women's Auxiliary dinner, Stina Johannesen (center) proudly displays the charter from the National Association of Home Builders recognizing the Women's Auxiliary of the Seattle Master Builders. Holding the charter with her are Fred Dally, Mrs. Bass, Mrs. Slabaugh and Mr. Rosian.

On occasion of their first anniversary, April 28, 1951, Stina reported:

It took a long time and lots of hard work to get the ball rolling. But we have had a very successful two years on our program of self-improvement. In August we had an all-day picnic and are now making this an annual affair. We've had some brilliant speakers on interior decorating, designing, electrical equipment in the home, the value of advertising. The General Paint Company sent us a factory representative to tell how wallpaper is made, how to use it, and how to decorate around it. We also had an expert on baseboard heating.

Our Associate members have proven invaluable, and we have taken them in as full members – and are we glad, since they are some of our best supporters. One of them gave us a talk on insulation – how it is made, and its value to the home. The City Light Company showed us movies on the workings of our Diablo Dam called "More Power to You." We also had a demonstration of flower arranging, a book review, a report on glass panel heating, a talk on the new use of linoleum and how it is made and one on Formica and its uses. One of our largest nurseries sent us a speaker on landscaping.

In June 1954, the National Association of Home Builders of the United States approved an amendment to their by-laws establishing a National Women's Auxiliary. Its members would be composed of local and state Women's Auxiliaries. At the annual convention of the National Association, the Auxiliary would elect its officers. The Auxiliary's Board of Directors meetings would coincide with spring and fall meetings of the National Board of Directors.

This was immediately followed by Seattle Master Builders President Dan Narodick's resolution that "the Women's Auxiliary of the National Association of Home Builders is a regular adjunct of the National Association. During the last few years in which the Women's Auxiliary of Seattle Master Builders has been active, it has helped the Association tremendously."

The Seattle Auxiliary became active members and continued to promote their stated objectives:

- To promote goodwill, loyalty and friendship among its members;
- To assist, when called upon, in those activities of the local or state associations which normally fall within the province of women; and

- To obtain a better understanding of the problems of homebuilding; to assist in producing more attractive housing by reflecting the woman's viewpoint; and to promote with other women's organizations the private enterprise objectives and ideology of the homebuilding industry.

Stina Johannesen was active in the establishment of other local auxiliaries. In August, 1954 she received a letter from Lucile Yates of Sherman Oaks, CA, inquiring about the involvement of husbands and wives in the Auxiliary. She responded, "We have your card of August 1, in which you ask for the names of husband and wife teams. You are practically asking for our roster! In Seattle Master Builders we don't actually have a woman builder as such. Nor do we have a firm that is listed as husband and wife. But I think there is scarcely a name in the roster in which the wife is not considered as part of the team. You can comment on some special feature or bit of decoration on almost every house and the builder comes up with 'Oh, that was my wife's idea.' Then there are several wives who do bookkeeping, payrolls, etc. for their husbands."

In each instance, only the men were actually members of the Association. The opportunity of

Suburbs usually have a prevalence of detached single-family homes. Both of these homes display the contemporary styles popular in the early 1950s in the ever-growing suburbs near Seattle.

engaging couples together promoted the growth of the Auxiliary and their attendance grew. The wives would hold their business session and often the men would join the meetings for the speakers and social hours.

Later the Auxiliary by-laws were amended to include honorary membership offered to those women whose husbands had withdrawn. They could still fully participate in all the activities of the Auxiliary, but did not have voting rights nor did they pay dues.

Suburban Trends

In the race to build houses after World War II, developers were no longer constrained by issues of proximity. Most families had a car, and were willing to drive it ten or fifteen miles each way to work, whether their work was in the industrial Interlake area, the Boeing plant in Georgetown or the office buildings rising in downtown Seattle. Contractors sold homes as fast as they were built,

At the opening of the Lake Hills subdivision in 1955, Washington Governor Arthur Langley and a local beauty queen dedicated the community, which would become part of Bellevue in 1969.

the first time the government was an ally. This historic shift in housing policy was the Housing Act of 1954. The Eisenhower administration had succeeded in creating consensus around urban redevelopment policies, stressing the importance of state institutions. It placed the federal government in an alliance with mayors and business groups by requiring communities to adopt code enforcement and other measures to prevent the spread of urban blight.

sometimes before the foundations were poured. Even as the real estate market showed signs of faltering due to a tanking economy, Seattle was still considered an expensive place to live. Suburbanization reached a fever-pitch as veterans looked for affordable homes on affordable land. Until the 1950s, suburban development had been dependent on public transportation. Now, the popularization of the automobile made it even more feasible to live farther from the city center.

Not only were developers looking to open up new land to meet the increased demand, but for

The community of Mountlake Terrace began in 1949 when the development team of Peterson-LaPierre, Inc. bought an old, unused airport north of 244th Street Southwest in south Snohomish County. Albert LaPierre would become Master Builders President in 1955. The abandoned airport reminded the developers of a terrace and from parts of the property, they could see Lake Washington and Mt. Rainer. Hence the appropriate name, Mountlake Terrace.

With the booming post-war economy trying to meet the housing needs of veterans who were starting families, Mountlake Terrace mushroomed from a few scattered homes in 1949

As potential homeowners took to their cars in search of the best deal in a new house, new model homes were open to show. The sign inside the window says, "Your home comes first."

the model homes over the first weekend. The Lake Hills community was marketed to middle-class families, and was marketed in the *Seattle Times* as a "self-contained city in a country atmosphere." Homes were priced at $13,000 and were rapidly sold. All the homes looked alike, and new residents joked about driving into the wrong garage by mistake. By 1955, there were planned developments all across the Pacific Northwest.

The same year, Bellevue, which had incorporated in 1953, was chosen as an All-American City by *Look Magazine*.[4] The Bellevue Chamber of Commerce used the award to promote suburban life, issuing a booklet that featured the prestige of being able to hire an architect and build your personalized, distinctive home.

Master Builders member George Bell's company Bell & Valdez developed most of Bellevue, including the Crossroads Shopping Center. His contributions were extensive – from Eastgate and Lake Hills to Tam O'Shanter and Brae Burn and south into Fairwood , Renton and Federal Way.

to a population of 5,000 in just five years. On November 29, 1954, the community was formally incorporated. However, the infrastructure was unable to keep up with the rate of growth. Many residents felt like pioneers, moving into the new areas before there were water and sewer services; before there were basic amenities like fire stations, schools and telephone service.

Builders cleared farm lands and replaced them with new communities as fast as their last harvests were trucked out. When Lake Hills, originally named "Eastgate Hills," opened with six ranch houses, 45,000 people shuffled through

Maps had trouble keeping up with the new suburbs. Properties with vistas that overlooked downtown Seattle or the Puget Sound or Mount Rainier or the Olympic range became highly desirable communities for custom building.

The natural terrain of the region allowed builders to respond to consumer demand for homes with sweeping views and large lots. Homes constructed on hills commanded higher prices, and builders rushed to take advantage of that. One of the highest hills in the area surrounding Seattle was located near Newcastle, one-half mile south of the Sunset Highway (now Interstate 90) and one-half mile east of the Bellevue-Renton highway (now Interstate 405). This land became the sought-after residential community called Somerset. Its appeal was its comprehensive and spectacular vistas of Lake Washington extending to the Seattle skyline and the Puget Sound.

National Convention

The September 5, 1952 *Seattle Times* lead headline screamed: "Builders Hit High Down Payments."[5] The occasion was the coverage of the National Association of Home Builders' Fall Directors' Conference and the Pacific Northwest Conference of Home Builders, both happening concurrently in Seattle. The meetings occurred at Seattle's Olympic Hotel September 3 through 11. The main topic was discussion of the government's Regulation X, the legislation which regulated loan-to-value ratios for FHA-insured housing. Under the regulation, many veterans had difficulty raising the money for the required down payments.

National Association President Alan E. Brockbank said, "The Korean veterans are eligible for G.I. home-loan benefits, but that puts them in the position of a man with a hunting license but no gun. Under the inflexible interest schedule set up by the government the needed capital is not available."[6] Brockbank led discussions on the regulation and hoped for its removal as early as the fall.

SEPTEMBER 3-12

Pacific Northwest
CONFERENCE AND
1952
FALL DIRECTORS
MEETING

NATIONAL ASSOCIATION
HOME BUILDERS

"The government has set us a goal of 1,200,000 homes a year," Brockbank said. "Our investigation shows we cannot reach the quota under the regulation's demands for high down payments, particularly in higher-priced homes, and its many other restrictive phases." His belief was that the 875,000 Korean War veterans were ill-served by this act.[7]

In addition to the immediate market, Brockbank urged builders to look ahead cautioning, "We must get a head start on the housing problem before then, or the homebuilding manpower and products simply will not be available." These fears were based on the fact that the present inflation trend was not over and the cost of labor and materials would continue to rise at two to three percent a year. Also predicted was a current slack in demand for new housing followed by a huge boom. For now, housing inventory looked favorable, but looking ahead to the "depression babies" marrying by 1960 who would need housing for their families. Brockbank forecast, "By 1970 we will have to build in the neighborhood of two million homes a year." He urged builders to renovate and replace existing housing to meet the future demands of public housing. Seattle was one of three community projects recognized at the housing conference.

The members from the National Association of Home Builders were happy to travel to Seattle for the Pacific Northwest conference. It wasn't all work and no play. The Board of Directors was treated to barbecued salmon at Golden Gardens park in northern Seattle with its spectacular waterfront views. Buccaneers of the Rotary Clubs barbecued 500 pounds of choice salmon for the guests. Of the salmon, one Texas delegate

Members were excited to register for the many events
and activities at the National Convention.
One was the presentation of the first fifty member Spike
award presented by Seattle Master Builders Association
President Don Wick
to Lloyd Clarke of the
Tacoma association.
Of course, king salmon was
always a Northwest hit,
whether to catch or eat.

said, "It's the first time I've ever seen anything like this."

The festive mood was enhanced by the announcement that the government was going to lift credit controls on homebuying. The government was changing its position on Regulation X. The consensus at the convention was that lifting the credit controls would permit current renters to be able to own their own home. They also unanimously agreed, "You've got a wonderful city here. We've never been treated so royally."

Both Seattle and the National Associations were urging Washington to terminate the Defense Production Act, to which Regulation X was attached. Without wartime defense needs, continued restrictions were choking the home-building industry. In November, 1952, the order was revised when the Housing Act of 1954 was signed into law. There was substantial modification to the mandatory warranty requirements. The Act once again improved the housing market, making it possible for more low- and middle-income families to obtain financing.

The Russians Are Coming!

The United States went from World War II quickly into the post-war negotiations with countries that had so recently been allies. The disagreements continued to create a state of tension and competition to the extent that the conflict between Communist countries and the U.S. became known as the Cold War. The Cold War would last into the early 1990s.

Though there were never any direct military actions between the United Sates and the Soviet Union, there was the constant threat of nuclear war. It wasn't uncommon for builders to offer homes with an attached fallout shelter. Usually the shelter was an enclosed space to protect the residents from radioactive debris. In actuality it usually consisted of a basement concrete-block room. It was furnished with two bunk beds, a portable toilet and the shelves which the homebuyer was to stock with supplies. With nuclear war a far-fetched fear, fallout shelters often became Dad's workshop, or the family storage room, as few people could maintain a lifestyle on high-alert.

DAN NARODICK

ACHIEVEMENTS:
President, Master Builders, *1954*

Dan Narodick moved to Seattle to practice law, but quickly realized it wasn't a profession he could stick with. He didn't like working with people who were unhappy. "He wanted to make them smile."

Born in Naywood, Illinois, Dan got a pre-law degree at the University of Illinois, then moved West to attend the University of Washington to get his law degree. He loved water and fishing, so it was not surprising that after working eight years as an attorney with the U.S. Supreme Court, Dan and his wife Maxine moved back to Seattle. He was struck by the lack of apartments in the growing city. This interest in real estate led to forming a partnership with Ross Hebb. They began Hebb and Narodick Construction and his new career was launched. They built custom homes, apartment buildings and even built the first two-story building in Honolulu and a hotel in Fiji.

Narodick was featured in a 1942 *West Seattle Herald* story. Neighbors were amazed: they saw a house placed on its waiting foundation in about two hours. "The home is factory built complete with plumbing and wiring and cut into three sections. These sections are transported to the home site by truck where they are lifted off by a crane and set on the foundation. The roof is put in place, the sections pushed together and fastened permanently and then the home is ready for the finishing touches." Narodick told reporters, "When we get going full blast, we will be able to erect three ready-built houses in a single day.

As President of the Association in 1954, Dan endorsed the proposal to incorporate the Women's Auxiliary of the National Association of Home Builders. "During the last few years in which the Women's Auxiliary of Seattle Master Builders has been active, it has helped the Association tremendously." In 1955, he received the first prize from the National Association of Home Builders in a nationwide contest for best celebration of National Home Week. Dan was a strong voice against more regulation of industry contractors and builders.

After his year as president, Dan continued to work with the Association. Dedicated to educating the public, he built a skeleton house where people could come and see what a house looked like. He built the outside, completing the exterior, but the inside had no drywall, so people could see what was in the walls. He was the 1966 chairman of the Festival of Homes Committee, and chairman of the Puget Sound Better Housing Council in 1967.

Dan loved to entertain, and especially loved entertaining his friends that he met through the Association, until his death in 1981. The company he started was sold to Weyerhaeuser, and became part of Quadrant Homes.

There were also periods of reduced tension. In 1955, the National Association of Home Builders extended an invitation to Soviet housing officials to tour housing projects in the United States from New York to California. Seattle was selected as one of the thirteen cities to be visited over the month-long tour. The State Department approved the invitation by the private builders and on October 2, the delegation from Russia arrived. They were taken from New York City to Washington, D.C. to participate in the dedication of the National Housing Center. The builders hoped to show the Russians all types of private homes, public and private apartment housing developments. It was the second organized visit of Russian officials to the United States. The first was an agriculture delegation which had visited the previous month.

The Russian group consisted of architects, builders and city planners. Perhaps to keep a degree of affluence hidden from the delegates, their city tours would include low-rent developments, middle-class suburbs and slum clearance projects but no high-end homes. In Boston, the homebuilders association arranged for visits to see low-cost, single-family housing as well as visit the Massachusetts Institute of Technology. In Fort Wayne, Indiana, they viewed prefabricated housing and in nearby Chicago saw massive suburbs. They also saw samples of industrial workforce housing built for the miners of Tucson. In New Orleans they visited a "Negro" housing development.

Seattle Master Builders' Executive Officer John Reuter, who had recently taken over the reins from Vyvyan Dent, co-chaired the visit with President Al LaPierre. They supervised the Association activities as they hosted the two-day visit of the Russians to the Puget Sound. The visitors were taken to see the Weyerhaeuser lumber mill at Everett, several housing developments in the north end and east of Lake Washington. The Master Builders entertained them with dinner and the following day took them to Seattle's Kaiser Gypsum Company plant. Before leaving to catch the plane for San Francisco, the head of the delegation and head of all urban construction in the U.S.S.R., I.K. Kozuilia, granted a newspaper interview. When asked how American housing compared with housing in Russia, he answered through his interpreter that he would leave the comparisons to the Americans who'd been invited to visit Russia. When asked if he had gained any new impression about the American way of life, he answered no because he had been here several times before. When further questions were asked, he replied that the interview was over.[8]

Nevertheless the purpose of the visit was realized. They had invited the Russians to view "the American way of life in its true setting, the American home." ❖

STONEY *Says:*

SEATTLE MASTER BUILDERS ASSOCIATION

SMB

WE'RE PROUD TO BELONG

*Members' pride was evident when they displayed the
Seattle Master Builders Association logo on their truck.*

CHALLENGE

CHAPTER 6

Managing Expansion

1956 – 1960

The year began with the reformation of a unified Association: the Seattle Builders & Contractors Association merged back into the Seattle Master Builders, and the homebuilding industry in the Puget Sound was again able to speak with one voice, under the name of the Home Builders Association of Greater Seattle. The combined Association moved into the building at 170 Mercer Street, and was able to host a number of social functions there, in its expanded basement. One "Old Timers Dinner" was held in the New Washington Hotel to honor men who had been active in the early days of the Association. After Joe Martineau was hired in 1956, the Association took on a broader role in membership recruiting, and reached out to Associate members more actively. Master Builders members were constructing houses with ever-increasing automation, so the woman of the house could relax while her self-cleaning oven did the dirty work. Marketing was touted as the new skill builders needed to learn as they sold homes to a more savvy buying public. Members were exhorted to do business with other member companies to strengthen the bonds between and the benefits of being members.

(Left to right) C. Fred Dally, Don McDonald, E. L. "Buzz" Flowers, Don Chapman and Howard Schroeder.

Fred Dally, outgoing President, is presenting the gavel, symbol of authority, to Buzz Flowers, newly-elected President of the Association (HBAGS) for 1958. Other newly-elected officers are Howard Schroeder, Vice President; Don Chapman, Secretary; and Don McDonald, Treasurer. Schroeder is holding the Charter of the renamed local Association as an affiliate of the NAHB

Reunited

The first permanent Manager of the Seattle Master Builders was Vyvyan Dent, who held the position from 1948 to 1954. Because of illness, it became necessary for Dent to retire, after which John Reuter, a retired Marine Colonel, was hired. He didn't fit well with the culture of the Association, and was only in the position for a few months. Then in February 1956, Joe Martineau came on board. He would remain in the Executive role for eighteen years, and be involved in the industry for even longer.

While serving in the Army Air Corps during World War II, Joe was injured in combat. He returned to Seattle to fight for veterans' housing rights by serving on the Veterans of Foreign Wars housing committee. There he got to know some of the men from the Home Builders Association of Greater Seattle: Dick McAbee, Dan Narodick and Axel Thornberg. Later Martineau went to work for the City of Seattle in the Building Department and then for King County as a county clerk. When Reuter didn't work out, former President Dick McAbee knew that Martineau would be the right man for the job.

Joe took care of the office, and he would also spend a lot of his time assisting builders in finding the right contacts to solve their problems. One builder was in disagreement with the Federal Housing Administration over the placement of porch railings. Joe remembers, "I went out with a representative of the FHA and we settled for a railing down the middle of the stairway so people could use it coming or going. It was just crazy."

Martineau nurtured contacts in the Federal Housing Administration. He was able to accompany the Director of the Federal Housing Administration to Washington, D.C. where he was helpful obtaining statistics for many of the cases that were being considered back in Seattle.

Martineau's first challenge proved to be a major one – the merger of the Seattle Builders & Contractors with the Seattle Master Builders. Since the split in 1949, each organization maintained a separate board of directors and their own headquarters. The Seattle Builders & Contractors Association had constructed a brand-new building at 170 Mercer Street while the Seattle Master Builders maintained the office at 1930 Sixth Avenue. The Master Builders had begun building a new office at 1920 Dexter Avenue North. Members were not united on the decision to move. Many of them belonged to both organizations, and most were tactfully trying to not offend either organization.

Many builders believed the post-war construction boom was beginning to slow. Interest rates, material and labor costs were rising. Associate member Clifford Olson, who was working for Pacific First Federal Savings & Loan Association, organized a meeting of both organizations. Seattle Master Builders President Sid H. Brase advocated, "It is imperative that [builders] strongly support an associated industry so that it might ultimately support us through the promotion of intelligent housing legislation and sound money markets."

A formal joint committee, chaired by Brase and Edward E. Roman, Seattle Builders & Contractors president, held their first meeting on "neutral" ground at Jim's Steak House in Lake City on February 13, 1956. Joe Martineau and Ken Mauck, the chief executives of both associations, participated, as well as prominent members from both groups.

The discussion focused on legal problems as well as the operational issues of having separate headquarters and sites. Dick McAbee believed these problems could be solved for the good of the industry and proposed a new organization with a new name that surpassed self-seeking interest.

The work continued by the joint committee, but it was then referred to as the Board of Trustees of the general membership. After only two meetings of the new Board, the members agreed. Details of the meetings were never made public. The official merger was March 2, 1956 and the new name was Home Builders Association of Greater Seattle, genially known as "H-Bags."

Brase and Roman remained as co-Presidents until the January elections. Mercer Street was the office servicing the 160 members. The Master Builders sold the land and the plans for the building on Dexter to the Swedish Club.

The builders immediately challenged the associate members to a softball game. Joe's first act as the new organization's Executive Secretary was booking the game and picnic at Magnuson Park. He wanted to be on the builders' team, but since he had never built a house or swung a hammer, the builders insisted Joe be on the associate team. Joe's pitching resulted in a formidable win for the associates.

This was just the beginning of Joe's eighteen-year career with the Association. "When I came to the newly merging Home Builders Association of Greater Seattle as Field Director/Executive Vice President," says Joe Martineau, "they were in the midst of a building doldrum. Most people had a very busy concern with just staying alive.

Some of the founding members of the Seattle Women's Auxiliary Club. The Women's Auxiliary were responsible for the social life of the Master Builders Association. They hosted cocktail hours, golf events and also were often responsible for their husbands' companies bookkeeping.

The club was formally organized as a National Affiliate in 1956, though the women had been formally organized in Seattle in 1950, and had been working behind the scenes for many years prior.

This beautiful new building was the headquarters of the Home Builders Association of Greater Seattle, at Mercer and Second Avenue North, had 4,000-square-feet in area. The first floor was devoted to display space and offices, and the basement was occupied by an auditorium, capable of seating 500, a kitchen and meeting rooms.

Civic Involvement

The building industry used to follow some very severe thirty to thirty-six month cycles. You'd be going great guns then all of a sudden you'd start back down, hit bottom, then start back up again. So when I joined, things were not all that bright in the general business sense."

In the years ahead, the Home Builders Association of Greater Seattle would be awakened to the responsibilities affecting their industry. The 1950s were heading into an era of political activism.

By the mid 1950s, the country was literally moving forward. On June 29, 1956, President Dwight Eisenhower signed into law the National System of Interstate and Defense Highways Act. The Seattle Freeway, which eventually became Interstate 5, was built by funds the State of Washington solicited from the government under this act.

The same year, the Washington Home Builders Association was coming into its own also. Portland and Seattle were the two biggest local associations. There were smaller Washington associations such as those in Tacoma and

Harold Larsen, 1950 President of Seattle Master Builders, takes a group of Norwegian builders to visit a Bellevue-area apartment project built by member Al Birkland.

Spokane, and Oregon had smaller ones in Salem and Eugene. It almost became a joint regional situation, until the organizations became organized strictly by state. Joe Martineau and other members began to build a good relationship with the Washington State Association. Joe was spending a lot of time lobbying in Olympia. He would go down for a session every year.

The Home Builders Association of Greater Seattle had committed to electing a new President every year, and Joe's frequent travels made these relationships challenging. Joe remembered how hard it was, "I was gone almost immediately, and I traveled back and forth. I'd be back in Seattle for a week, at times three or five days. We used to work with a committee chairman down in

Olympia and try to find out what they were going to discuss. And if they weren't going to discuss it, and if they weren't going to work on anything that involved us, I'd go home and take care of things."

In the beginning the Association's involvement in Olympia was simple. There weren't many people lobbying, and the lobbyists could easily approach a legislator's desk. A lot of business was conducted over a dinner or on the golf course.

The Association formed a number of committees to monitor and act on growing concerns: Technical, which combined Federal Housing Administration and Veterans Administration programs; Labor Relations; Entertainment; Programs; Attendance; Apprenticeship; Building; Zoning; and Membership. It was essential the Association learn how to deal with government departments. The general economic stability of the Seattle area depended on a high rate of housing production. Lack of rental housing, local and state sanitation and health codes, public housing, all these issues demonstrated the need to maintain a direct conversation with Olympia. Martineau noted, "Ours was never a fraternal organization; it was designed for member service. Once again, our

Member Roy Fassini and his family were toasting marshmallows in their new fireplace, and featured as the center spread of the November 1956 Master Builder *magazine.*

service base needed to evolve with the changing economy."

Jack Sylvester came to work for the Home Builders Association to represent them in Olympia. His law firm was Diamond & Sylvester. (He would continue to represent the Association until 1980.)

How the state computed worker's compensation rates became a major legislative battle in the 1950s. Joe explained, "Our builders were paying the same workmen's comp as the guy building the Grand Coulee Dam."

Seattle builders were able to get the legislators to consider the number of floors on the building when determining the class of the building. The Association always negotiated together with the Associated General Contractors, but this meant separating from the AGC on industrial insurance workmen's compensation.

Another concern that went to the legislators was the increasing rate of destruction of new property. Vandalism was a growing trend as Baby Boomers reached adolescence, and the public seemed apathetic. It was often malicious, so the Association sponsored the Parental Responsibility Act. Martineau remembers this as the Vandalism Act, and as a very emotional issue which completely enveloped the legislature.

As the membership was educated to the personal and professional importance of involvement, members began to participate at a civic level. Home Builders Association members were encouraged to seek seats on local water, building code and sewage commissions. Active members began to serve on King County and Seattle planning commissions, and in the Burien city government. Participation didn't stop locally. Other members sat on state building code and advisory committees.

"We had strong leadership and very active members," attorney Sylvester remembered, "and the Association was effective. It overcame opposition...that usually carried a lot more political clout, because the builders were so tenacious."

There was a time in the homebuilding industry where unions had firm control. In 1958, the Home Builders Association of Greater Seattle's formed the Associate Advisory Committee. Its first

STINA JOHANNESEN

ACHIEVEMENTS:

Founder, Seattle Master Builders Women's
Auxiliary, *1950*

Stina Johannesen thought of herself as a tomboy, when she was sixteen years old, she married William Johannesen. Stina remembered, "Billy was 21, a builder with a sound head on his shoulders. From the beginning he wanted me to do things. He insisted I pick the color for a house he was building, I was shocked — frightened to pick colors. In those days when we married, girls weren't allowed to continue school," Stina mused. "So while washing my pottery dishes after meals I got my first ideas for room color plans. The colors were used, the houses with them sold without delay, I gained confidence, and my ability grew."

In 1927, The Johannesen Brothers firm joined the Seattle Master Builders as part of a huge membership push. Bill joined on October 27, and his wife attended the meeting with him. That is the first record of a woman present at a Master Builders meeting.

During the Depression, Stina was able to take the courses the W.P.A. (Works Progress Administration) offered. "One exciting seminar series at the University of Washington included as lecturers world-famous Charles Eames, the interior designer who created the famous chair; Frank Lloyd Wright, architect, and Lawrence Halprin, one of the foremost landscape architects in the world." Then her husband decided that she should learn to read commercial building plans and learn about construction. Bill wanted Stina to "use imagination in designing different types of houses; we were successful because we dared to do them — ignorance is bliss." Stina did layouts of wiring, placement of outlets, plumbing, windows and doors. Her husband believed

a woman would know best where outlets for the vacuum would be needed, where a sink should be, or windows and doors, so a nice arrangement of furniture inside the house would be possible. By the early 1940s, Stina began to buy blocks of lots and build on her own, even while she was doing her husband's projects as well. "I had a ball," she said.

In 1949, Stina founded the Seattle Master Builders Women's Auxiliary. She then became active in forming other women's auxiliaries in other states and was also responsible for forming the national auxiliary to the NAHB in 1954.

The objectives of the Women's Auxiliary were to promote good will, loyalty and friendship among its members; to obtain a better understanding of the problems of home building; to assist in producing more attractive housing by reflecting the woman's viewpoint; and to promote with other women's organizations the private enterprise objectives and ideology of the homebuilding industry.

By 1977, the Auxilliary had grown nationally to 5,000 members, and Stina was still actively involved. She was also active on the Board of Directors of the Washington State Chapter of the American Society of Interior Designers, and was many times an officer for the state chapter of the National Society of Interior Designers.

chairman, Russ Miller, was committed to making progress toward better inter-industry relations. Together with the Labor Committee and its chairman, Dick McAbee, they were working with the Home Builders Associations of Washington and the Carpenters Union locals. The seeds were planted for a new carpenters' contract, which was signed the following year. However, it still took an additional five months to negotiate extending the contract through 1965. It would not be until the 1970s that the Association would have an exclusive contract with the Carpenters' Union.

Joe Martineau recalled there was only one strike during his tenure. "It got to the point where there were too many people in the business who were non-union. On the occasion of the strike, it was quite a laugh, because they [Carpenters Union] had given us the contract. So I called Jack Sylvester."

Jack responded with a smile on his face, "Well, I'd tell you to sign this, but it's pretty hard for me to say that." He went on to tell Joe that he didn't think the contract would stand up in court. "This is a case of the union drawing their own contract and writing it out. They know how to write these things up, they got a lawyer, but they didn't bother to contact him."

The carpenters had people line up around the whole block. The Association decided that if they didn't sign, the carpenters would be out to picket whoever was building. Joe recollected, "They didn't do a very good picketing job, because they hired laborers to be their pickets. They didn't picket themselves, they were too busy going out and starting houses."

Joe called the president of the State Contractors Union and Harry Carr, the president of the King County Labor Council, and said, "You know legal counsel has told us not to sign this agreement." They were sweating as Joe pointed out the union contract wanted a raise, but it indicated no time limit. Once Martineau pointed out this error, an agreement was reached.

"It was time-consuming and very frustrating," Joe remarked. The irony of doing labor negotiations on a big scale, he pointed out, was that even when there was agreement, was the weeks it took for the process. He had met in a bar with the President of the Carpenters Union, Harry Carr, and Dick McAbee. "We got talking, and he said, 'Why don't you two guys do this, you write down on a piece of paper what you think it will be settled for. Put it in an envelope and seal it and I'll hang on to it.' And we did that. With God as my witness, we both had written the same figure. I think we spent weeks getting to where it just turned out that we got what both of us thought we would get, and it was the same."

Martineau lamented the frustration of negotiating with the laborers, but at the same time it was hard on Association membership. Many Seattle Master Builders members belonged to a union themselves, or had employees who did.

There were other issues, on which Joe did not have as much luck striking a bargain. "I had tried for years to get an agreement with them to have not only the apprentice, but to have specialty workers. We were talking about the framing contractors, because that's all they did. One crew went in to set up the forms for the footings, and then the cement men would come in and fill the footings. The cement men would move on to the next job down the street with the guys doing the framing. You had specialized workers. You had one guy on the job who, if you had to cut a stair tack or something, he knew how to do it." An agreement was never reached.

Building community pride included building support for each other. In 1959, the Seattle Association organized a new department, The Builder's Manpower Exchange. When contractors were unable to keep key personnel working, the new service became a central place to list qualified personnel. These employees could be available to other builders until the time the contractor was ready to resume business.

Social Functions

During the 1950s, builder meetings were held in Joe Martineau's office. The idea was that way he would know how many people showed up. Social dinner meetings were monthly and usually held in a hotel. However, there was a meeting room downstairs at the Mercer Street office, which also had a bar and a kitchen. Martineau remembered, "For a while all the meetings were catered, even though the caterer preferred taking all the dishes back to Kirkland and washing them there." But it was hardly a kitchen for a big affair.

After the meetings, some members would stay and play cards, or they would want to keep the bar open. Joe protested, "This is not my job. I don't want to be here until three o'clock in the morning or whenever they decide to call this off." 1957 Association President Fred Dally listened and moved the socializing to the Swedish Club.

The Association was hungry for new members. To Joe Martineau, associate members were just as important. "I had a system where I would go out to the builder, and I'd say, 'Okay you give me a list of your suppliers, subcontractors, all these people. I'll write them the letter and here's the letter we'll send them. It will be over your signature on your letterhead. I need your stationary and your envelopes and this will be going from you out to them.'" It wasn't a hard sell. Members just didn't like to write letters.

The National Association of Home Builders wanted to come up with a fun way to reward members for recruiting new members to the organization. Playing off the concept of a "spike" in membership, and the "spikes" (nails) used to build houses, from then on anyone who recruited was called a Spike. It became an occasion for an annual banquet.

Kick-off dinners for the Parade of Homes, Golf Tournaments and Women's Auxiliary events – there were many opportunities to get to know fellow members outside of work.

The National Association formed the Spike Club Program. This grassroots effort awarded credits to members for every member recruited and retained. Once they earned six credits, they were a Spike and a member of the club. To remain a Spike, a member had to continue to earn at least one credit yearly. After earning 25 credits, Life Spike status was achieved.

The 1950s were a social time, and many grand events were sponsored by the Home Builders Association of Greater Seattle Women's Auxiliary. Chairperson Mrs. E. L. Flowers announced a fall Mardi Gras Cabaret Dance. It too was held at the Association headquarters. There were Christmas balls and golf parties.

An all-member dinner meeting at the Windsor Room, at the New Washington Hotel was planned on April 2, 1959, to honor the "old timers." The theme, "Hail! Hail! The Gang's All Here," summed up the anticipated atmosphere. The invitation read, "Names, faces and people will blend together again to relive a little of the past, with such old stalwarts, whose names are synonymous with the building industry, as Stanley Long, Sam Andersen, Harold Reinertsen, Bernard Dahl, Harry Forsman, Lyle Henton, Ole Bardahl, and many, many more to be invited guests of honor." The program promised to be filled with entertainment, humor, memories, and nostalgia to pay tribute to "those whose labors and efforts gave the industry the Home Builders Association as we know it today." One of those "old stalwarts," Ole Bardahl, had left the homebuilding field for chemical manufacturing, and became quite infamous for his high-speed boat racing, made possible because of a new adhesive oil he'd discovered how to produce.

As Joe Martineau was introducing the evening skit, he was interrupted by Fred McCoy telling him Sam Andersen had collapsed. The attendees tried to revive him, but he died before the paramedics could get to him. Sam had been a member

for over forty years, and his family remarked that "he wouldn't have wanted it any other way."

Two years earlier Sam had been honored when Association President C. Fred Dally announced Sam Andersen along with Stanley Long to Life Memberships in the Home Builders Association. The revised by-laws approved issuing Life Memberships to builders or associate members who "have devoted for many years, unselfishly of their time and efforts toward the best interest of the construction industry."

Keeping up with Changing Technologies

In 1958, the hula hoop craze hit the United States. The plastic toy was released by Wham-O and sold 25 million in the first four months and over 100 million in its first year. The newly created plastic industry had also made its way into plumbing. The availability of many different materials was a challenge to the building industry. There were hearings on copper plumbing and plastic plumbing. This plastic pipe reminded Joe Martineau of "hoses you put in a car and you could do bends and turns and stuff into your plumbing. It was quite odd looking." The flexible piping didn't last very long.

With lobbyists active in local government, the Association was poised to become an advocate for safety standards. The newest trend in housing was also dangerous – sliding glass doors caused a lot of accidents, some of which were fatal. Adults and children who were unfamiliar with the new technology didn't see the glass, so they'd just run into it, sometimes walking through the doors. The thin glass would shatter and would cause life threatening situations such as slicing an artery. Accidents would occur as simply as someone going back in the house to retrieve something then return only to find the door had been closed. Expecting the glass door to be open, the unsuspecting victim would walk into it and the glass would shatter.

E. B. "Tug" Vaughters, 1960 Association President, said, "We'll go ahead with this." So the answer had to be found through a cooperative effort – not only the Home Builders Association and the legislature, but industry had to invent a solution.

Martineau began to spend time in the library researching different types of glass. "One was a double sheet of glass with a piece of plastic

in between it. They used them in windshields of cars, so-called safety glass. If you ever stick your head through one of those from the inside, you don't pull back. And the other one was wire glass, which we knew would not be welcomed."

Owens-Corning and Pittsburgh Glass engineers came to Seattle for a meeting. Joe remembered, "They brought a couple of engineers with them and books on glass, and we met up in the County Engineer's Office in King County, and they had just redone his office, and we were breaking glass all over the place. He said, 'Don't worry about it. Don't worry about it, this is important.'"

The engineers demonstrated what happened and why the glass was called guillotine glass.

Glass was broken in every conceivable way. As a result, the first safety glass legislation in the United States was drafted locally in the law offices of Diamond & Sylvester, under the sponsorship of the Home Builders Association of Greater Seattle. National laws did not follow until twenty years later in 1979.

After the bill was written, the Association brought in door and window manufacturers. In addition to the type of glass used, work continued to standardize where and how the glass was going to be installed. Joe tells, "A supplier had a whole lot of old doors and the law would not become effective until January of next year." The Federal Housing Administration stepped in and saw that the law was put into effect immediately.

They added that any window below a certain height had to be tempered glass.

In 1956, General Electric launched the Live Better Electrically campaign. They produced a gold medallion that could be affixed to the all-electric home. The company was sponsoring the "General Electric Theater" weekly on television. The show's young hosts, Ronald Reagan and his wife Nancy, treated their audience to television tours of their all-electric Pacific Palisades home. The sales pitch declared, "by Thanksgiving, there should not be a man, woman or child in America who doesn't know that you can 'Live Better Electrically' with General Electric appliances and television."

All-electric houses included electric washers and clothes dryers, garbage disposals, refrigerators, stoves and heating systems. The General Electric campaign was supported by the nation's 300 electric utility companies and 180 electrical manufacturers.

The campaign's goal was to reach 100,000 homes by 1960. In Seattle, 1960 residential use set a new high record for per-capita electrical use, which caused a celebration. City Light Superintendent Paul J. Raver reported customers used an average of 9,133 kilowatt hours in 1960 as compared with 8,660 in 1959.

The average Seattle residential bill for 1960 was $88.13 as compared with $84.63 in 1959, reflecting the extra kilowatt hours used. In 1958, the average bill nationally was $89.78, for which the customers received only 3,577 kilowatt hours, only 2/5 as much electricity.

Raver concluded by pointing out that "just 21 years ago, in 1940, Seattle householders used only 1,703 kilowatt hours and paid an annual light bill averaging $35.93. In 1960, they used nearly five-and-a-half times as much, but because the cost had dropped from over $2 to below, they paid an average bill of only $88.13."

George Bell

ACHIEVEMENTS:
Board Member, Master Builders
Founder, Bell & Valdez
Major builder in Bellevue

Known for his hard work and commitment, George Bell's legacy can be found all over the Eastside and South King County. For over thirty years, beginning in the late 1940s, Bell built 15,000 mostly single-family homes. Bell served on the Master Builders Association board for many years.

George Bell was born in 1917 in Boise, Idaho, moved to Seattle, then graduated from West Seattle High School in 1935. During World War II, he was a civilian contractor for the Navy in Honolulu, repairing aircraft. Returning from the war, George and his wife rented a house in the White Center neighborhood, and Bell learned that there weren't enough houses to meet the demand. So the couple built their first house in 1947 for George's mother. He built another and another, and after a few years formed Bell & Valdez with his son-in-law Ted Valdez. Within five years, they became the top name in Northwest home construction.

Through the G.I. Bill, Bell constructed low-priced homes, selling for as low as $12,000, with as little as a $200 down payment. His ads promised "nothing down if you paint the interior walls." Bell tried hard not to have a cookie-cutter design, offering more than 15 floor plans. He specialized in ramblers and split-level homes, giving suburban families a downstairs "rec" room where the kids could hang out. In the 1950s, Bell even offered a home complete with a basement fallout shelter. As his success grew, weekend sales were so high that Bell hired a traffic policeman to direct traffic through his subdivisions.

In October, 1959, Bell & Valdez won honors in a nationwide competition sponsored by the *American Home Magazine* for a Colonial house built in the Bellevue area. They shared the honor with E. B. Vaughters. Each had homes named a "Best Home for the Money," The homes were chosen by a panel of judges from hundreds of houses submitted from seventeen states and the Washington, D.C., area.

Bell was very involved in homebuilding industry. with estimates that he had interest in 42 companies. One partnership was in the Crossroads Shopping Center, built in Bellevue in 1962. George sold his firm in 1965 to go into business with Dick Willard to form Quadrant Corporation, later sold to Weyerhaeuser in the 1970s. They built stately golf course communities: Tam O'Shanter, Brae Burn, Fairwood and Twin Lakes. Thus Bell served the consumer who had raised his income and tastes and wanted to move up.

After suffering a stroke in 2000, George Bell died July 17, 2006, at age 89 at his home overlooking Fairwood Greens in Renton, one of several golf communities he developed.

Housing Seattle

The history of humankind is full of examples where one group profited at the expense of another. Or someone or some groups were treated differently because of who they were, rather than on merit. Discrimination in the housing industry took national attention in May 1948 when the United States Supreme Court declared racially restrictive covenants to be unenforceable in court. The Seattle Housing Authority had been ahead of the rest of the country when they, along with Master Builders members, constructed Yesler Terrace, the first racially integrated housing project in the country. By May, 1954, the Court made a decision in Brown v. Board of Education, declaring segregation in public schools unconstitutional.

Society in the 1950s continued to break down the racial barriers. In 1955, a social and political protest campaign began in Montgomery, Alabama. In oppostion to the city's racial segregation on the public transit system, there was a boycott of the buses. Rosa Parks refused to give up her seat on the bus to a white man.

Her arrest led to the Montgomery bus boycott and encouraged civil rights leaders to challenge segregation in court. A United States Supreme Court decision one year later in December 1956 found the Montgomery transit segregation laws unconstitutional.

The same year, the Civic Unity Committee in Seattle created the Greater Seattle Housing Council. Its purpose was to encourage open dialogue between proponents of open housing and the real estate industry. Unfortunately, the efforts were unsuccessful. Though some progress was made when the following year the State of Washington passed the Omnibus Civil Rights Act, which made discrimination illegal when federal and state government loans were still in place.

This marked the beginning of Seattle Open Housing Campaign to put an end to housing discrimination and to pass open housing legislation. In 1959, the Omnibus Civil Rights Act was challenged in King County Superior Court, O'Mearas v. Washington State Board Against Discrimination. The Robert L. Jones family filed a complaint with the Washington State Board against discrimination. The seller, John O'Meara, had financed his home through a private loan insured by the Federal Housing Authority. The Board upheld the complaint saying the O'Meara family had refused to sell their home to the Joneses because of their color.[1] The case was taken to the King County Superior Count in January, 1960, and the court found the law unconsitutional. In September 1961, the case went to the Supreme Court of Washington. The Supreme Court ruled on a five-to-four vote in favor of the O'Mearas, judging that the state law did not apply because a Federal House Administration loan was not considered "publicly assisted housing."

"Open housing" or "fair housing" were becoming the terms used in connection with the rental or purchase of homes. The terms spread to be applied to any house-related transaction such as advertising, mortgage lending, homeowner's insurance and zoning.[2]

Attempts at the state level to pass broad anti-discrimination in housing laws were vigorously opposed in the late 1950s and early 1960s by apartment-building operators and real estate representatives. The open housing legislation went before the voters on March 10, 1964, and was defeated by more than a two-to-one margin, 115,627 opposed to 54,448 in favor. Attitudes were slow to change. The Seattle Real Estate Board issued a Statement of Principle in June 1965, stating that it was the policy of the Board that members should show all listings without discrimination.[3]

Not until April 19, 1968, three weeks after the assassination of Martin Luther King, did the Seattle City Council unanimously pass Ordinance 96619, "defining and prohibiting unfair housing practices in the sale and offering for sale and in the rental and offering for rent and in the financing of housing accommodations, and defining offenses and prescribing penalties, and declaring an emergency therefore."

The ordinance had been sponsored by six of the nine council members, but the chief architect was first-term council member, Sam Smith, the first African-American to sit on the council. Smith had previously been a tireless advocate for open housing and fair employment while serving as the first African-American member of the Washington State Legislature. [4]

The Home Builders Association of Greater Seattle's membership remained somewhat removed from the issue of discrimination. They were concerned with constructing houses for all, or so the documents of the period assert. Housing was generally constructed of a "traditional" style. With the influence of television, which exploded on the scene by the mid-1950s, life imitating art seemed to be the case. Shows like *Leave it to Beaver* featured the Cleaver family, who exemplified the idealized suburban family. It ran from 1957 through 1963. This lifestyle was also highlighted in *Father Knows Best*, which ran from 1954 through 1960.

Life in the suburbs pointed toward the importance of the car. The 1950s home usually placed importance on the double attached garage. The rambler, a one-story house, became the most popular house for homebuilders. Other features were central heat, cedar roof, brick and stone trims, large lots with trees, covered porches and spacious rooms. Popular also were brick fireplaces, hardwood floors, ranch-style kitchens with garbage disposals. Families were looking to be conveniently located near schools and fire stations.

A New Skill: Marketing

The Home Builders Association, though they had been sporadically producing magazines, finally had firmly committed to a monthly production schedule. In October of 1957, the magazine proclaimed, "For many years, the four 'M's' stood for the essentials of the homebuilding business. They were Markets, Methods (which includes Materials), Money and Manpower. Now they number a fifth – Merchandising."

Following World War II, the demand for houses had exceeded the supply. Builders had no problem selling a house. As the 1950s progressed, there was a lot of competition for consumer dollars – people wanted to buy television sets and new cars. Mortgage money became scarce, as larger down payments were required, and interest rates rose. The National Association of Home Builders began to educate builders on how to sell the homes they were building. The NAHB formed a Merchandising Committee to train builders in sales techniques. It offered a three-day Merchandising Short Course at the National Housing Center in Washington, D.C. It encouraged members to advertise by participating in National Home Week and the Parade of Homes. Based on the success of the national programs, the local Association reproduced a series of articles, "So You Want to Sell Houses!"

The national Merchandising Short Course engaged experts in the field. They applied proven merchandising techniques to the homebuilding business. Builders learned the best techniques for marketing, advertising, promotion and selling, all tailored to the homebuilding business from initial planning to closing the sale, and how to keep your customers happy. The builders

FOSTER and KLEISER

SEE THE 1960
SEATTLE
HOMES...
GO BUY!

KAISER ALUMINUM ...ER VALUES FROM PROFESSIONAL ABG BUILDERS

Left to right: Dave Cost, Kaiser; Frank Perkins, Seattle Real Estate Board past president; and Buzz Flowers, 1958 President, Home Builders Asociation of Greater Seattle

were given specific details on the fundamentals of site selection, design, color, financing, market research and the use of trade-in houses. The organization had brochures available illustrating how to do a good brochure, signage, and paid advertisements. How to show your model home focused also on taking advantage of home shows. The best avenues for sales were the satisfied buyers. Succinctly stated, "take

care of your owners, and your owners will take care of you."

The Home Builders Association of Seattle made public relations the topic of their monthly dinner meetings. The November 1957 *Home Builders Magazine* announced, "Public relations – a modem, dynamic sales tool – will be the topic discussed by the round table at the monthly dinner meeting of the Home Builders

greater seattle
home builder

NEW HOUSING IDEAS

HAVE COURAGE, FAIR DAMSEL, 'TILL MARCH 5TH TO 13TH INCLUSIVE!

I'VE GOT YOU IN MY POWER! HEH! HEH!

1960 SEATTLE HOME SHOW

OLD HOME BUILDING METHODS

SEATTLE HOME BUILDING

OCTOBER, 1959

Chambers®
QUALITY BUILT-IN

959 HOME SHOW GUIDE
HOME BUILDER'S

...twins" re...t ovens, the 42-inch "In-A-Top" broiler-...utomatic ...asher in luxurious antique Copperlux. The ...ator-freezer ...s wood panels.

...ly Living that's

...sales peaks

...rofit

TERRACE		
COVERED PORCH	LIVING ROOM	
TERRACE	DINING	
BEDROOM	KITCHEN	OVEN
FAMILY ROOM	REF.	FURN.	ENTRY
BEDROOM		BATH	MASTER BEDROOM
BATH	UTILITY	
COURT		
CARPORT		

...e color kitchen with
...erie, surface range, hoo...
...eezer. Custom-planned ...

Chambers custom-matched kitchen includes oven, surface range, ventilating hood, disposer, and 17-cubic-foot refrigerator with "Decor Door" which can be finished in matching woods, plastics or colors.

Association. Four experts, all members of the Public Relations Round Table of Seattle, will relate how public relations can effectively be put to work in the homebuilding industry."

Panel members were Byron H. Christian, professor of journalism and public relations at the University of Washington; Dave Wood, public relations representative for the Northwest for Bethlehem Pacific Coast Steel Corporation; Ken Sorrells, public relations director for Northwestern Mutual Insurance Company; and Carl Robertson, advertising and public relations executive with Penman-Neil Advertising Agency. "Question and answer period will follow the talk by the panelists."

E. L. "Buzz" Flowers, 1958 President, praised members in his monthly message. "Public relations and promotion saw most outstanding results in Parade of Homes." He congratulated co-Chairmen, Jim Burns and Mike Cooke-Dallin. The Public Relations Committee under Archie Iverson's leadership presented a Model Home Contest. Flowers promoted several upcoming events: the Women's Housing Congress, Builders' Business Management Course, and the Home Owner's Service Policy Program. Praise was given to Omar Brown, for leading "Operation Face-Lift" through the remodeling program.

Efforts of the organization were concentrated in co-sponsoring the Seattle Home Show and the Parade of Homes. Buzz Flowers encouraged participation by noting, "The Home Show, held each year just prior to the opening of the spring building market, is the one program which provides the necessary impetus to kindle the fire of buyer enthusiasm. A pageant of modern building products and equipment, the Seattle Home Show provides a most excellent opportunity to manufacturers and suppliers for public display of the myriad of new products and materials awaiting today's discriminating home buyer."

These efforts were acknowledged nationally, when *American Builder* magazine awarded the Seattle Parade of Homes "best parade" among major U.S. cities. The magazine said of the Seattle event, it was "the most comprehensive promotion in the history of the award." The 1950s saw this recognition not once, but twice.

The Home Builders Association of Greater Seattle was gearing up for the next decade. The skills needed by contractors would include the ability to conduct sound market analysis as well as an ability to predict future housing trends. ♣

CHAPTER 7

It Happened at the World's Fair

1961 – 1969

In *1961, Seattle again played host to the NAHB Convention, with salmon bakes and "Indian Princesses." Legislatively, the "H-Bags" fought for plumbing regulations, anti-vandalism laws, and financing regulations. In 1962, the East Side Builders and the Renton Builders merged into the Greater Seattle Association. Also in 1962, the region gained international attention as Seattle entertained the world at the Century 21 Expo. The Master Builders had a front-row seat to the action, as their headquarters were just across the street from the Space Needle. By 1965, there were a total of 448 member companies. The Association voted to rechristen themselves as the Seattle Master Builders Association. The late 1960s were a period of economic boom: "You couldn't get an apartment's foundation poured before it was rented." Outsiders moved to Seattle in record numbers, perhaps due to Century 21. Land use was discussed intently, predicting much of the Growth Management Act's eventual legislation. Construction prices in Seattle rose at a record rate, and builders had a hard time keeping up with the demand for their product.*

The "plywood house of living light" was one of two display homes constructed at the 1962 Century 21 Expo. The Plywood Home was a joint project of the Douglas Fir Plywood Association and *Practical Builder* magazine. The cones you see were intended to rotate on circular tracks, so the modern family could choose whether they wanted to follow or avoid the sun.

The House of Tomorrow

The "House of Tomorrow" was quickly becoming the norm of today. Interior decorators were purchasing record numbers of ads in the *Master Builder* magazine to promote a dazzling selection of colors for exterior and interior paint, tile, linoleum, and wallpaper. Kitchens featured built-in electronic ranges and microwaves, which boasted that the harried housewife could thaw a frozen meatloaf in two minutes, and would allow her to quickly cook foods before browning them in the oven. Maybe due to the microwave, but definitely due to other time-saving modern appliances, electricity use was at an all-time high.

E. B. Vaughters and Bell & Valdez, two regional builders, won honors in a nationwide competition sponsored by *American Home Magazine* for building the "Best Home for the Money." The winners were chosen by a panel of judges from hundreds of houses submitted from seventeen states and the Washington, D.C., area. The home that won the prize for Bell & Valdez was built in Bellevue, and featured a decorative quarry-tile split level entryway, oversized closets, sliding-glass doors leading to a patio for outside living, a rec room and two-car garage. Its price tag was $17,600.

Seattle-area builders were thinking about the Home of Tomorrow and other future gizmos. They'd been thinking about that since 1959, when the Seattle Planning Commission signed the contract to bring the World Expo to Seattle in 1961. Perhaps because Boeing was an integral part of the country's future or perhaps it was as simple as Kennedy's Space Race, but the Fair's theme would be centered on the Future. Century 21 aimed to "show the real things of the 21st century to the world": Man in the Space Age. Predicting the near-term future wasn't as easy as the planners had thought, though: the fair opened behind schedule.

The Century 21 Expo opened April 21, 1962. The exposition was an investment of $7,500,000 by the City of Seattle. In addition, the city got $9,000,000 from the U.S. Congress, the largest amount ever donated to a state fair. The State of Washington put up another $7,500,000, earmarked directly for construction of Coliseum 21, which would house the World of Tomorrow. It was to be designed by Paul Thiry of Seattle. The Coliseum afforded almost four acres of unobstructed floor space during the operation of the exposition.

Construction projects ranged from the Seattle Space Needle to the Alweg monorail, Seattle Center, the Pacific Science Center, and the unforgettable Bubbleator ride. Howard Wright, the largest local contractor, built the Space Needle.

Nearly ten million people attended the fair, and in the end, the Expo was in the black. The lasting profit was the revitalization of Seattle's economic and cultural life. Seattle Opera and Seattle Repertory Theatre now had a home. Speight Jenkins, who came to Seattle as opera director in the early 1980s, recalled, "Before the fair, we had a small symphony and the art museum, which was run as if it were a private affair. After, we had the basis for everything that has followed. (English conductor) Sir Thomas Beecham is said to have called Seattle a cultural dustbin. He never said that. He said if Seattle didn't create its own art institutions instead of relying on touring companies, it would become a cultural dustbin. After the World's Fair, we put that prospect behind us."

The H-BAGS suddenly found they were in the midst of the excitement, not only from the increased construction, but their 170 Mercer Street office was located across from the Space Needle. Joe Martineau remembers watching the Space Needle go up. "I sat in my office and the Space Needle was just about at a thirty-degree angle. I could sit there and watch it go up. It was kind of an exciting time, and we had far fewer visitors. However, the Association was disappointed at the lack of traffic through their office. We anticipated a lot of builder visitors, but we didn't get very many in the office."

Joe remembers The House of Tomorrow, featured at the fair: "It was kind of interesting, because of the cabinets in the kitchen. If you pushed a button, the cabinets came down to you." That didn't make it to the market, but Joe said, "A lot of little things made the market. It was all right." Other wonders which awaited us in the future were homes with changeable color schemes, gyrocopters, and the 24-hour workweek, which would earn a whopping $12,000 per year salary.

(Following page) *The House of Tomorrow featured moveable walls, automatically height–adjustable countertops and spartan decoration. Visitors saw displays on the future of interior decorating, which both echoed the Bauhaus movement of the 1930s and predicted the utilitarian aesthetic of Swedish funiture warehouses.*

NAHB Convention Held in Seattle

In August 1961, the National Association of Home Builders staff members and officers began to arrive in Seattle from all over the country. The Spanish Lounge of the Olympic Hotel filled rapidly. Name badges were issued to representatives of at least 45 states and Canada. Over 1,200 eventually registered, including 160 children. There was so much excitement, even with the Century 21 Expo behind schedule, there would be plenty for the group to do.

Seattle, not known for its sunny days, had serious downpours on the morning of Wednesday, August 16. Spirits weren't dampened. Hospitality desks served the guests hot coffee and hot clam nectar with assorted bakery goods. Though there were plenty of meetings and presentations, the organizing committee made sure there was time for exploring Seattle, and distributed maps, pamphlets and tour brochures as well as menus from Seattle's best restaurants.

The national convention sponsored nine entertainment events. The women were hosted at a "Mad Hatter" champagne brunch, while the teenagers participated in a Splash Party at the Washington Athletic Club. The youngsters were treated to a tour of the Woodland Park Zoo. Hawaiian entertainment was the theme of the opening reception for the entire convention.

Seattle *Master Builder* magazine reported:

> As originally conceived, the Friday morning Fishing Derby on Shilshole Bay was probably intended to be a stag affair, and it was estimated that only about fifty stalwarts would get up (or stay up) at the ridiculous hour of 3:30 a.m. Provisions were made for that number, and then several things happened. First of all, since the convention was billed as a family affair, there was no keeping it from being just that. Wives and children were as anxious as the men to test the murky morning waters of Puget Sound, and in several cases, the women went alone and left the men behind. Tickets for the fiasco were well exhausted as early as Thursday morning and the waiting list swelled to well over 300. Emergency measures were instituted, but the demand continued. Ticket requests were eventually honored on a first-come-first-served basis and the committee prepared to handle about 120 delegates. More than 180 showed up... some fish were actually caught. A fourteen-pound salmon took top honors.

sitors to Seattle's 1961 NAHB convention passed a peace pipe in front of a teepee up to demonstrate the housing style and handicrafts of the natives.

The Women's Auxiliary club hosted a number of different events, including this "mad hatter" champagne brunch at the Olympic Hotel Georgian Room, a "sherry flip" luncheon at the Seattle Tennis Club and a shopping trip to Nordstrom.

On the business side, the convention predicted that western states would experience a sharp recovery of homebuilding. The report forecasted a 26 percent increase (71,460 units) in apartment construction in 1968 and an 8.5 percent increase (93,000) in single-family homes. Leading the forecast was Seattle, with single-family starts of 10,500 homes and 13,000 apartment units.

Saturday morning's highlight was the appearance of Federal Housing Administration Commissioner Neal J. Hardy, who joined with several other national dignitaries in a discussion of opportunities offered by the new housing law. It was a free day for the women, who utilized the occasion for shopping and sight-seeing, or scenic tours and side trips to Victoria and Mount Rainier.

FRED BURNSTEAD

ACHIEVEMENTS:
President, Master Builders, *1984*
Hall of Fame, *2006*

With over five decades of experience in the building industry and involvement in three building companies, Fred Burnstead has a proven record for staying successful through challenges in the construction market. The Burnstead family name and reputation is based on the premise that "the Burnsteads don't simply build homes, we build vibrant neighborhoods." Fred has been involved with the Master Builders Association since the 1960s and has remained an active member for most of the time since then, including his term as President of the Association in 1984.

Burnstead was introduced to the Northwest region through service in the United States Navy post-Korean War, and after a stint at Boeing, he got into building in 1957 through a friend. He recalls that the building climate during that time included a lot of smaller builders, with ramblers and one-story homes averaging at around 1,700-square-feet. His company grew and expanded its building areas to Mercer Island and Bellevue. When the housing market took a turn for the worse in the late 1950s, Burnstead's company stayed strong by focusing on custom-built homes. This approach also worked well during the 1980s downturn, when Burnstead's model home in Bridle Trails brought in business.

The Burnstead building tradition continues with Fred's two sons, Rick and Steve, who each run their own construction companies under the Burnstead name. Fred and his sons share an office and use their individual strengths and interests to promote the Burnstead umbrella company.

His wife, Joan, designed interiors when the company first started and participated in women's auxiliary meetings at the Master Builders Association.

When asked about his membership in the Association, Fred emphasizes the professional relationships and helpful information that is shared between members, "a whole variety of different people doing different things; the interaction gives you a lot of contacts. You get friends." He also has enjoyed the several trips that the Master Builders Association has sponsored for its members to worldwide destinations. "We did a lot of trips with our associates under their sponsorship to lots of places in the world." These places included London, Spain, Greece, Tahiti, Japan, and Hong Kong. Fred continues, "And that was a strong learning experience, they did a really attractive job on them. We had a good time on all of them. You learn a lot, you learn about different cultures and different peoples."

Along with a history of family-owned building and Master Builders membership, the Burnsteads' triad of construction companies also strongly supports the Built Green program, a program that would have probably been unheard-of when Fred started building in 1957. Looking ahead to similar initiatives, and back over the several business cycles that he has experienced, Burnstead reflects that up and down turns in the market are just parts of the larger cycle. Fred concludes, "It's been a good business and I've liked and enjoyed it. It's satisfying to provide a home for people to live in and enjoy."

Changing the Landscape

The exposure Seattle had gotten on an international stage with the Century 21 Expo was driving a huge number of people to move into the region. The monthly *Greater Seattle Home Builder* magazine introduced a new word to its readers in 1961 – "condominium." Member Harry Pryde had seen them in Perth, Australia, and knew they were going to be a problem-solver for the Puget Sound's challenging building landscape.

The May issue of the magazine talked about the Federal Housing Administration's approval of condominium style financing, but in order for that to be meaningful, the editors thought the need to give its readers a dictionary lesson, beginning with the origins of the word. "Condominium is a term derived from old Roman law providing for common ownership of common land... Each buyer has independent ownership of his dwelling unit and plot of ground, plus an interest in the common areas. The buyer is responsible for only his own mortgage."

The National Association of Home Builders advertised the idea. Congress supported the idea with federal financing for a trial venture named the "guinea pig," a project set up in Richmond, VA. The units sold for $10,000 with $300 down and $95 in closing costs. Condo monthly dues were set at $72.50, which included $2.50 for maintenance of the common recreational areas and swimming pool.

The concept of the condo was an old concept and suddenly its time had arrived. In some places, such as Puerto Rico, condominiums had been legal since 1955. Yet here in the United States, they did not have the backing of the Federal Housing Administration.

As with unfamiliar concepts, there was much skepticism, drawn from the comparison between a condominium and the more familiar cooperative. The *Master Builder* magazine article noted, "Unfortunately, a true comparison is not possible at this time inasmuch as both seem to be operating satisfactorily at the present time under entirely different circumstances. When a cooperative and condominium can exist economically in the same community under competitive circumstances, then some of the doubts may be cleared up. For the present, however, those doubts exist."

The Golden Trowel Award was a popular program in the early 1960s. The award was made as part of the 1966 Parade of Homes by the Unit Masonry Association. The winning choice was based on "skilled selection and use of masonry materials" under a four-part grading system. Executive Vice President Joe Martineau (left) looks at a plan showing how one company used masonry in their home construction.

The confusion centered on the organizational setup of the condominium and the role of the governing board and its legal liability. The cooperative was able to borrow money and likewise be held accountable through lawsuits. The only experience drawn on was Puerto Rico's "Horizontal Property Law" under which condominiums existed. Unlike traditional real estate law, which took for granted that when you purchased a property, you had legal ownership of the earth up to the sky, the Horizontal Regimes Act of 1963 delineated new boundaries. By creating discrete and horizontal properties, the condo owner would not have any legal right to claim that the upstairs neighbor's property was also his. The law also required 100 percent owner approval for expenditures in excess of general building maintenance, a possibility that many assumed was unreasonable. Another difference between cooperatives and condos was that co-ops had control of occupancy, requiring approval of prospective tenants by the board of directors. The condo, like any other single family home, required only owner's right of refusal.

The 1960s were the perfect moment for a residential building boom. After the successful Expo, Seattle had a growing reputation as a high-tech, forward-thinking city. By 1966, Washington State saw the creation of 80,000 new jobs, followed by yet another 80,000 the following year. The State of Washington was experiencing the largest migration wave since World War II. Bill Conner, who was elected to the Association's presidency in 1975, remembered. "The late 1960s were boom times. You could just pour an apartment's foundation and you'd rent it, sometimes three months ahead of completion."

The 1967 Association President, Al Mullally, wrote, "Builders have done well housing the masses. Even the critical shortage in apartments in this area is rapidly being overcome for the lower and upper income groups."

Indeed, Seattle builders had finally hit an up cycle. Builders were boasting of "Building a New Seattle" to the Chamber of Commerce. The building industry was in a period of recovery. There was an increase of available mortgage credit, a healthy national economy, and implementation of the housing legislation enacted by Congress. On the local front there was active attention given to updating outmoded building codes and other regulations.

By 1967, Boeing's commercial-aviation business was soaring. Boeing's non-military work saw the production of the 707 and the new 727. With the increased labor force, Boeing opened its own housing office and officials contacted the Home Builders Association of

Greater Seattle to promote more residential construction. They also held public meetings to express the urgent need for at least 10,000 rental units. The Association responded, and fully 56 percent of building permits issued in Seattle in 1967 were for apartment construction. With the housing boom came supplemental needs – new shopping facilities, office and medical buildings, hotels, motels, warehouses.

Mullally continued to write in the Association magazine. This time his topic was the successful builder. "It is no small matter to be a successful builder… To succeed, a builder must be courageous and always optimistic, willing to take risks investing at times all of his working capital. Banks, mortgage companies, suppliers, and subcontractors anticipate progress payments as the homes are built and sold."

During Mullally's term, the organization established a retirement program for the Association's staff members. Public relations and educational programs which focused on the economics of homeownership proved to stimulate the local economy. On the legislative front, Master Builders were working with the state association to develop the political platform for residential construction. One of the immediate concerns was plastic pipe acceptance. Joe Martineau prepared to defend plastic pipe for

plumbing and the Association eventually won after appearing in hearings in the City of Seattle, Snohomish County and also in Bremerton. Other concerns were the amendment of the proposed low-income Turnkey Housing Program as well as tax- and building-code reform.

In January 1968, Don Wick was elected President. During his term, Association efforts in public relations and educational programs further stimulated the local housing market. With the further growth of the area came a new jump in membership. As the expansion continued, the Association began to further compartmentalize. In addition to the Remodelors Council, the Association formed the Labor Council, the Carpenters' Council, the Insulation and Truss Manufacturers' Council. The Snohomish County builders also formed a separate council within the Association.

In 1968, a study by Owen Corning Fiberglass Corporation predicted single-family units would increase by 28 percent. Then over the next five years, grow by over eight percent, whereas apartment construction was predicted to jump to more than fifty percent in the same five-year period. There were two reasons for these predicted trends. First, the Baby Boom, six million additional young adults ages 20 to 29, would be entering the market. Second, the study showed that people over 55 prefered apartment living. C. E. Peck, vice president of Owens-Corning's Home Building Products Division said, "The older group will be more independent and more financially secure than ever before. Greater numbers of older people will be seeking more convenience without the responsibility of single-family ownership."

The study was the subject of *Master Builder* magazine's January 1968 article entitled "New Apartments to Swing with Younger Swingers," and several trends were noted. Other factors cited in the apartment trend forecast included that more than 45 percent of the 20-to-25 age group moved each year. This mobility made apartment rental more attractive. Because of longer educational periods, people were beginning to marry at a later age. More single people were seeking to live away from parents and school. Also noted were divorce, movement from farm to city, decrease in the number of rooming houses, and the desire to be close to work; all expected to produce a higher rental market. With the majority of existing apartments aging – some were sixty years old – new construction was imperative. The report cited low-maintenance materials, central air conditioning and noise control systems as features which would be attractive to the younger generation

Reorganization

Meeting the challenges of the early 1960s had served to bring builders together on common causes and concerns. The East Side Builders and the Greater Renton Community Builders saw the advantage of strength in numbers, so in 1962, they joined the Home Builders Association of Greater Seattle. The combined membership totaled 396 – composed of 210 builders and 186 associate members.

After the merger, the Association's name once again came under scrutiny.

The name of the Seattle Master Builders Association had a history of varying opinions, and over the years battles had sometimes become intense. Memories of the conflicts over the name when Seattle Master Builders merged with Seattle Builders & Contractors in 1956 were still vivid. The factions had come to an uneasy truce at the request of the National Association of Home Builders – they preferred that all locals be called "HBAs" – so the Association became the Home Builders Association of Greater Seattle, and members often referred to it as "H-Bags." However, copyrights were still carried and maintained on the state department's registry under both names – the Seattle Master Builders Association and the Seattle Builders & Contractors Association.

The official name, Home Builders Association of Greater Seattle, did not encourage pride or independence for the local organization, even though the national organization's pride was quite satisfied.

In 1965, "We had a big struggle with the national organization," recalls Joe Martineau. "NAHB wanted unity on a national scale and felt similar association names promulgated it. Regional names were divisive, breeders of autonomy."

Other associations around the country dreaded losing their names once they affiliated with the national association. Majority rule was usually the philosophy of the National Association of Home Builders, and consequently, they had to cede to the numerous local groups who applied pressure to keep their local pride by keeping their original names.

The official re-adoption of Seattle Master Builders Association was unanimously selected by vote on July 15, 1965 to be effective January 1, 1966.

The merger of East Side Builders and the Greater Renton Community Builders with the Seattle Association was only the beginning of a broader wave of Puget Sound communities

Throughout the 1960s, builders worked hard for a few weeks out of the year constructing their home show model house as well as keeping their regular projects going. These cartoons from Master Builder magazine poke fun at the lengths that builders would go to in order to complete the houses on time.

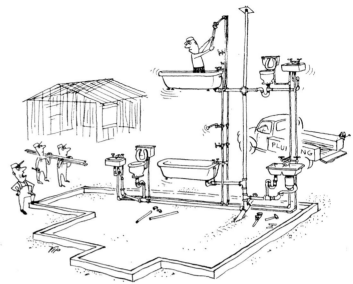

"We all know this Home Show Home has to be completed in days, and we admire your enthusiasm, but if I might mak slight suggestion . . ."

"When the hell are you painters going to start on this garage?"

Home Show Enters Final Stages

banding together to work for regional good. More than ever, communities needed to look out for the area's benefit as well as their own. The need to preserve the environment created the regional Forward Thrust movement, formalized in 1966. This initiative created public transportation systems, bus systems, and then a regional sewer system which cleaned up the region's lakes, and passed the largest parks bond issue ever seen. Until the 1960s, Lake Washington, Lake Union and Lake Sammamish all posted signs: "contaminated water." Surrounding jurisdictions emptied all their sewage directly into the lakes; consequently the lakes were unfit for swimming and the habitats were threatened and damaged.

Forward Thrust was a regional plan in which all the jurisdictions participated to keep everyone from dumping sewage into the lakes. The result was that eventually, a freshwater recreational lake environment could exist in the middle of a populated urban area and the beginnings of a regional transportation system to get people from place to place.

Cecil E. Powell, 1966 President of the newly rechristened Seattle Master Builders Association, set two goals for the year: "An increase in membership and the improvement of the Association's image in the industry." Starting on a positive note, his first Association gathering on January 13 was the largest Builder-Associate business meeting every held. More than 300 attended the yearly Beer and Crab Feed at the Swedish Club. Cecil took this opportunity to kick off his President's Membership Program for 1966. He challenged the organization to solicit 100 new members by the March 17 meeting. To reach the goal, each past President had to get three new members to join. He kept track with a Membership Thermometer. To entice members to bring in even more Spike credits, Powell changed the March 22 meeting's location to the Sand Point Golf and Country Club. He later said, "This change was necessary because of the increased attendance at our monthly meetings. Some of the locations where we had planned to meet simply would not accommodate the number of members and guests attending."

By the end of Powell's year as President, there were over 400 members of the Association. In addition, Powell worked with the Public Relations Committee to polish the Master Builders' image. Efforts resulted in the record attendance of 112,593 visitors to the Seattle Home Show.

BILL CONNER

ACHIEVEMENTS:
President, Master Builders, *1975*
President, BIAW, *1979*
Hall of Fame, *2006*

A Master Builders Association member from 1959 until his retirement in 2000, Bill Conner played an active role in the building industry. In 1959 he joined his brother's construction business, then five years later founded Conner Development Company. The business is still family-owned and run, with his son Charlie as the current president and owner of Conner Homes Company, Inc.

Based in Bellevue, Conner Homes designs and constructs custom-built, single-family homes and condominiums throughout King County. Conner says from the beginning his company was dedicated to providing exceptional customer service. This included soliciting home buyers on feedback on the homes they had purchased. With incentives for filling out the questionnaires, there was an eighty percent return rate. Currently, service representatives at Conner Homes conduct a walk-through with homebuyers after the sale to show them the house's many features.

Connor Homes initiated the Zero Lot Line Concept in Seattle, in which individual units are built on separately platted lots. Bill remembers, "In about 1979, we built small houses in eastern Kirkland, and we could get eight lots to the acre, and we were selling those houses for around $50,000. They were cheaper than anything else around. That was a great benefit to us." Conner Homes also prioritized environmentally responsible homebuilding long before it became popular to build green. The company constructed its first Earth Sense Home years ago, and encourages homebuyers to reduce, reuse, and recycle. Conner Homes received a number of awards for outstanding environmental efforts, including recognition for stream rehabilitation. The company recycles by restoring and preserving historic hotels in Seattle and its surrounding areas.

Bill's experiences as President of both the Master Builder Association and BIAW, as well as presiding over many committees and serving on numerous boards, has led to many professional and social contacts within the building community. Conner reflects that being a Master Builders member provided "a better view of what was going on in the industry and a better overview of the market" than he would have had otherwise. He recalls many international trips sponsored by the Master Builders Association to such places as London, Acapulco and Rome. These trips were not only for social purposes; rather, the excursions involved promoting builders and businesses.

After retiring from building, Bill was "still interested in improving the environment" and continues to remain involved in environmental and public policies. Bill currently serves on the board of the Washington Policy Center and is the chair of the Evergreen Freedom Foundation.

Legislative Battles

Don McDonald, 1963 President, appreciated having the Association's longtime attorney, Jack Sylvester, as a mentor. Sylvester helped Don to lead a case all the way to the State Supreme Court. The Spokane Homebuilders Association was suffering the effects of regulation dictated by the Contractors Registration Act, which dictated the laws under which industry contractors and builders could operate. The Spokane Association was attempting to take the case all the way to the U.S. Supreme Court. But the issue was not theirs alone.

McDonald remembered, "There were three positions. There were those who didn't want any regulation, and then there were those who wanted very strict consumer regulation and professional regulation, education and all that jazz. Then there was the middle ground and I was able to create the middle ground with our Association attorneys."

The Association attorneys became involved in the negotiations. The debate over the process to obtain a permit and the number of inspections required during construction was thoroughly vetted. Many felt there was no need for yet another administrative group to impose their will. This view was certainly not shared by labor. The Department of Labor and Industries wanted more control over the industry in the hopes to unionize.

Builders began to suffer the effects of regulation. No longer were they able to, as one builder later remembered it, "fill out a permit application on a blank piece of paper and go to the counter, and hand it in, and [get] a permit to build a home."

Sections of the 1963 Contractors Registration Act related to the bond requirement, proof of insurance, and the annual registration fee. These became part of a legal snarl, but attorney Sylvester advised the contractors to pay the registration fee when they registered. He based his recommendation on decisions in recent cases in King County. Whereas the State Supreme Court had ruled the law constitutional, an order issued by the Superior Court in Spokane County required the state to issue registration certificates even though the applicants did not comply with regulations. This court order could not be withdrawn until the case went back to the State Supreme Court.

The Association supported the enforcement of the state statute which required anyone taking a building permit to have an industrial insurance number or a receipt from the industrial insurance division. This indicated an estimate of industrial insurance on the proposed construction, and the receipt proved it had been paid.

The Master Builders Association was already involved in a direct petition to the State Department of Labor and Industries' Industrial Insurance Division. The Association was seeking legislation that would provide for changes in the industrial insurance statutes, creating a merit system for experience ratings within the building industry. To prove that point, the building industry was the only one of sixty categories which did not realize savings from safe operations. Experience ratings would be a quantitative measure, which the insurance company would use to determine how much a given policy should cost. It would be calculated using historical data to determine the risk of future claims.

The Association, together with the BIAW and others in the industry, wanted to determine the practicality and advisability of pursuing an "experience" rating in the residential and light construction industries. Interactions with the state Department of Labor and Industries led to a cooperative study with the Industrial Insurance division, and eventually resulted in the Return on Industrial Insurance Program.

Urban Renewal and the Changing Nature of Housing

In March 1959, the Association magazine featured an article, "Seattle has active Urban Renewal Group." It praised an organization, Seattle Urban Renewal Enterprise (SURE), which would be financed by voluntary contributions to assist neighborhoods develop a comprehensive city-wide program, encourage improvement in the quality of housing, promote home rehabilitation and conservation, encourage clearance and acquisition of extremely blighted areas to be redeveloped for the best land use, and analyze the plans for needed improvements.

As happened around the rest of the country, "Urban Renewal" functioned as a way to push African-Americans out of central city areas. The first renewal project undertaken in Seattle was the 63 acres around Yesler and Cherry. The next project outlined would be the central part

The 1969 Tour of Homes was the first to feature "condominiums" as well as single-family detached homes. Beneath is an advertisement from the same month's magazine for a champagne gala.

of Jackson-Atlantic Streets area. SURE adopted a three-part program: Conservation, Rehabilitation and Clearance. One of the first steps was to draft a Minimum Housing Code.

The National Association of Home Builders had as part of its mission the promotion of housing-friendly legislation. Builders worked on the Minimum Housing Code in response to President Dwight D. Eisenhower's 1959 veto of the Housing Act.

H. D. Schroeder, who was 1959 Association President, wrote in the July 7, 1959, magazine, "At this writing, the President of the United States has just vetoed the 1959 Housing Act. Immediately upon being advised of this action, I conferred with Mr. Carl T. Mitnick, President of the National Association of Home Builders and after thorough consideration we've jointly issued the following statement to the press—

"We feel that it is incumbent upon the responsible leaders of our government to settle promptly on a housing program that will meet the needs of the American people.

"The Federal Housing Administration, which has been a bulwark of our housing progress for the past 25 years, must not be allowed to die because of failure to provide the additional insuring authority it needs. And the time is long overdue for modernization of the credit terms upon which both FHA and the Federal National Mortgage Association operate.

These are the bare minimum essentials which the interests of all the American people demand. Without them, hundreds of thousands of families will be deprived of their chance at homeownership.

"Without them there is a very real danger that housing production may suffer a serious decline in the months ahead with consequent repercussions on employment and the whole national prosperity.

"May I most urgently request that all parties concerned with the housing industry immediately contact the members of the Washington State delegation and urge our congressmen and senators to exert every effort possible to accomplish the passage of a housing program that will meet the needs of the American people."

Newly-elected President John F. Kennedy listened to the building industry. As one of the first acts, his administration outlined a housing bill to include defining a new mortgage plan, and plans for urban renewal, low- and moderate-income housing, home improvement, housing for the aged, college and hospital housing, and financing. The Housing Act passed in June of 1961.

Short-term, the Act seemed to help the lagging housing industry, but builders headed back to Washington D.C. to look for amendments. It was feared there was just too much federal government control. Critics charged the bill placed the federal government in the role of benevolent landlord.

Other critics believed the bill was going once again to lead the country into inflation.

The *Master Builder* magazine of July 1961 outlined the $6.1 billion Kennedy Housing Bill. It noted that the new mortgage plan was the most controversial section. The Federal Housing Administration was allowed to insure 35-year mortgages with only a three percent down payment. The result would mean equity would be painfully slow, and consequently, funds available from moneylenders would dry up. Another problem was the cost of urban renewal. Cities would buy up decaying sections, and then sell them at a loss to private developers. It would cost over $2 billion to reimburse cities for the losses they would incur. Other items – low-income housing, housing for the aged, moderate-income housing, home improvement, college and hospital housing, veterans' housing – all came with either government financing or government guarantees. In conclusion the article said, "Even the most sanguine backers of the Administration's housing bill recognize the cold fact that private lenders will be reluctant to tie up funds for as long as forty years in the controversial home-mortgage plan or to lend money at below-market rates for home improvements and for housing for moderate-income and elderly persons. To encourage the money to flow,

the Federal National Mortgage Association can buy up the loans from private lenders, thereby giving the lender a quick profit. The bill boosts the mortgage-buying fund of FNMA (popularly known as "Fannie Mae" in the trade) from $950 million to $1.7 billion. Kennedy's program should help the lagging housing industry shake off the after effects of the recession."

A year later in March 1962, Neal Hardy, Commissioner of the Federal Housing Administration, credited the Kennedy Administration for helping create the best year the Housing Administration had experienced: applications for mortgage insurance were up seventeen percent from the previous year; there was a reduction in the interest rate; and the annual service charge of one-half of one percent formerly permitted on mortgages of $9,000 or less had been eliminated. The enactment of the Housing Act of 1961 "liberalized and broadened FHA mortgage insurance programs and provided authority for FHA to enter new areas of housing market." And Hardy also praised a reduction in processing time and increased efficiency of the agencies' operations.

To undertake urban renewal, the Association had to get its membership ready for all the issues – local zoning codes and requirements, land use, access and community relations. And all over the country, the burgeoning preservation movement was coming head-to-head with the goals of urban renewal. The demolition of the Occidental Hotel in 1961 drew attention as Pioneer Square might become the next target for urban renewal. Support for balance between historical preservation and urban renewal was a growing interest throughout the United States, as cities experienced a loss of their historic buildings. The Century 21 Exposition which looked to designs for the future was located on the opposite end of the city from historic Pioneer Square, where turn-of-the-century architecture was in poor repair.

Past Association President Harold Larsen stepped on to the Building Code Advisory Board of the City of Seattle in July 1967. He was replacing Carl Tshudin, who was the former Association representative on the board. Tshudin resigned to accept a position with the city's Urban Renewal Department.

By 1967, Archie Iverson was honored as the Chamber of Commerce "Construction Man-of-the-Year." Iverson had served two terms as Association President, 1961–1962. Among his many accomplishments, Archie was one of the original sponsors of Urban Renewal for Seattle, and built several apartments to encourage the upgrading of Cherry Hill.

Master Builders would be involved on both sides of the issue for many years, and ironically much of the culture which was destroyed in the rush for urban renewal would be rebuilt over the next decades at great cost to everyone. ♣

At the 1969 induction of officers to the BIAW board: from left, vice president, John Bozick of Tacoma, president Harry Pryde of Seattle, immediate past president Don Rasbuson of Brementon and, secretary/treasurer, Ralph Lindsey of Longview

CHAPTER 8

Will the Last One in Seattle Turn Out the Lights?

1969 – 1976

Rising construction materials cost, inflation, and the loss of Boeing jobs all added up to create tough times for builders. The Association created campaigns to encourage the public to consider buying new houses, and they also worked hard to create compromises in the governmental arena. As the decade progressed, the Association launched a Home Owners Warranty program, modeled after the highly successful British one, and the Association gained a lot of new members. The public was convinced that Master Builders members built quality houses, and as they purchased homes, the economy began to turn around. By the end of 1976, there were a record-setting 669 member companies.

1976 Home Show floor
The local economy stabilized a bit in the early 1970s, then went up and down, but
throughout the Northwest, builders and architects experimented with modern homes.
The public continued to enjoy the Home Show and builders continued to support the
Association. Even in the downturn of the mid–1970s, the number of members quadrupled.

Better Living Starts with Looking

Nearing the end of the turbulent 1960s, Seattle felt a sense of optimism. There was a robust economy. The building industry was bragging that the city would see 10,500 single-family homes and 13,000 apartment units. This wasn't just wishful thinking; in one year, 56 percent of permits issued were for apartments. To keep up, land developers were opening new areas and builders, suppliers and subcontractors were working to keep up with new shopping facilities, office buildings, medical facilities, hotels and warehouses.

In the spring of 1969, the American League brought in a professional baseball team, the Seattle Pilots. Perhaps forecasting the difficult times ahead, the team became known as the major league's One-Season-Wonders. The losing season was plagued with low attendance, the team was forced to file for bankruptcy, and the next spring the Pilots moved to Milwaukee and changed their name to the Brewers.[1]

The Home Show, on the other hand, was enjoying its success as the longest running home show in the country. It celebrated its silver anniversary under the same family management as had started it in 1939. The Seattle Master Builders Association and the Seattle *Post-Intelligencer* had worked together with the McDonald family to establish one of the most successful promotion efforts Seattle's building community has ever known. Proudly, the 25th anniversary event featured some of the same exhibitors from the first show.

"In the years of rapid growth, the Master Builders Association has met many housing challenges," 1969 Master Builders President Vern Gambriell pointed out. "Today we again see a changing focus as interest is heightened in the second home or the recreation property. We find tremendous mobility as younger families move to the suburbs or upgrade their living levels and older families transfer back to smaller quarters, to townhouses or city condominiums. Home shows give these people an

Better Living starts with Looking!

Seattle in the 1970s was a much smaller city. This photo from 1971 was taken looking north from the site where the Kingdome would be built. These tideflats were just north of where First Avenue's Hooverville had sat forty-odd years earlier.

opportunity to preview new ideas and items they want for new homes, new apartments or rustic cabins they expect to build." Throughout the years, the show was a way to increase not only public awareness of the advances in methods and materials, but at the same time inform the industry of customers' expectations and demands.

During Gambriell's year of leadership, the building community faced increasing material costs, higher land costs, wage increases, property tax increases, which in some cases could be 25 percent of the gross income of a building. The availability of money with its ever-increasing costs added to the difficulties. He wrote, "1969 may prove to be a year to test not only our desire but also our capabilities... The homebuilding industry faces the greatest challenge of all times – the big question is how we can best meet this challenge, and meet it we must, for all people shall be adequately housed. The direction our country takes in solving this problem can be greatly influenced by our industry, if we are 'involved' in policy making decisions. We will be involved only if we care enough to make that special effort. We have the talent – do we care enough? We'll be calling on you!"

In this year, Harry Pryde, the Bellevue-based homebuilder who was now the state association's president, trumpeted the need for greater political involvement. "The industry itself must become not only more sophisticated, but knowledgeable and active in all phases of legislation and on all levels."

A position paper was presented to both state and national legislatures in September 1969. After presenting the urgent need, the Home Builders asked for two immediate actions: "immediate implementation of effective controls on consumer credit, and an immediate rollback in the Prime Interest Rate to 7.5 percent."

While waiting for change on the governmental fronts and riding the turbulence created by the financial ups and downs of the 1960s, the Seattle Master Builders Association had one ace-in-the-hole – the Boeing Company, with its apparently inexhaustible demand for workers and their need for adequate housing. Suddenly and with drastic consequences for the economy of the entire region, its largest employer went from a peak of 100,800 employees in 1967 to a low of 38,690 by April 1971. The primary causes of these drastic cutbacks were the slow demand for the new 747 airliner and the decision by the U.S. Congress to stop funding the development of the supersonic transport, a project that had been awarded to Boeing in 1966.

February was declared Better Living Month by Seattle Mayor Wes Uhlman (center). Uhlman was elected mayor in 1969 and reelected in 1973. During his administration he worked to preserve historic Pioneer Square.

The magnitude of the looming crisis was driven home to 1970 Association President John Nord during a plane ride. He was traveling from Seattle to Houston for the 1970 NAHB meeting, and Nord struck up a conversation with his seatmate. Soon the topic turned to Boeing, and discovering that the man had connections there, Nord asked him if he knew why the Boeing Housing Office had stopped answering the phones. The man shared with him that the Boeing workforce was about to be drastically cut, he thought it would end up being about 70,000 workers. By July, Nord feared that the region's residential construction industry was "in the midst of an economic famine."

Indeed, starting in January 1970 and extending into December 1971, Boeing reduced its workforce by 65,000. The ripple effect of this massive layoff led to the loss of an additional 40,000 jobs in the regional economy.

Seattle Master Builders responded to the economic crisis triggered by the Boeing layoffs. Joining with material suppliers, the real estate industry, and banking institutions, they formed the Better Living Council. The council's objective was to promote the value of home ownership and to offer fact-based research to counter the "doom and gloom" rumors that only served to add to the real economic woes. The council coordinated monthly promotions, issued informative news releases, and aired public-service spots on local radio. They also had a few gimmicks that they used to keep buyers optimistic, like wearing rose colored glasses in ads in the papers. The January 1970 local issue of *TV Guide* featured two full-page ads inviting readers to call the Master Builders office for information about recommended home-improvement contractors. The picture caption read, "It's Great! More 'living' room for your family, and lasting value for your home."

These concerted efforts helped stimulate new building starts and played a role in lifting

Setting up for a national ad to run in the January 1970 issue of
TV Guide, *the photographer coaxes a pose from models Nick and Carol*
(left). Larry Henderson, the Seattle Master Builders Field Services Director,
discusses the layout with decorator Bette Anderson, who worked with
the advertising agency to set up shots promoting the Home Improvement
Contractors Division. Junior model Tami Hinch looks cozy on the bed.

IT'S A GOOD day
for buyiNG A HOME

moratoriums on state and federal projects. The Association turned its efforts to public relations campaigns to promote home ownership. The Better Living Starts with Looking campaign focused on convincing people that their current living spaces were obsolete and old fashioned, and they needed to buy a new home, now. By 1970, the labors proved quite successful and helped to stimulate the local market. The trend in home values was continuing to sharply rise, by 1970, the median home value was at $21,700.[2]

As part of these campaigns, sixteen Association directors and representatives traveled to Washington, D.C. on two occasions to lobby the state congressional delegation and officials of Housing and Urban Development, Veterans Affairs, and other agencies. These efforts generated several direct benefits, including a federal commitment to build an additional 235 low-income housing units; a $250 million appropriation for the Federal Home Loan Bank system to lower interest rates; and efforts to curb inflation in wages and building material costs.

JOHN NORD

ACHIEVEMENTS:
President, Master Builders, *1970*
Builder of the Year, *1984*

A builder from the beginning, construction has always been in John Nord's blood. "My dad was a carpenter, so I always had a hammer in my hand." His family settled in the Seattle area during the 1930s, and John worked with his father on construction projects after school. Nord formed his own company, Parkwood Homes, in 1960, which built single-family homes, residential buildings, and the occasional apartment building throughout Snohomish, King, and Pierce counties. John eventually sold his company and is currently retired.

Throughout his long history with the Master Builders Association, John was a driving force in steering builders through rough economic times, and helping the Seattle Master Builders to grow into the largest association of its kind in the country. John recalls the earlier days, when a smaller Association meant even more hands-on participation in policies and programs. The Association was valuable in connecting builders to other builders. Nord became friends with Bill Conner, with whom he shared a common vision. He explains, "We became very good friends over the years. We both believed in giving something back to the industry that we made our living in. The Association was good, because it brought people together, builders together."

In 1970, Nord was elected President of the Master Builders. This was a challenging time: building business was down, interest rates were skyrocketing, and Boeing had massive layoffs. Nord warned that the region's residential-construction industry was "in the midst of an economic famine." Despite all of these conditions, Nord remained optimistic and initiated programs to support builders and keep their spirits up. To help accomplish this, Nord and his team established the Better Living Council. "The idea was to advertise houses as still being great buys, and it turned out to be a successful campaign." This campaign included a few offbeat and creative tactics. "We'd wear rose-colored glasses and things like that, to try to get a better feel from people."

John Nord was the first builder in the Seattle area to introduce the ten-year Home Owners Warranty program (HOW). Along with fellow member Pete Hansell, John traveled to England to research their program. "We structured ours with the information we got from what they had done, looked at their product, and we did what we wanted to do. But we wanted to make sure that it was going to be something to be around for awhile." And it was a program that did stay in Seattle for many years.

"Those experiences were important to me. It was just a lot of good things that would come out of there. We had good people on staff and good officers that ran that part of it. It was a good living."

1970 Master Builders President John Nord lamented, "We were over-regulated and the time element for permits, etc. was getting so elongated. We must keep [the building industry] a part of the free enterprise system. Without the Seattle Master Builders Association, we'd have been zoned and controlled out of business a long time ago."

Costs rose to keep up with the demand of government requirements. The Federal Housing Administration had raised the cost of getting money, and as builders had to pay more, they then had to charge more for their houses. Homes became too expensive for many people to buy. It was easy to place the blame for the ensuing building recession on the government.

The Iconic Billboard

It was the worst time in Seattle Master Builders Association membership. At the start of 1970, there were 400 members still on the rolls, but building in Seattle had all but stopped. With the Boeing crash, membership fell another 35 percent.

Seattle ranked the highest in the nation for unemployment, with thirteen percent of the region's workers looking for a job.

"In 1969 I built an apartment building in Bellevue at 140th and S.E. 6th," says Bill Conner, who would become the Association's President in 1975. "It was the last thing I built for over a year. I did nothing during 1970, except build a road in Hawaii."

To the rest of the world, Seattle's misery appeared desperate. London-based magazine *The Economist* featured one Seattle journalist's point of view in a May 1971 article headlined "City of Despair." He wrote, "The country's best buys in used cars, in secondhand television sets, in houses, are to be found in Seattle, Washington. The city has become a vast pawnshop, with families selling anything they can do without to get money to buy food and pay the rent."[3]

Bob McDonald, left, and Jim Youngren just wanted to poke fun at the "pawnshop" mentality of outside investors.

Photo © GREG GILBERT/The Seattle Times

It never hurts to tackle problems with a sense of humor, or so thought Bob McDonald and Jim Youngren. The young real estate agents, who worked for member company Henry Broderick Realty, responded by renting a billboard for $160 and wrote: "Will the last person leaving Seattle — Turn out the lights."

The billboard was displayed for only fifteen days in April 1971 near Seattle-Tacoma International Airport. Ironically, even decades later, other cities have had occasions to pick up their hastily thought-out slogan.

It was one of the first sights for arriving visitors. McDonald said their out-of-town clients "were amazed that Seattle wasn't a ghost town with weeds growing in the streets. We wanted to counteract that attitude with a little humor." The purpose of such a broadly displayed message was to point out to the arriving clients and investors that even though the news from Seattle was bleak, they would arrive and see a city with plenty of life.

"It went over real well, once people understood the motivation behind it," McDonald says. "But there were definitely people who disliked the sign." It certainly caused attention and the two men were not popular – they were frequent recipients of mail addressed to the "two idiots."

The Boeing recovery began slowly. By October 1971, the company was back up to employing 53,300 workers. However, the early 1970s weren't bleak for everyone. Some were able to turn woes into easy profits. Realtors McDonald and Youngren were able to pick up bargains and prospered in real estate. "You could buy an apartment building for less than construction cost, with virtually nothing down," McDonald says. Jim Youngren went on to co-found Cornerstone Development and Bob McDonald was able to get out of the industry entirely, retiring in 1983 at age 46.

Nevertheless, even with declining membership, the Association stayed on firm financial footing. "We were always solid financially," says John Nord. "The key was, is, good management. No matter who your president is, he changes every year. But your executive officer looks at that budget year after year. They provide the continuity. We've had good Executive Officers." An additional layer of continuity through these difficult times was proved by Jim Burns, who served two terms as the Association President, from 1971 to 1972.

The Seattle Master Builders Association recognized that membership was their future. They sponsored a one-day membership drive and urged builders to support each other. The

Association regrouped, and working through the Better Living Council, pulled together member representatives, and representatives from real estate boards, savings and loan associations, mortgage banking institutions, title insurance companies and building suppliers to work together to move the economy forward. They launched this endeavor to counteract negative public opinion of homebuilders by concentrating on researching and presenting the facts. Once again it was a multi-pronged attack, combining public relations, education and political strategies. On the political front, the Association successfully opposed a rent-control ordinance in Seattle. And the Association continued its industry leadership with former Seattle Association President Don Wick elected to be a national vice president of the National Association of Home Builders at that organization's national convention in Houston, Texas.

Taking every opportunity to educate, the May 16, 1971, *Seattle Times* featured an article about a new program at Franklin and Rainier Beach High Schools. Students were given the opportunity to build houses. Students at the schools were provided with all the tools, training and materials to construct a 1,100-square-foot home. The homes were fully functional, and were to be sold for money to fund the project's continuation. Students had fun building the houses, and the projects also functioned as a way for the next generation to get interested in the construction trades. The Seattle Master Builders worked with other industry groups, such as the Building Construction Trades Council and the Carpenters' Council to accomplish the initiative.

These educational efforts led to the formation of the "Building and Construction Trades" educational program in partnership with the Seattle Public Schools. President Jim Burns told the *Times* that the program's goal was to "challenge more students, not only to remain in school, but to seek additional training in a specialized trade."

Warranties and Security

When the numbers were released for the 1970 census, they proved something that locals had been noticing for years: the suburbs were growing. More than half of the King County residents no longer lived within the Seattle city limits. Bellevue was growing at a gangbusters pace: for the first time, it had cracked the "largest

Bill Winn congratulates John Nord, president of Parkwood Homes, for being the first registered HOW Builder in Washington State, as HOW Council Chairman Pete Hansell presents the Builder License Certificate.

Association staff member Falk Kelm manned the Home Show's Home Owners Warranty Display. HOW was promoted by saying,"Gives you the selling edge…avoids misunderstanding by reducing call backs."

cities in Washington State" list, with 61,196 residents; it was also now bigger than Everett.[4]

By 1972, there was a steady upward trend in the aerospace industry, and optimism began to seem a little less foolish. By year's end, Boeing was employing 46,000 with $1.5 billion in commercial transport orders and had won several major government contracts. Residential construction was up again, resulting in an additional creation of 14,000 jobs. But the decade continued to be a roller-coaster ride with brief upturns in the

economy counterbalanced with brief recessions. And the recessions were lengthened, in many opinions, by the intervention of governmental agencies intent on enacting new rules.

The National Environmental Policy Act was signed into law by President Richard Nixon in January 1970. It was sponsored by popular Washington State Senator, Henry M. "Scoop" Jackson, and it required that federal agencies prepare environmental impact statements before authorizing major projects. Washington then followed up with its own reform package called the State Environmental Policy Act (SEPA) which mandated that governmental agencies consider the environmental impacts of public or private land development matters in making decisions on actions. Next came passage of the 1972 Federal Clean Water Act, which eventually led to a host of regulations governing stormwater runoff from construction sites.

These government regulations imposed new rules on how housing was constructed, where it was to be built, development density and also levied new fees and taxes on the builders to pay for public infrastructure.

Adding to the building industry's economic woes was a rapid increase in lumber exports. Harry Thornberg, 1973 President of the Seattle Master Builders, warned the state congressional delegation on the "crisis situation in lumber [and the] worldwide softwood shortage." He emphasized that the Japanese were buying a "tremendous quantity, and paying up to 100 percent above acceptable prices."

The Association sent a delegation to Washington, D.C., where they met with 2nd District Representative Lloyd Meeds to discuss the log export situation. Meeds responded, "The problem is larger than just log exports. We are not managing our public lands wisely and we are depleting our timber."

The severity of these years, 1973 through 1975, was the most challenging yet for the local building industry. Bill Conner, 1975 President, observed, "The 1973 through 1975 housing slump differed from previous cycles. The energy crisis and double-digit inflation coupled with a rising unemployment rate and a general slowdown in economic growth created new and unforeseen problems that caught us off balance."

In 1974, homebuilders were caught off balance again by a Harris poll, which indicated that more than seventy percent of those surveyed had no confidence in the workmanship of homes. John Nord and other leaders of the Master Builders Association traveled to London, where a Home Owners Warranty program had reinvigorated buyer confidence, and in the ten years since its expansion, home warranties had become so beloved that they were required for 85 percent of mortgages being written in Britain.

John Nord's company, Parkwood Homes, was the first in the nation to offer a ten-year Home Owners Warranty. The warranty guaranteed against major structural defects in new construction. It was attractive to both builders and consumers. Under the program the first two years of warranty coverage would be provided

HARRY PRYDE

ACHIEVEMENTS:
President, Home Builders Association
of Greater Seattle *1965*
President, Home Builders Association of
Washington State, *1969*
President, NAHB, *1983*

Born to a farmer in the Yakima Valley in 1930, Harry Pryde grew up to become a national advocate for affordable housing. After completing his degree in Economics and Business and serving two years as an officer in the Air Force, Harry earned a Master's degree in Public Administration from the University of Washington. Following graduation he worked with the Association of Washington Cities and the Institute of Governmental Research. Harry left non-profit work in favor of the business world, and became a homebuilder. He started with a few houses in the Northgate area, and soon thereafter founded the Pryde Corporation, which he led for more than forty years. His company built more than 3,000 homes, apartment complexes, health-care facilities, office buildings and condos, including one of the first condominium buildings on Seattle's Capitol Hill overlooking Lake Union.

Harry enthusiastically joined the Master Builders Association in 1959. Pryde was elected President of the Home Builders Association of Greater Seattle in 1965. He believed that future success for the industry depended upon greater political involvement, stating that "the industry itself must become not only more sophisticated, but knowledge-

able and active in all phases of legislation and on all levels."

In 1969, Harry served as President of the Home Builders Association of Washington State. He continued to expound his belief, "The opportunity to meet and discuss the issues of the day with members of our State Legislature and to represent our industry has been indeed a challenge. During our recent and long tenure in Olympia, our Legislative Team has reached at least one basic conclusion and that is the residential construction industry, both on an Association level and as individuals, must become more politically involved if we are to insure the survival of our industry as we know it... The time has come, my friends, for us to consider whether we shall continue to be the captains of our ship, or merely the crew." The concerned builders acted in September 1969, forwarding a position statement on their financial crisis to both state and national legislatures.

Harry Pryde was the first member from the Pacific Northwest, and the only member from Washington State, to be elected President of NAHB, in 1983. He advocated for regulatory reform and bringing the nation's budget deficit under control to alleviate rising interest rates, carrying those concerns directly to President Reagan. He advocated that interest rates were too high for a sustained economic recovery, and federal deficits projected at more than $200 billion were threatening to devour most of the capital available in the credit markets. "Unless those deficits are reduced," Pryde said, "there will not be enough money to go around; thereby pushing interest rates back up."

During his presidency Harry established a Deregulatory Task Force. The Financial Institutions Deregulation Act of 1983, Pryde said, "strikes dangerously at the heart of the housing finance system as we have known it for the past forty years." NAHB believed that regulatory barriers between commerce and finance should be maintained in the case of real estate development. Deregulation in this area would be detrimental not only to homebuilders but could jeopardize the soundness of bank or thrift subsidiaries. NAHB also opposed the legislation because it would consolidate financial institutions into fewer, larger entities controlled by large holding companies. President Reagan called homebuilders "the heroes of today's economy," noting builders' accomplishments again three years later when presented with an NAHB report summarizing recent achievements.

Other initiatives under his leadership were a Monetary Task Force Forum and continuous support of national membership drives. Harry's motto when he was the president NAHB was "shelter for the people, jobs for the economy."

He served on boards of the Seattle Housing Authority, Washington State Affordable Housing Commission, Washington State Housing Finance Commission, and the Washington State Housing Task Force. He was a founder of Enterprise Bank, and on the Board of Directors of both the Seattle and Bellevue Chambers of Commerce. He was a Director of Federal Home Loan Bank of Seattle and DASH (non-profit housing for low income families). Harry was inducted into the National Housing Hall of Fame, as well as the local and state Master Builders Association Hall of Fame and the University of Washington Construction Hall of Fame.

Harry Pryde valued principles of hard work, established in his early childhood on the family farm. He constantly sought to expand his and others' knowledge of the world until his death in March 2009.

Vote With
PRYDE
for a better NAHB

HARRY PRYDE
An Outstanding Candidate for
Vice-President/Secretary
NAHB

"Harry Pryde is a man of leadership for NAHB and for our industry"

directly by the builder, while the remaining warranty period of eight years would be covered through a national insurance plan. *Master Builder* magazine explained, "Builders generally agree that the biggest problems that occur between builder and buyer are not structural problems or problems of allowable tolerances, but simple communication lapses between the two parties. Conflicts arise over just what is covered and what the builder actually promises to do. For this reason, a consumer's walk-through inspection and an itemized check-off system will be established to eliminate confusion, to let both builder and buyer know where they stand."

Within five months of its inception, 240 new homes were registered under the HOW provisions, and by mid-1975, more than thirty of the Master Builders member firms were participating, the highest rate of participation of any builder group in the nation.

"The homebuilder ranks just above the used-car salesman in terms of consumer confidence. HOW is designed to change that image, to make the builder a good guy – and to do it without government interference in our business," said Pete Hansell, who would become President of the Association in 1979. The program gained acceptance and was even endorsed by Ralph Nader, consumer protection activist.

Some of the houses covered by this warranty program had added levels of security. Builders advertised "unpickable" magnetic locks, and some laid-off Boeing engineers developed a home security system which was installed in houses throughout south Snohomish County.

Despite the decreased demand for housing in the Northwest, builders and architects experimented by building homes with a more modern flair. The Seattle Home Show attracted more than 120,000 visitors. This annual opportunity to connect building industry with consumers presented innovative ideas, including modular housing and Recreational Vehicle homes. Other houses were starting to be built in a style dubbed "neo-eclectic," meaning that they didn't conform to one specific architectural style. These houses could combine elements of historic styles, but were not tied to the building materials of the past. So you might see a new house constructed with a Craftsman-style porch, and Colonial windows, with Mediterranean roofing, but these houses were constructed using very modern materials like vinyl and composite resins.

In 1972, Herb Chaffey was featured in *Master Builder* magazine, and was asked about modular constructed houses. While Chaffey felt there was definitely a market for modulars, his company,

Above is the model home featured and built for the 1975 Seattle Home Show. Interior design ads showed the hottest new colors and carpets for the modern decorator.

Wick Homes, was still producing conventional construction. He thought modular homes would take off in areas where labor and materials were expensive or scarce. He maintained that in the Northwest, you wouldn't see many modular homes. Chaffey stood by the assertion that on-site stick building would always make the customer happier.

The stick-built houses that Chaffey was constructing now featured the "technological wonder of the decade": the trash compactor. They came in the standard appliance colors of the day: avocado, harvest (yellow-orange), coppertone (brown) or plain vanilla white. Self-cleaning ovens were also a big hit for the lady of the house. Some ladies didn't even need to use the oven enough to make it dirty, as their kitchens had the newest in high-tech gadgetry, the microwave.

Growing the Association

In 1974, Omar Brown was elected President of the Association. He emphasized the need for increased communication, and vowed to lead the Association to a more profitable place of legislative influence. Brown was a strong advocate of members doing business with other members, and worked tirelessly to recruit new members.

The Association immediately felt the impact of spike drives that Brown instituted. By the end of his term, the Association has grown from 380 member companies to 523. To spur membership, Brown and Executive Officer Joe Martineau created four geographical divisions within the Greater Seattle area to compete against one another in membership drives, and that brought recognition from NAHB for being the best recruiting organization in the country. On that high note, Joe retired from his position and handed the reins over to his second in command, Bill Winn. ♣

Even in economically tough times, the Association made sure that all its members had a good time.

BICENTENNIAL BASH

NAHB SPIKETTE

Annual HOLIDAY *Christmas* BALL

LET'S ALL GO

FRIDAY, DEC. 14, 1973

HOSTED COCKTAIL HOUR — DINNER BANQUET DELUXE —
ENTERTAINMENT — MUSIC
Dancing to the ever swinging music of ED ALLENBACH & his Orchestra
GRAND BALLROOM — OLYMPIC HOTEL
FEATURING "The Frye Family" AND THEY'RE GREAT!!!

RESERVATION FORM — SEATTLE MASTER BUILDERS ASSOCIATION

Please send _____ tickets for the CHRISTMAS BALL,
Friday, December 14, 1973

Signature _____

Firm Name _____

Address _____

Check enclosed for $_____ at $12.00 per person or please bill.

170 MERCER ST. SEATTLE, WASH. 98109 — AT 4-4114

The Associa
Advisory Comm
invites YOU
to their Hoste
Cocktail Hour
at 7:00 p.m.

RESERVA

CHAPTER 9

Elevating the Association

1977 – 1983

Area housing markets were reinvigorated by the popularity of the HOW program, the FHA programs allowing five percent down payment on homes, and the secondary mortgage market. However, the multifamily situation was dire, and builders had to work to accommodate those who needed to rent. The Seattle Master Builders Association split into three "councils" – Snohomish, Seattle/Eastside and South King. There were over 1,100 member companies by late 1977. The Asssociation realized that they were not effectively lobbying in Olympia and formed a Political Action Committee, called Builders for Better Legislation. In February of 1978, the Association formed a regional "sensible growth" committee to help municipalities plan for how to manage the inevitable population growth. As the building industry dug in its heels to weather the storm of high interest rates and low demand, political actions took more and more of the Association's energy. The Association battled the state legislature, and emerged victorious against development fees and against artificial energy standards for new homes. But the economic challenges hit builders hard, and membership levels hit a low of 768 at the end of 1982.

Because organizations like the National Association of Home Builders and the Seattle Master Builders Association provided professional safety training to members, those members were eligible for a return on their industrial insurance premiums.

The Perfect Storm

The nation's unemployment rate was high; ten percent of the country was jobless, and many others were afraid they might lose their jobs. There was also fear that inflation would spur higher interest rates. Nevertheless, the construction of single-family homes was experiencing one of its cyclical growth spurts. The Tax Reduction Act of 1975 provided a rebate on the previous year's taxes paid, along with increasing the annual deduction. The effect was a stimulation of the Puget Sound housing market. Builders produced more than 15,000 living units, nearly a fifty percent increase over the 1975 total. However, there was no similar spurt in multi-family housing. As the price of homes increased beyond the means of many families, a shortage of new, affordable housing became acute. The majority of Americans who owned their homes wouldn't have been able to afford it, had they needed to buy it in the current market.

1976 Association President Dave Dujardin was concerned. "To sustain the production levels indicated by market demand, monthly payments needed to match consumer incomes."

Fueled by Boeing's incredible growth, huge numbers of people were moving to King County, and they needed someplace to live. With the newly immediate need, the multifamily housing situation was unprepared for the market demand. Builders were challenged to find ways to finance and build rental units. Some retained ownership, some "syndicated" ownership as a group, and still others sold to investors. The bureaucratic problems of land use regulations, together with inflationary costs of materials and labor, haunted builders.

But things quickly began to look up with several programs beginning to reinvigorate Seattle's housing market. After a Nixon-era scandal effectively shut down the Department of Housing and Urban Development, the new leadership was quick to react to the crisis they saw. In 1976, they reactivated both the Section 235 single-family housing program, as well as its sister program, the Section 236 multifamily housing program. These two programs were responsible for producing over half a million new housing units in 1976; 1,100 of them in the Puget Sound region alone.[1] Under 235, the federal government was able to guarantee financing for single-family homes at five percent interest.

Leiv Vikingstad took over as Seattle Master Builders Association President in 1977. During his term, the FHA programs were allowing five percent down payments on homes, and the secondary mortgage market allowed for greater creativity in financing. The Home Owners Warranty program continued to build in buyer popularity, and it also reached new heights in builder participation. Consumer confidence was up. The Veterans Administration encouraged the warranty program by accepting it in place of some builder requirements. Both of these incentives contributed to the rise of housing with 757 new houses in the first quarter of 1977, with a two-year total to over 4,500.

Promotion of new homes was high. The September 25, 1977, annual Seattle Master Builders Association-*Seattle Times* Parade of Homes expanded section featured homes in King and Snohomish counties ranging in price of $22,500 for a one-bedroom condo in south Seattle to a $250,000 mansion on Mercer Island. Not even a year later, the Seattle Home Show moved to the Kingdome, in March 1978. The move to the Kingdome allowed for fifty percent more display area, and even more parking for visitors. The growth continued to March 1979 when the 35th Annual Seattle Home Show featured a "Leisure Living" theme and entertained and informed more than 135,000 people.

By January 1979, Pete Hansell, the newly-elected President of the Association, lamented the industry's continued focus on single-family homes during the last decade. Hansell observed, "A builder's greatest problem during the late seventies boom was an inability to provide housing for a great portion of society." Many families could not afford a single-family home in the rapidly inflating housing market; in fact, by 1980, the median value for a house in Seattle was $65,000.[2]

The limited number of buyers created a competition between builders. The competition focused more on obtaining building sites, rather than competing for the customers. The cost of developing a raw lot skyrocketed, so the cost of housing necessarily had to follow. The answer was to increase the lot supply.

"Once the lot supply was increased," Hansell predicted, "builders would be forced to broaden their markets by developing lower priced housing."

Land use and growth management have always been two of the most political and controversial issues in the building industry. Everybody had their own agendas, and growth management was fodder for front page news stories. It seemed

Even through the 1970s, most meetings were held in the basement of the building at 170 Mercer Street, with cocktails provided. Here, GE hosted the bar for a 1979 Remodelers Council meeting.

everyone had opinions, not only the local officials, and builders and developers, but also school board, media and local citizens.

1978 President Ed Dean remembered, "But it wasn't a good guy versus bad guy situation. Our industry strongly supported the idea of sensible growth and land use planning. Without it...chaos would result. We didn't, and do not, challenge the motives, reasons, or special interests in the land use issue. The public is concerned and so are we. We do, however, hold highly suspect the unrealistic approach and needless procedures of many proposed policies to control growth."

The resulting high costs incurred by the builder were ultimately passed to the buyer. Nevertheless, the public only judged from their perspective and the building industry was cast in the role of the bad guys.

Organizational Restructuring

The King County population was growing. It had increased by more than 145,000, with the entire county population reaching 1,269,749 by 1980. Seattle-proper was shrinking as the population moved to the suburbs.

The organization was growing, too. By 1978, there were over 1,000 member companies, who began feeling some disenfranchisement. Builders in Bothell had different concerns from builders in Burien. To address those concerns, the Association decided to strengthen the organizational division they'd started in 1976.

The builders split into three councils: the Eastside Council (which included Seattle), the Snohomish County Council and the South King County Council. The divisions would allow member companies to effect change in a more geographically focused manner, and enjoy the strengths of the organization as a whole.

"With the three-council concept, we can better position ourselves to respond to the continually changing aspects of our industry; we can work with and for each other, and yet strive individually to improve it; we can exercise the autonomy of a growing council and at the same time enjoy the strength, continuity and singularity of the 'parent' SMBA. It is truly the best of both worlds," wrote President Dujardin at its inception.

Don Davis was one of the field directors working with the councils. "I staffed our

The South King County Council of the Seattle Master Builders Association didn't always meet at restaurants, sometimes they met in hotels' banquet facilities, as in the photo on the left.

land-use and multifamily committees as well as our South King County and Eastside Builders councils. I thought the council system worked well – members participated in whichever group made the best sense for their business, then the staff was able to take the groups' positions and effectively advocate on the members' behalf."

John Bratton was part of a group, started with Dave Main, called the South King County Builder Group. The group met once a month for breakfast, rotating restaurants in the south end. John says that over time the group "had gotten more focused and directed toward the political side and was willing to understand how the process works and how you get things done in a political world."

The Master Builders already had made extensive use of its committee Builders for Better Legislation, but as the 1970s came to a close the committee renewed fundraising efforts to investigate which political candidates would be sympathetic to the industry. The philosophy behind which candidates would receive the industry's support was based on the personal integrity of the individual, their open-minded-ness, and their dedication to preserving free enterprise as well as a commitment to housing. The Association would choose candidates to support, and suggest to members that they make

contributions to that candidate, rather than donating money directly through the PAC.

In 1979, the Association started a Speaker's Bureau. Spokespersons went out to talk about new methods of construction, and supported their speeches with a multi-screen audio/visual presentation. They gave speeches at Rotary Club meetings, or maybe they'd go to the Fraternal Order of Eagles, and spoke during lunches and other informal meetings. The Public Awareness committee worked to be sure the Seattle Master Builders scheduled a spokesperson at every major public and industry conference.

The Association was in full gear and now needed more professional help, so they embarked on a process to find staff who could juggle new responsibilities and do so with an increasing level of professionalism. In 1978, for the first time, the Association introduced a new Group Insurance Program designed exclusively for members, whereby they could purchase health insurance as a group, and receive discounts on premiums. As the 1970s came to a close, Association membership reached its highest level to date, 1,152. The organizational staff grew to eight full-time staffers.

General Electric Director, associate member, and 1979 Secretary of the Master Builders Roger Shaeffer applauded, "We became an organization that could accomplish more for our members than ever before. In 1979 alone, we were out in front on all the major issues: land use, financing, usury, building codes, energy, community plans, up-front fees, and all forms of government overregulation."

Along with the increase in staff and members, it was time to look for another location for the Association. The headquarters at 170 Mercer Street was too small for the expanding organization, and with construction focused more and more on the eastern side of Lake Washington, the location at Seattle Center wasn't so central any more. The decision to relocate was unanimous and land was purchased in Bellevue, though it would take until 1983 to make the move a reality.

It wasn't all work and no play for the Seattle Master Builders members, as this prize from a 1981 golf tournament shows. Whichever builder got the first hole–in–one would win the new car pictured. There's no record of whether anyone pulled it off.

Builders for Better Legislation

At the end of the 1970s there were signs of a turning economy, but signs are not always clear. Visible realities of the current economy were sale signs everywhere – on resales and new houses. Money was tight and interest rates still on the rise. Consumers were nervous. To the south, there were signs that Mount St. Helens would erupt. On May 18, 1980, the signs couldn't be ignored. The mountain was no longer threatening. The volcano erupted and the landscape changed literally and figuratively. Seattle-area voters were becoming critical of Forward Thrust, and the political landscape was changing, but the future was unclear.

Builders predicted (rightly) that government influence on land use issues was increasing. Jim Harkey, an Auburn developer, and Norm Davis, a Seattle remodeler, led an intensive effort by the Builders for Better Legislation Political Action Committee. Committee Chair Norm Davis believed, "Strong and active participation in government is the only way we can have a voice in making the laws that we will have to live with and work with."

Harry Pryde speaks on behalf of the building industry testifying before Congress on the national deficit.

They recruited 45 members to work for the cause. They increased available funds for their work by co-sponsoring a huge sale of surplus building materials in 1979, which lasted for three days. The Builders for Better Legislation also suggested to member companies that they make semi-annual contributions. Funds were raised for lobbying activities, and a Legal Action Fund was established to finance court actions and protect builder rights. Now, builders were active in politics, so it wasn't only funds they were raising, but greater political awareness.

Paul Nolan, the 1980 Association President, emphasized the "tremendous need for you and I to become directly involved in the political

process...It is not a matter of choice but of survival." By August, 1980 the membership in the Builders for Better Legislation PAC had grown to 107.

The Master Builders were ready to proactively get in front of an issue before the public had a chance to react. They were quickly put to the test in two cases. One opportunity was presented because Seattle Master Builders did not want homebuilders to be charged "front-end" fees. The Association introduced its first bill to the state legislature and for the first time, hired a full-time state lobbyist, Mary Mauerman. Mauerman, along with former executive Joe Martineau, who was lobbying on behalf of the state association, attended legislative hearings in Olympia. They were joined by volunteer members, and together they cultivated a network of other lobbyists.

After tireless lobbying for two years, on July 1, 1982, a new law (HB 1014) prohibiting cities and towns from charging "front-end" fees to homebuilders went into effect. Bringing the law to fruition was filled with drama.

This case was extremely difficult because cities, counties and homebuilders couldn't find a compromise to identify monies to replace the development fees. "It became the most complicated bill I'd yet seen," says Mauerman. "Starting as a half-page, it ended up 64 pages long. By then everyone and everything was in it."

An agreement was reached on the final day of the House session, only to die in the Senate's special session. That action did not defeat the Association. Work continued for another year to establish base support for the Association position against development fees. During the 1982 session, HB 1014 was enacted into law. Then the educational arm of the Association held seminars so members would understand the business implications. The final decision supported the Association's position on front-end fees, the ruling: charging of such fees by counties was a form of taxation, and not permissible under the general grant of police powers.

"It was a once-in-a lifetime experience," Mary Mauerman recalls of that two-year political struggle.

The other opportunity was on July 31, 1980, when the Association filed suit in King County Superior Court. The complaint was against the Washington State Utilities and Transportation Commission and the Puget Sound Power and Light Company. At issue was the recent decision by the commission to allow Puget Sound to restrict electrical hookups for space and water heaters in their western Washington service area. It was ruled Washington State Utilities and Transportation Commission had acted beyond its authority. In addition, it was discriminatory and did not comply with the State Department of Ecology's State Environmental Policy Act (SEPA).

"Master Builders' political success," concluded Jim Summers, 1981 Association President, "is attributable to the tremendous financial support of our members, the hard work of many people in drafting and advocating our legislation and, above all, electing to office representatives and senators who would listen and act favorably on our proposals."

ROB STEWART

ACHIEVEMENTS:
President, Master Builders, *1982*
Builder of the Year, 1983
President, BIAW, *1997*
Hall of Fame, *2007*

Rob Stewart has a long and established history of leadership within the Seattle Master Builders Association. A son of a homebuilder, Rob worked his way through college as a carpenter, then gained valuable experience in the Army Corps of Engineers. In 1972, Stewart founded Greacen Homes, which custom-builds single- and multi-family homes in King County.

The following year, he became a Master Builders Association member, initially because as a small-business owner, he was looking for help that supported independent entrepreneurs within the building industry. King County was one of the first metropolitan areas in the country to enact growth management legislation; Stewart had faith that the Association would be a crucial resource for homebuilders in this region as they locked horns with local and national politicians in favor of builders' rights.

Stewart's interest in supporting local builders through professional solidarity was apparent from the get-go. Stewart has served on numerous Association committees. As Stewart points out, "I have probably been on every committee they've ever had."

Stewart became President of the Association in 1982. Among the issues on his agenda for that time was energy.

Concerned that unfair standards regarding energy would negatively affect the builders' ability to provide cost-effective housing, Stewart spoke out against energy conservation rules which he said lacked serious scientific testing and investigation.

Under his leadership, the Builders for Better Legislation committee changed its name to the Affordable Housing Council. This indicated the committee was not solely composed of builders, but represented a wider and more diverse membership. Today, similarly, Stewart is interested in how the Association has evolved from a builders' association into a members' association. With an ever-expanding membership base, Stewart believes that the Association is doing a good job of focusing on the needs of builder members and associate members alike.

Rob feels that the organization should remain "aggressive" in confronting and challenging the city and county land-use policies. He emphasizes that an industry association such as the Master Builders Association has to "take care of the builders" as well as its associates. Because of his strong commitment to the Association, Stewart was among the first builders inducted into the Hall of Fame in 2007.

No Growth is No Good

Fear was high that suburban sprawl would have a negative impact on the region. Would strip malls and subdivisions take over the Northwest lifestyle? The issues were complex, the stakes high, and virtually any outcome was destined to be controversial. Many diverse groups – citizens, local officials, the media, and, of course, builders and developers – were drawn into the issue.

The No Growth movement gained traction, as popular *Post-Intelligencer* columnist Emmett Watson wrote about an organization called Lesser Seattle, more colorfully called "Keep the Bastards Out." He wanted to create an opposition to the boosterism of groups such as the Chamber of Commerce, and, vocally, wanted to fight the "Californication" of the Puget Sound. Watson said that Seattle was an Indian word for "stay away from here," and he urged that *real* Seattleites fight tooth and nail against growth of any kind.[3] He championed affordable, small-scale housing on large lots, so we didn't have to see our neighbors when we didn't want to.

Although the builders were often portrayed as villains in the land-use debate, Association Executive Bill Winn explained that their concerns extended beyond the interests of the building industry, "Home builders opposed actions that would severely regulate land availability, adversely affect the economic structures of the areas in question and place an inflated price on available land and thus substantially increase the cost of housing."

While not opposing reasonable land-use and growth-management legislation, the housing industry felt threatened by many of the proposed policies. One example was a procedure which imposed lengthy delays in plat approval. It also became a separate cost factor in subdivision developments, increasing cost which was passed on ultimately to the consumer.

As the primary spokesperson for the housing industry, the Association, in February of 1978, established an industry-wide committee to develop a growth program for the Puget Sound region. The committee solicited input from builders, developers, engineers, realtors, title companies and financial institutions. Its intent was to put its recommendations before relevant government agencies. The Association's campaign actively defended against policies which, once enacted, would include discriminatory, exclusionary zoning, unreasonable limitations or moratoriums on rezoning, and issuance of building permits. The campaign looked to remove needless administrative delays and excessive fees and charges.

In late 1979, Leiv Vikingstad, 1977 Association President, got the news that the discount rate – the rate that banks pay on the money which they borrow to lend back out – was up to thirteen percent. He remarked, "The *discount* rate! Well, I had four houses I was working on at the time. Three were already sold. The other sat for a year at eventually 23 percent payment...I went on a three-year vacation."

1975 Association President Bill Conner remembers his experiences of the late seventies. "King County had passed an ordinance that you could build houses on very small lots, and we got approved to build an eight-lot-to-the-acre project in eastern Kirkland. We were building those, and even when the rates were at eighteen percent, people were buying them because they were cheaper than anything else around, about $50,000." Conner says that he was able to work out a deal with his bank where his company could buy loans and then loan homebuyers the money to purchase the house directly.

Unfortunately, the No Growth movement gained popularity and the cost of constructing homes rose quite dramatically. Interest rates hit sixteen to seventeen percent. Plus the inflation rate had reached double-digit figures and was still climbing. In this environment, homebuilding in general faced trying times. 1980 Association President Paul Nolan had his work cut out for him. By 1982, membership had fallen back to 1977 levels, 768 companies. To weather the difficult time, there were budget cutbacks and staff realignments, along with some Seattle Master Builders staff members volunteering to take a five percent pay cut.

Energy Crisis

Nationally, energy had been at the forefront of consumers' minds as early as the 1973 oil crisis when members of the Organization of Petroleum Exporting Countries proclaimed an oil embargo. For the most part, industrialized countries relied on crude oil from these suppliers. As a result targeted countries turned their attention to finding ways to develop new systems to support energy conservation.

In 1977, in fact, the Women's Auxiliary of the Master Builders Association had made energy their top priority. They not only had conservation-minded speakers, but also produced

Balancing efficiency with inflation costs
and environmental concerns, all kinds
of energy producers were competing for
builders' and consumers' dollars.

principles, responsible environmental stewardship and account-ability to the region." However, the result of the interpretation of their mission was to enforce excessive conservation at an unacceptable cost.

The Association had set out to prove that the new standards were immeasurable. Complicated issues involving land use, growth management, and energy conservation dominated the concerns of the building industry and would be the over-arching challenge of the 1980s.

Builders took personal responsibility and made small steps forward in individual ways. Snohomish County builder and Association President of 1988, Larry Sundquist, remembers, "The energy code was a big issue, and there was a program back then called Super Good Cents, and they were trying to push very energy-efficient houses and getting everybody to build them." The program made good progress particularly in Snohomish County, because Snohomish County houses were usually either heated electrically or by oil, whereas there was a lot of natural gas in King County.

"energy efficient" desserts, fruits and store-bought cookies, for their meetings all year.

Washington State signed into law The Northwest Regional Power Act in 1981. The Bonneville Power Administration, headquartered in Portland, Oregon, was the federal agency under the U.S. Department of Energy serving the Pacific Northwest. It operated an electricity transmission system, which included several different types of production facilities. Bonneville Power aimed "to be a national leader in providing high reliability, low rates, consistent with sound business

Rob Stewart's 1982 year as President of the Association was in the middle of the most economically devastating years. Membership bottomed out at 768, and it was a struggle for Spikes and Spikettes alike to recruit new companies. Nevertheless, the March 13, 1982, annual Seattle Home Show opened at Seattle's Civic Auditorium, featuring five model homes, and drew the second highest attendance ever with 145,220 visitors. Then on September 26, 1982, the annual Parade of Homes drew a record number of 228 entries.

The popularity of these events may have profited from the 1982 Seattle-King County Convention and Visitors Bureau tourism campaign. To promote the city, the Bureau adopted the epithet "The Emerald City."

The "Computer" is Coming

As 1983 came to a close, there seemed to be a glimmer of hope. Redmond, a one-stoplight town on the Eastside, welcomed a new business – Microsoft, founded in New Mexico but relocated to Bellevue in 1979, was expanding from Bellevue into Redmond as well. The age of the personal computer was exploding upon the world. Already, the Puget Sound region had been the birthplace of some of computing's most important milestones. In April 1980, for instance, a Tukwila man wrote QDOS, the "Quick and Dirty Operating System," which he sold to Microsoft in October of that year, before developing the language that would become MSDOS.

The impact of the business to the region was unimaginable. Earlier, in April 1978, builders

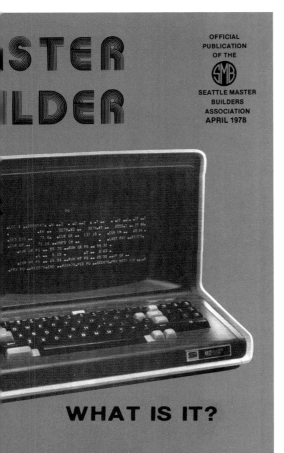

OFFICIAL PUBLICATION OF THE

SEATTLE MASTER BUILDERS ASSOCIATION APRIL 1978

The early computer terminals had small screens with only black and one other color. They functioned as combination typewriter and calculator to many; others liked to play text–based games.

WHAT IS IT?

had opened their mailboxes to find a *Master Builder* magazine with a photograph of an early PC, headlined "What is it?" Data service centers joined the Association, hoping to aid builders in computerizing job functions and cost analysis. However, judging that there is no record of wide scale computerization until 1988, members did not appear to welcome the service.

National Stage

The dual challenge of "expensive money" and rapid inflation was taking a major toll on homebuilders and homebuyers. Bill Winn, who had been Executive Officer since 1976, retired in 1982, and passed the reins to Falk Kelm. Falk had experience as the Executive Officer of the state association as well as having successfully helmed both the Snohomish County Council and the HOW program.

By mid-1983, inflation had slowed substantially, and lending institutions had money available from new money market deposit accounts. The local housing market began to stabilize, but new homebuilders were still hampered by the FHA interest rate, hovering at thirteen percent with conventional rates a point or two higher.

The new money banks were lending to homeowners became a boon for remodeling. By July 1, the Association's Remodelors Council reported a fifty-percent increase in activity over the previous year. As often is the case, when homebuilding is slow, many builders turn to remodeling as a source of income.

By 1983, it was time for an extensive membership drive to overcome the slump caused by the housing slowdown of the previous three years. A logical start was with the Associates Council. Their main focus was to ensure that members would do business with other members.

Former Seattle Master Builders President Harry Pryde was elected 1983 president of the National Association of Home Builders, after a contentious election. During his term, he focused on issues of regulatory reform and established a NAHB Deregulatory Task Force. He also met with President Ronald Reagan to discuss growing concerns over rising interest rates and high budget deficits.

As the only Northwest builder to have been elected to the presidency in the forty years of NAHB history, all eyes from the state were on

JOHN BRATTON

ACHIEVEMENTS:
Remodeler of the Year, *2004 & 2007*
President-Elect, Master Builders, *2012*

John Bratton has been an active leader in Master Builders since he joined in 1972, with the sole intention of displaying in the Seattle Home Show. As a subcontractor material supplier, John knew the show would be a very good source of sales and exposure to the general public. He worked for several larger builders, then started his own custom homebuilding company in 1982.

His construction company started building small ramblers and eventually ended up in the custom home market. In 1992, with his building slowing down, he got into the remodeling field. "I got started in remodeling and never looked back."

When Bratton moved to Seattle, one of the first things he saw was the billboard asking "Would the last one leaving Seattle please turn out the lights?" After starting in business during a downturn, and then weathering several more, he tells people in the industry, "this last four or five years of growth was not a normal market. You have to prepare for a downturn." Bratton credits the Master Builders Association for preparing members for a recession or depression through the networking established with fellow members over the years. "The members will openly share anything because we all go through the same experiences, we're all suffering the same consequences now. People who are outside of the organization in today's economy are really suffering because they have no place to go. That's a big problem and that's why I've been a strong promoter of the Association."

John received the bulk of his education basically through Association-sponsored classes, receiving Certified Graduate Remodeler designation and Certified Aging-in-Place Specialist designation. "I've probably over the years taken 25 different classes through the Association."

John worked on the Education Committee for a number of years and also teaches courses on Customer Service and Sales and Marketing for Remodelers. However, he gradually moved to the political side, working with the Housing Policy Committee and the South King Issues Group. On the state level, Bratton worked as the chair of the Legislative Policy Committee in 2007, BIAW's Affordable Housing Council and has been active in the Remodelors Council and Executive Committee on both the state and national levels.

Even after all that, Bratton says, "My position is that I would rather be a foot soldier than leading the charge. I'd rather be a support to those people that are going to do it, and be friendly and offer conversation based upon an understanding of how things work."

John thinks builders need to better leverage technology to find new employees and to engage young people in the industry. "The use of the social media, it's tremendous."

As President of the National Association of Home Builders, Harry Pryde introduced President Ronald Reagan. Pryde believed that political participation was absolutely a necessity for individuals, as an industry and as Associations.

Pryde. He stepped up to the challenges at hand. He worked directly with President Reagan to craft a new plan for housing; Reagan told him "You and your industry have just struggled through your toughest, most painful time since the Great Depression; and you did it without bailouts, boondoggles, or big brother. And here you are today leading America's economic recovery by the strength of your nerve and the sweat of your brow."[4]

President Reagan had drastically reworked the FHA program for homebuyers. A homebuyer in 1981 needed an income of $43,000 per year to qualify for a $60,000 mortgage; by 1983, they could qualify with just $31,000 annual income. Pryde travelled extensively, talking to homebuilders' associations around the country about how to weather the economic downturn and how to strengthen their associations using tricks of the trade he'd learned in the Seattle Master Builders.

Harry's motto was "Shelter for the People, Jobs for the Economy," because he believed strongly that the housing industry could help turn around the nation's economic woes. In his travels, Pryde was always on the lookout for the next big thing in real estate, something that he could bring back to the Seattle area. But his wife, Ann, said, "You couldn't afford to make many mistakes up here. Harry would travel around and see what other builders were doing, and just laugh. He said they could never get away with that here." ♣

CHAPTER 10

Riding the Wave

1984 – 1989

Economic indicators were on a big upswing, and their effects reached the majority of builders and others in the Puget Sound. Seattle became an increasingly white-collar town, and the Association opened their Bellevue office in 1984. Efforts were redoubled to promote doing business with members. In 1985, the Master Builders hired Don Chance to be Executive Officer; he quickly got the books back in the black with member spike drives. Not only was the Puget Sound area's housing industry strong, but developers were building downtown-Seattle housing for the first time in decades. The average King County home price increased to over $100,000 for the first time in 1987, spurring further discussion in the Association about what "affordable housing" meant. The Political Action Council was renamed the Affordable Housing Council to reflect that concern. In 1988, the Seattle Master Builders, along with the National Association, funded scholarships for nine students interested in the construction field. The Seattle Return on Industrial Insurance program was merged with the state's, bringing financial stability to BIAW's program, and a more consolidated functionality to the local chapters.

Homes constructed in the 1980s were not locked in to any one style, and reflected the growing desire for more space. Homes such as these two, built in Klahanie by Burnstead Construction in 1988, typically had more bedrooms, more bathrooms and more amenities than did older homes. Klahanie, a master-planned community in the Sammamish Plateau, was begun in 1985 and completed in 1998.

Moving & Shaking

Seattle and the Northwest were finally breaking the dependence on Boeing jobs. White-collar businesses were moving to town, attracted by the growing import of Microsoft and other high-tech firms. With the majority of King County construction happening on the Eastside, leaders at the Seattle Master Builders had been planning for several years to move to a more central location. Those plans had been put on hold, though, by the economic downturn. In July 1983, a piece of land at 2155 112th Avenue NE, Bellevue, was acquired and the ground was broken. By December, the 2,200-square-foot, wooden two-story new office building was ready. At first, the Association would only need the first floor and rented out the second. They were excited by the surrounding wooded area and accommodation parking. It was so different from the Mercer Street office with its view of the Space Needle and city congestion; its lack of parking, with members complaining that their cars might be broken into by the panhandlers.

The building was built, owned and operated by the members of Seattle Master Builders Association. Fred Burnstead took over as President and immediately embarked on a long-range plan to broaden membership participation. If an association is to be dynamic and effective there has to be a large percentage of volunteer member involvement. "At that time," says Burnstead, "the Association had some 240 members working on committees, council executive committees, and the Board of Directors. That represented about 24 percent of the total membership. When compared to other homebuilder associations, the Seattle Master Builders Association ranked among the biggest and best *involved* in the country." The first action was to restructure and develop goals for each Association council and all standing committees. The Association committees were reorganized to better serve the membership.

Foreshadowing the 1984 restructuring, in 1982, the Builders for Better Legislation changed its name to the Affordable Housing Council. This name clearly defined that "affordable housing" was the political aim of the Association. "Better legislation" was too general for a political action committee. At the same time, the committee set up a fund for future legal expenditures.

Similarly, Seattle Master Builders Association had created the Public Awareness Committee in 1981. Now three years later, Chairman Bill Hurme

The Remodelers Council sponsored improvement projects of all sorts for the Association. Here, a group of remodelers pressure-washed the Master Builders parking lot at 112th Avenue in Bellevue.

was looking at how he could make his committee more effective. The committee had begun with the objective to inform and educate members on marketing new construction by understanding the needs of promoting new home sales. As a means to acknowledge and celebrate the best work and achievements in quality by member builders, the committee decided to begin an annual awards program, MAME, which stood for the Marketing and Merchandising Excellence Awards. Seattle took hints from other cities such as San Francisco, Dallas, Denver, Miami and San Diego to fashion the awards. By showcasing member talent, their outstanding product, and innovative merchandising, MAME aimed to reinvigorate the building community.

Susan Wells, chairperson of the MAME committee, reported, "We achieved all we had expected, including a more positive public image, industry pride, and increasing Seattle Master Builders Association stature." The members were revitalized from the positive results of increased press and public awareness, and of course, they also enjoyed the opportunity to dress to impress their compatriots. The first overall MAME award winner was Pembrook Meadow in Mill Creek, built by Northward Construction.

MAME would continue for many years, with members competing against their peers in building, design and marketing skills. Contestants were evaluated by professionals from other parts of the country, so the Oscar-like trophy became more than just a gold statue. This competition pushed members to stretch their boundaries.

By 1985, Bill Hurme reported to the Public Awareness Committee that a Sales and Marketing Council was being formed, and after being approved by the Seattle Master Builders

Falk Kelm worked for the Seattle Master Builders Association from 1983 through the end of 1985. Tragically, he died at his home just two months after stepping down from the Executive Officer position.

Association Board of Directors, the council would take over the responsibilities of the promotional programs such as MAME and the new Spring Designer Showcase. The Public Awareness Committee would concentrate on local media relations for the Association. At that time, the Association had a small staff, so when the membership decided that something had to be done, they would have to do it themselves. From public relations to local lobbying, members were responsible for implementing many of the Association's activities.

Awareness of quality campaigns highlighted the need for a greater emphasis on education, so the Seattle Master Builders Association also formed an Education/Leadership Committee in 1984. It developed a series of workshops and seminars to provide members with an in-depth look at subjects such as marketing, building technology, builder law and computers.

It was the year of committees. In addition to the ones mentioned above, and the always active Remodelers Council, the Seattle Master Builders Association formed the following committees in 1984: the King County Land Use Committee, Housing Crisis Task Force, Energy and Building Codes Committee, Education Committee, Government Affairs Committee and the Past Presidents Council.

By 1984, the economic pendulum was back on its upswing, and for the majority of builders and others in the Puget Sound area, business was strong. Developers were remaking the city's skyline and building downtown housing for the first time in decades. The average Seattle home price increased to over $100,000 for the first time. When Executive Officer Falk Kelm left the Association, the Master Builders launched a national search for their new Executive Officer. They found him close to home. Don Chance's previous experience was as Director of Land Use and Environmental Affairs for the Washington Affairs for the Washington Forest Protection Association. He was hired as the new leader effective January 1, 1985.

Chance brought strong organizational skills, and he quickly got the books back in the black with membership drives. Over the next two years, the Association embarked on a campaign to modernize: records were computerized, functions updated and management structures reorganized. Chance described it thusly: "The administrative regrade of the Seattle Master Builders Association could be likened to the refurbishing of a Korean War-era cruiser into a modern missile frigate."

Don Davis, who came on board with the Association in 1983 as Land Use and Technical Services Director, remembers that time period as being fairly intense. "The title didn't actually relate to what I was doing," Davis laughs. He described the atmosphere of the Association at the time, "It was relaxed in the fact that you could smoke in the building, they'd sit around and smoke cigars. Sometimes even grab a bottle of scotch and drink at some of these meetings. But, it was intense. I remember our board meetings were filled with high-level debates. I think our internal politics were very polarized then."

Indeed Chance and the other six staff members had challenges. Revenues had fallen well below expectations and together with the deficit spending in the budget, the reserves were dangerously low. By late 1986, the Association had made management changes by juggling personnel to different job functions and computerizing records, and they were finally able to increase revenues.

Membership drives remained the key focus. 1986 President Bud Tynes complimented the Spikes for bringing membership up to over 900 companies. Executive Officer Don Chance, proud of the job accomplished, retired in early 1988 to Montana. James Williams took the helm.

BILL SHERMAN

ACHIEVEMENTS:
President, Master Builders, *1989*
Builder of the Year, *1991*
Hall of Fame, *2006*

Bill Sherman has a building history steeped in family tradition and years of experience in the industry. His company, Sherman Homes, constructs luxury homes in Washington and Oregon. After earning a degree in chemistry, Sherman worked for Union Carbide, a consumer chemical company. In 1971, he served as a commissioned officer in the army, before getting into construction through his father-in-law, George Bell. When Bell decided to sell off a few of his subsidiary companies, Sherman bought a building materials firm, and later also acquired a cabinet operation and a countertop operation. In 1984, Sherman started Sherman Homes. Bell's reputation solidified the new venture since both Sherman and Bell positioned themselves in the industry with a long-standing local legacy of building homes and building multi-family projects.

Joining the Master Builders as an associate member in 1970, Sherman immediately became active in activities and committees. He appreciates the work of associates for all they do in bringing together valuable resources, formulating policies, promoting the building industry, and endorsing quality, affordable housing. Sherman transitioned to a builder member when he began Sherman Homes. Bill definitely values his involvement and the relationships he has established. "I have been able through that, to create all kinds of relationships at both the local, state, and national levels. To me, you cannot put a price tag on it."

During Sherman's tenure as President in 1989, the Association was growing to 1,000 members; a "pretty good-sized organization." Some challenges facing Sherman during his presidency were the creation and development of the ROII program and further development of the medical program for members. He came to realize how much value the medical program brought to individual members, but especially to the Association as a whole. According to Sherman, "The medical program also could become a revenue stream for the Association. We knew we needed not just the dues that were collected, but also other sources of revenue."

Bill says the Master Builders have contributed to his professional success, particularly in the relationships that he has cultivated through the organization, which can make or break a business during lean economic times. Sherman feels that the housing industry is essential in contributing to the country's economy. He explains that his personal philosophy is to stay hopeful, despite what happens. "Just keep the positive attitude. When I'm being challenged, I remember that I've got to have a good attitude, and the good attitude will take us to the next day, the next step, the next project, and solve the issue. No matter what that issue is."

Builders partnered with the Snohomish County Public Utilities Department and the Bonneville Power Administration on the "Super Good Cents" program, which let potential buyers know they were looking at energy-efficient housing. Here, in 1984, Larry Sundquist (far right) poses with his Super Good Cents Certification and a group of builders outside the sign for Harvest Glen in Bothell.

Legislative Battles

During the early 1980s, the Association established the Remodelors Council Referral Service, put the final touches to the Remodelors One-Year Limited Warranty, the Parade of Homes, produced dinner and breakfast meetings, coordinated booths for Seattle Home Shows, builder's surplus sales and continued to take up the fight for builders' rights. The pursuit of legislative rights for homebuilders at the local level in both Snohomish and King Counties was extensive and comprehensive.

In 1984, the struggle for builders' rights was underway with efforts in Bellevue, Renton, Kent, South King County, and Snohomish County. These local issues included: the Housing Preservation Ordinance and amendments that affected parking access and minimum dimension standards; correcting "major flaws" in the Natural Determinants Policy; affordable housing studies used to streamline Renton's city's regulatory system; changes to the proposed Solar Access Ordinance; and Public Utility District line extension and hook-up charges; and alleviating the backlog in land-use hearings.

Another major accomplishment in 1984 was the adoption of a one-day permit-processing service by the Seattle Department of Construction and Land Use. Frustrated by lengthy delays in permit processing, the members of the Association met with the department to advocate reform. Multifamily Council vice president, Dick Rokes says, "Builders often support certain regulatory concepts but, by nature, cannot tolerate the additional paperwork, needless rules, and lengthy time delays. Permit processing at the City of Seattle was getting out of hand."

The committee members set up a meeting with the director of Seattle's Department of Construction and Land Use to suggest "fast-track" and "self-certification" methods. After long discussions, the city responded with a one-day permit-processing service and accepted the Association's permit suggestions, unless conditions warranted review.

These exchanges between the Association and government resulted in the adoption of several industry recommendations. For example, one of the most important issues of 1984-85 was a General Development Guide which was being developed by King County. The new guide was going to be a new comprehensive land-use plan, which would propose growth controls on future housing, subdivision and commercial developments. The Association put together the Alliance for Sensible Growth, a group meant to oversee King County's proposed guide. Working through the alliance, the Seattle Master Builders Association used all its influence to create a plan for managing growth that was not only clear, but could be implemented while still providing diversity. The alliance asked the county for more time to perform a detailed study before implementing its General Development Guide.

At the same time, conservation standards were set forth by the Northwest Regional Power Act. Signed into law in 1981, the Act was designed to answer the growing problem of meeting the region's electrical energy supply needs. The Act established a commission to create a conservation plan for the Northwest and asked it to predict future energy supply and demand for the next twenty years. The building industry was anticipating a negative impact based on the requirements the Act might impose on excessive conservation, growth and power usage, as well as incentives for utility companies. Builders and suppliers immediately formed a coalition to challenge the Act.

Once again, the members undertook an intensive study by going out into homes and buildings to measure heat loss. The conservation plans underestimated the costs; the study demonstrated the proposed standards would increase construction costs of a 1,350-square-foot home by about $4,000. Additionally, the plan overestimated the savings in electricity use. In essence, the study challenged the validity of the plan by asking, "How could conservation and weatherization be effectively mandated when no one could prove that the proposed savings were real?" The Association position was that energy conservation makes sense in housing when it is cost effective, so the conservation standards needed more scientific testing and investigation. Energy use continued to be a primary building issue.

Nevertheless, the January 1, 1986 adoption of the Northwest Power Planning Council's Model Conservation Standards for residential construction would mean increased construction costs. Before its passage, in 1985, those costs had reached an additional $8,500 for the average 1,800-square-foot house. Additional costs were viewed by 1985 Master Builders President Don Dally as "not cost effective in decreasing a homebuyer's energy expense. It was a ludicrous demand for government to place on our industry."

The Association tried to point out alternatives, but was defeated. There was no other choice but to take the Northwest Power Planning

Homes' interiors were constructed with energy-saving appliances and heat-conserving windows.

Photo courtesy The Burnsteads.

Council to court to oppose the standards. The lawyers argued the case on three issues: the lack of cost-effectiveness, its constitutionality and the lack of environmental accountability. It was first heard by the 9th Circuit U.S. Court of Appeals on May 9, 1985. The court denied the Seattle Master Builders Association's plea and its decision upheld the Northwest Power Planning Council's Model Conservation Energy Standards.

These battles only fueled the resolve by Seattle Master Builders to continue to take on legislative issues that affected its members. The Association was ready to step up. In 1987, Jim Halstrom and Bob Austin were contracted as lobbyists, replacing Ed Moger. These new lobbyists were ready to put pressure on local government as well as the state legislature.

Larry Sundquist took over as President of the Master Builders Association in 1988. He was instrumental in hiring the new executive officer. Sundquist had known Jim Williams in Olympia, where Sundquist had spent four years as Legislative Chairman for the Building Industry Association of Washington. Larry had worked in that volunteer capacity with the state home-builders and was aware of the tension that could come between Seattle and the state association. He would use his presidency to build bridges between the two organizations.

Sundquist was soon battling not only political issues, but found himself locked in confrontations with the media. For years, the issue of sprinklers and where sprinklers were required by the government was raging. Despite their small size, sprinklers can add a lot of money to

Snohomish County Master Builders members met frequently with concerned community members and elected officials to talk about issues of safety and affordability.

the cost of a home. Sundquist's position was "It started out as a great idea for hotels and things like that and maybe for some apartment houses, but pretty soon, they pushed it down and out. Now, we're putting them in a lot of houses, and I think it's a totally unnecessary expense."

In 1988, on his way to work, Larry heard the radio news report a fire in a south King County apartment. A mother and several of her children had died in the blaze. The reporter on KIRO was talking to a fire marshal who was saying, "Well the Master Builders have been fighting this, putting sprinklers in apartments." The reporter indignantly responded, "You mean the Master Builders have been fighting this?"

Larry Sundquist learned quickly all about sprinklers and the industry position as he came to the defense of the Association's opposition to mandating sprinkler systems with the media.

One thing was certain: the Seattle Master Builders were learning that if change was going to come, they would need more support. The Association decided it was time to become directly involved in making election recommendations by forming the Committee to Elect in order to suggest which candidates deserved contributions from members.

Affordability

On August 10, 1988, Larry Sundquist's office put out a press release. "Rents will rise sharply under Tax Reform." The Tax Reform Act of 1986 drastically changed the way people could write off real estate losses. Prior to the Act's passage, investors could pool their resources and purchase rental real estate, then, at the end of the year, if it hadn't made money, they could each write off losses equivalent to their share in the property. Thus, investors were incentivized to keep rents low, and losses high, so their income would be offset by the rental property loss. Tax provisions were also made retroactive for all those who invested prior to enactment. The net result was that raising rents became the only way an investor would get a return. The nation's tax policy was striking the rental housing market squarely on the jaw. The Tax Reform Act's effect would stagnate the market for building new rental housing. Investors would be searching for more profitable, less risky investments. The release warned that multifamily units would decline by 36 percent. "And there's no turnaround in sight, which means that over the next few years the supply of rental housing will tighten, rents will go up and people on the bottom rung of the income ladder will experience even greater difficulty ahead finding decent, affordable housing."

The Association presented a study by the Joint Center for Housing Studies of Harvard University, which reported significant drops in home ownership among young households since 1980, with rental rates also rising to forty to fifty percent of the household income. Many Americans were unable to obtain affordable housing and lived in substandard homes. Now, the Tax Reform Act of 1986 would exacerbate the problem.[1]

The Seattle Master Builders Association had raised these issues in 1985 throughout the government's consideration of the Act. However, these concerns were obscured in discussions due to the popularity of the lower tax rates. Effective January 1, 1987, the Act became law and home equity loans became tax deductible if they were "less than or equal to the purchase price of the home plus the cost of any capital improvements." This was advantageous for the remodelers because it enabled homeowners to use home equity loans to embark on remodeling projects.

Crafting Compromise

Conflicts between the building industry and conservationists proved challenging when it came to finding common ground. Builders continued to argue that increased costs to them did not equate to savings for the homeowner nor measurable impact on the environment. Little had been done to implement the State Environmental Policy Act of 1971 (SEPA) until the adoption of the 1986 Northwest Power Planning Council's Model Conservation Standards. The requirements the standards put on new housing construction were severe: triple-pane windows, R-27 walls, R-38 ceilings, and the wrapping of homes to drastically limit changes of air and, thus, moisture. Alternatives existed, the industry pointed out to no avail.

After SEPA was adopted, it took over a decade for the state to figure out how counties would implement it. In the early 1980s, King County took on an evaluation of its use and they found enforcement was left to administrators. The administrators were responsible for making precise interpretations of vaguely written environmental policies. Without accountability, ecological damage was allowed to continue, undermining the purpose of the policy. The substantive, fundamental provisions were seldom used, and when enforced, environmental impact statements could allow a permit to be overridden without consideration of established zoning codes. The net result was that SEPA was not being used effectively. Administrative decisions had to be based on specific guidelines and backed by the impact of well-documented research and case studies of the environmental effects.

In 1985, King County unanimously adopted an updated Comprehensive Plan. The plan identified an "urban growth boundary line," which limited growth to areas with existing infrastructure for facilities and services. This way rapid growth could not impose on forests, farmlands and other natural habitats. Preserving the natural resources and beauty of rural areas could be realized while at the same time, cities could manage growth. Thus, the Comprehensive Plan attempted to balance the dual objectives of environmental protection and affordable housing.

Concurrently, the Seattle Master Builders Association was working with the state on the State Building Code Act. Passed in 1987, the Act established a residential construction category which included a merit rating system. This had a positive impact on industrial insurance payments. Additionally, an amendment was included clarifying that zoning rights were vested at the time of acceptance of a complete building permit application. For years, the permitting process had been murky regarding when zoning was vested, and it was hoped that the Act's provisions would clarify the issue.

Political activism was nothing new for the Association. However, the increasingly anti-growth, anti-building environment was going to be a challenge they would face for years to come.

Charitable Giving

Charitable efforts had always been part of the work ethic of Master Builders members, but had often been undertaken silently, or as part of members' other associations. In 1961, the organization had constructed a shower room, dressing room, and office for the Luther Burbank School gymnasium on Mercer Island. As a state-operated school, Luther Burbank had been unable to obtain funds to complete the recreational

facility. The Association members and friends donated materials and labor. This thoughtful aid and generosity was a tradition that was often repeated. Members formalized giving through the Remodelors Council.

Through the Remodelors Council, several outreach programs were started, and it quickly became one of the most visible councils in the Association. One way that the council was helping the less fortunate was through building ramps for people who had become disabled, and

Northwest builders have to contend with getting wet sometimes, as did this gentleman framing a house in the rain in 1987.

LARRY SUNDQUIST

ACHIEVEMENTS:
Builder of the Year, *1985*
President, Master Builders, *1988*
Hall of Fame, *2007*

Larry Sundquist owns and operates Sundquist Homes, a construction and development business under the umbrella of the Sundquist family of companies. Larry started the business with his father in 1974, and became its sole owner nine years later. Sundquist Homes builds residential living spaces primarily for Snohomish County in regions near its headquarters in Lynnwood, Washington.

He got involved with the Master Builders in 1977, when Jim Klauser, an Association member from Snohomish County, solicited his membership. At the time, the most important issue facing Snohomish County builders was agreeing on an energy code. A program called "Super Good Cents" advocated energy-efficient housing and promoted building growth in Snohomish County. The energy program was especially relevant to Snohomish County because of the lack of gas hookups available at the time. King County relied more on gas fuel; thus, based on available natural resources, it made more sense (or "cents") to endorse electrically heated homes in Snohomish.

Sundquist was named Builder of the Year in 1985, partially because of his work promoting sensible building and growth in Snohomish County. He became more interested in working with the Master Builders, and was eventually named its President. As Sundquist concluded his tenure as the Association's President in 1988, he experienced what he calls a "life moment" and started to question whether he

should move into new directions in his life and business. Larry says, "What we're doing right now is increasing our production, not because we have to. It's by design."

Just as Google has replaced the Yellow Pages for most of us, potential homebuyers are searching for houses online more than ever. Sundquist understands this fact well. The Sundquist Family of Companies' web site contains descriptions, photos, and layouts of its four subdivisions. Each community of Sundquist homes offers unique characteristics, such as a countryside appeal or a grander, more exclusive setting. Sundquist is excited about his soon-to-be fifth community, DiModa. Sundquist describes DiModa as displaying a "kind of urban, more edgy look" to attract younger homebuyers, and these sorts of buyers tend to spend much of their time online.

Keeping with family tradition in business involvement and ownership, Sundquist's son, Nathan, oversees the company's web site. Kristi, Sundquist's daughter, is the marketing manager of Sundquist Homes.

Though no longer spending long days at construction sites, Larry Sundquist continues to be active politically, both through the Master Builders Association and by working directly with Snohomish County.

were no longer able to get out of their houses. Omar Brown's phone rang off the hook with calls from Easter Seals representatives when he was chair of the council. They were trying to find qualified remodelers who could assist their clients in doing retrofits to their homes to make them fully accessible.

In the beginning, Omar Brown took the lead to get consensus on the proposed charity works at Remodelors Council meetings. Byron Vadset remembers, "Omar was just like a grandfather. He was very low key, very honest, very loyal. He would go to all kinds of meetings. He was a driving force for the remodeling council and he probably helped get the whole building association together to speak as one voice."

The Council was really struggling financially for a long time. To promote themselves they started the REX (Remodeling Excellence) Awards. They also started holding events to raise money. They put on wine-tasting contests, had pig roasts and picnics. The Remodelors Council proved they could

fund themselves, and eventually, the Association as a whole.

By 1988, the Association was invested in securing the future foundation for the construction industry by establishing a scholarship fund. The purpose of the scholarship program was to help youth become future builders, skilled tradesmen, and to train leaders in the construction industry. There were scholarships to universities and some grants given to some high school students as well.

The association was able to secure matching funds from the National Association of Home Builders in Washington, D.C. Nine scholarships were granted on the basis of academic achievement, financial need, and past experience in the construction industry. The scholarships were spread over three state colleges: University of Washington, Washington State University, and Central Washington University.

The Seattle Master Builders Association hosted the 1989 Washington State Home Builders Convention. The logo for the event, celebrating the Washington State Centennial, was a more colorful version of the one that the Association used for its own marketing.

More Robust Benefits

1987 President Dick Rokes and Byron Vadset, vice-president of the Remodelors Council and 1991 President, collaborated on how the Association could increase the amount of money available to it. They were mostly interested in supporting the political action agenda. The Association also wanted to provide help to member builders for litigation against frivolous lawsuits; being a friend of the court when it was needed for fairness. The answer to their problems was found through the Return on Industrial Insurance program.

There had always been an undercurrent of tension between the state organization, the Building Industry Association of Washington (BIAW) and Seattle Master Builders. Members have speculated that, due to the Seattle Association being the largest local in the state, the state association paid more attention to smaller locals, so as not to give Seattle undue influence. Political activism could give each side a negative spin of the other, depending on the aggressiveness of the tactics displayed, and that fractionalization spread down to the member builders.

"The Seattle organization was the largest in the state, and the state organization was small," explains Vadset. Members expect the Building Industry Association of Washington to get things done for them. "They can't do it themselves, or don't want to do it themselves or feel like they don't have the power." The differences around the state in lot prices and the cost of regulation are real, depending on where you are.

With the leadership of Dick Rokes and Byron Vadset, who represented the interest of the remodeling contractors, a good relationship between the two organizations developed. Together, the Seattle Association partnered with the State Association to combine their Return on Industrial Insurance (ROII) programs. Builders would get a larger check back, due to "merit ratings," and the state association was strengthened by the program's revenues.

The Department of Labor and Industries allowed organizations like the Building Industry Association of Washington and the Master Builders Association to pool their industrial insurance premiums, with the result of receiving a refund on these premiums. The organization bragged, "In each plan year, if the group's premiums exceed its losses, a refund is

CHUCK CROSBY

ACHIEVEMENTS:
Builder of the Year, *1989 & 1993*
President, Master Builders, *1995*

Chuck Crosby started working for homebuilders after school and on weekends while in high school, and became infatuated with building. Construction, he explains, "was outside. It was exciting. It was hands-on type stuff. All the stuff I enjoyed." Chuck built his first house in 1976. In 1978, he started his company, Crosby Homes.

Chuck joined the Association in late 1970s, and during the 1980s he saw a need for restructuring the Snohomish County chapter of Master Builders. "I was getting frustrated trying to get things accomplished at the county." Crosby continues, "We started organizing meetings for Snohomish County and putting things together and building it up."

During this period, there was discussion of breaking off Snohomish County into its own association. "It was decided that it would be better to stay here and be as one unit than to fracture it. Actually that is part of where the name change came from. I think the way it finally came down in my mind is we were better off strengthening the Association and making it stronger rather than fractionalizing it."

This background served him well as President of the Master Builders Association in 1995. Many previous presidents were based in King County, so Crosby brought a unique voice to leadership. "I think I had a lot of support in Snohomish County because of the involvement I have had

there." During his presidency, Snohomish builders became more prominent as Association members and he worked to get them more involved.

Crosby emphasizes the importance of Master Builders membership within local and state legislatures. "I think when you are active in the Association, especially when you are an officer or the president, or the immediate past president, when you need to get things done, especially governmental things, the Association name packs a lot of weight. It opens a lot of doors for you."

Chuck no longer lives in the Seattle area. He says, "I still do have an office here and we still do quite a bit of work out of my office. I still enjoy the benefits of the health insurance. I still enjoy the benefits of the Return on Industrial Insurance. I still enjoy the benefits of my past association with the Master Builders. People still recognize my name, I still get my phone calls answered."

Chuck has seen the Association grow and improve with each year. "It has gotten a lot bigger. It has gotten a lot more efficient and does a better job legislatively and working with the different counties and the different cities. From what I expected to see the Association do and be, it's just gotten better and better and better."

distributed to the participants. The refund for a plan year ranges between 24 percent and 30 percent spread over a three-year payout. Seattle Master Builders basically found that this partnership could bring not only benefit to our members, but also could become a revenue stream for the Association."

Not only did member companies get a refund from the state, but the Association received a percentage of the return, as incentive to make sure participating members were well trained, and thus less likely to make costly mistakes. To ensure that the training was up to snuff, the Association began, in 1987, the so-called Graduate Builders Institute. The first offering was a three-day seminar, held at the University of Washington, and its curriculum came from the NAHB. Builders would get an education on "Sales and Marketing, Business Management and Computer Applications" and they'd get a certificate through the UW.

Education had always been a priority of the Seattle Master Builders Association, but this marked the first time they were offering a professional designation. The continuing education of members was about to become even more important with the changes on the horizon. Builders would have to be highly adaptable, and responsive to changes that would come even more rapidly over the next decade. ♣

CHAPTER 11

Maturing through the Nineties

1990 – 1999

As the 1990s began, the Seattle area was growing rapidly. Due in part to its robust job market, the region experienced an influx of young adults as well as highly educated immigrants lured by the growing high-tech economy. With the expanding population, the suburbs began to sprawl as well. In 1990, the State of Washington passed the Growth Management Act (GMA), which identified goals counties and cities needed to meet in order to plan for growth; the implications for King and Snohomish county builders were many, and the impacts of the GMA would be felt for decades to come. The Association's leadership recognized the importance of getting out ahead of public opinion, and began to highlight the charitable activities of members. Sam Anderson was hired as the new Executive Officer in order to build greater consensus between different factions and change the industry image. The Association continued the tradition of throwing parties: they started the decade with a past-presidents' roast, and ended their first ninety years by throwing a Millennium Gala.

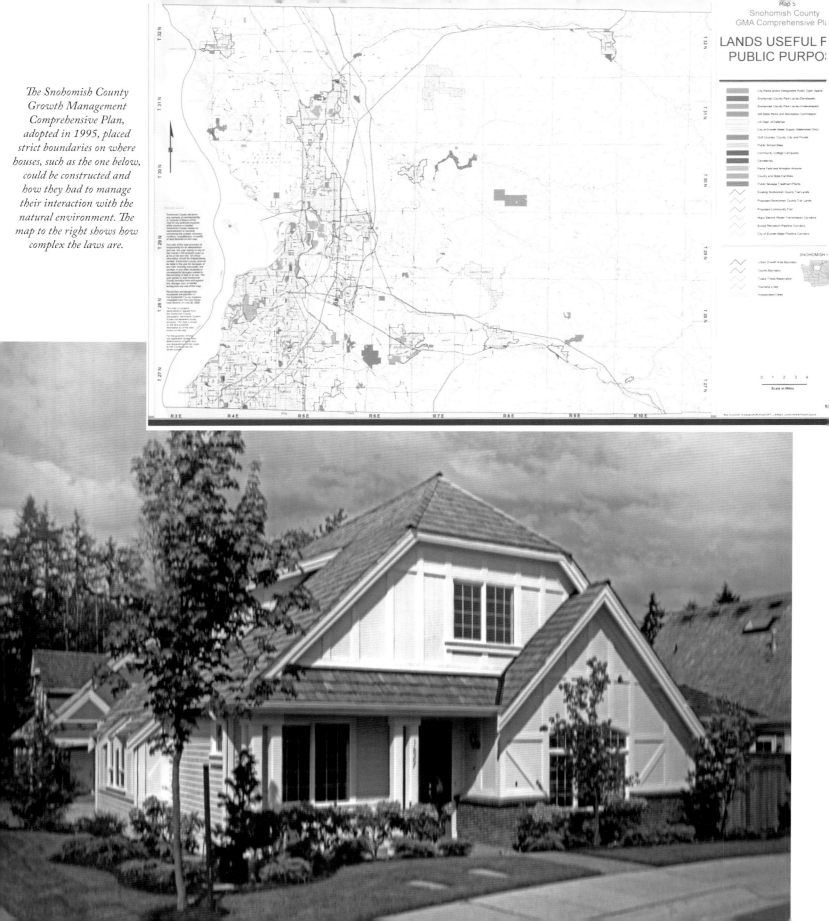

The Snohomish County Growth Management Comprehensive Plan, adopted in 1995, placed strict boundaries on where houses, such as the one below, could be constructed and how they had to manage their interaction with the natural environment. The map to the right shows how complex the laws are.

Map 5
Snohomish County
GMA Comprehensive Pla

LANDS USEFUL F
PUBLIC PURPOS

City Parks and/or Designated Public Open Space
Snohomish County Park Lands (Developed)
Snohomish County Park Lands (Undeveloped)
WA State Parks and Recreation Commission
US Dept of Defense
City of Everett Water Supply (Watershed Only)
Golf Courses, County, City and Private
Public School Sites
Community College Campuses
Cemeteries
Paine Field and Arlington Airports
County and State Facilities
Public Sewage Treatment Plants
Existing Snohomish County Trail Lands
Proposed Snohomish County Trail Lands
Proposed Community Trail
Major Electric Power Transmission Corridors
Buried Petroleum Pipeline Corridors
City of Everett Water Pipeline Corridors

SNOHOMISH I

Urban Growth Area Boundary
County Boundary
Tulalip Tribes Reservation
Township Limits
Incorporated Cities

0 1 2 3 4
Scale in Miles

Growth Management

On April 1, 1990, the Washington State legislature enacted a sweeping regulatory plan that builders in King and Snohomish counties would wish was just an April Fool's joke. The state had been considering for quite some time how to regulate growth, and had finally crafted an 89-section plan to do so. The Growth Management Act (GMA) had its roots in much of the same anger at disappearing farmland and rural area as had fueled the "Lesser Seattle" movement. In 1989, voters who felt that the environment and quality of life were being threatened ousted council members who were perceived as pro-builder, and replaced them with council members who supported growth management.[1] The Act stated that "uncoordinated and unplanned growth, together with a lack of common goals... pose a threat to the environment, sustainable economic development, and the health, safety, and high quality of life enjoyed by residents of this state. It is in the public interest that citizens, communities, local governments, and the private sector cooperate and coordinate with one another in comprehensive land use planning."[2]

Once the state legislature passed the GMA, legislators and builders alike had to figure out exactly what its implications were and what it meant. King and Snohomish Counties were considered "Fully Planning Counties." This meant that in addition to protecting wetlands, farmlands and forest lands and making sure that subdivisions were appropriately served by infrastructure, the Fully Planning Counties also had to agree on county-wide planning policies, create urban-growth boundaries, adopt comprehensive plans, and adopt development and zoning regulations which fit with the goals of GMA. (King County was able to pass its Comprehensive Plan in 1994, Snohomish followed suit in 1995.)[3]

Before the counties could fully react to what the GMA would require of them, citizens in King County took it on themselves to place an initiative on the November 1990 ballot: Initiative 547, entitled "Shall state growth and environmental protection goals be implemented by measures including local comprehensive land use planning and development fees?"[4] The argument for passage read, "If we want to protect Washington State from becoming another Los Angeles, we must act now to protect our environment and manage growth... Initiative 547 makes developers pay, not taxpayers." Developers, builders and elected officials alike knew that Initiative 547 would be a costly boondoggle that would set regional planning back decades.

Don Davis remembered, "Initiative 547 was initially very popular. We knew we needed to put together a strategy to defeat it, and we were ultimately successful." The strategy relied on simple common sense. If people actually understood the bill, they would see that it was detrimental to the quality of life in King County, as well as negatively impacting all construction. Davis continues, "We sent the initiative out to all the voters in the county with writing in the margin, *take a look at what this is really saying.* It was expensive, but we thought that if we let the public really know what it said, they wouldn't vote for it."

Chuck Henderson, President in 1990, led the fight against I-547. John Cochenour, who would be President in 1996, remembered that the fight against I-547 was the first time he had really felt engaged by the Association. "Chuck Henderson, I thought he did the most amazing job and went to bat for the industry." Cochenour was recruited to stand on the corner of 108th and Northup Way in Bellevue waving a sign in the dreary November chill. "I got really engaged. Of course, it

The fight against Initiative 547 was costly, but worth it. Here, Executive Officer Jim Williams (left) and 1990 President Chuck Henderson review a scrapbook celebrating their experiences fighting the anti-growth initiative. The fight was a success on two levels: one, the initiative did not pass, and two, the battle against a common enemy engaged builders to get involved in political actions.

helped that I-547 was resoundingly defeated in the polls, resoundingly defeated."

With much of the public against the so-called "Californication" of the Puget Sound, growth-management advocates on the King and Snohomish county councils had to get to work crafting their Comprehensive Plans for implementation of the GMA goals. Several member-developers were on the front lines of the fight – creating large-scale, master-planned communities had just gotten a lot harder. Peter Orser was working with Quadrant to develop Redmond Ridge in King County. The project had been platted and was in the early stages of development when, in 1994, the urban-growth boundary line was drawn straight through the proposed project. Orser fought King County over the right to develop what he calls "an urban island in what was going to be a rural zone. We envisioned Redmond Ridge as a fully-contained community with places to live, work and play. At these large sizes, you're not putting as much impact on the infrastructure as the typical subdivision would do, and we can dedicate fifty percent of the property to green space and wetland protection, and live to a higher standard because we had more space to work with."

The Master Builders Association fought to create comprehensive plans for both King and Snohomish counties that allowed for flexibility

like that required by the Redmond Ridge development. Unfortunately, the compromises reached were not as far-reaching as some of the members would have liked, and provisions were set in stone requiring where growth could occur. Also, the zoning for what could be built even within the growth boundaries was not always changed to match the desired higher density, and over time, this had the effect of creating an "artificial buildable-land shortage," according to past President Bill Conner. In 1998, Conner wrote, "The home- and shelter-building industry is obliged to operate under the philosophy of the state's Growth Management Act that presents a basically flawed & unbalanced approach. While on one hand it mandates unequivocally that planning districts set urban growth boundaries beyond which no urban growth shall occur, it provides no certainty of opportunity to build in the cities within the boundary."

The buildable-land shortage, whether artificial or not, had a nearly immediate effect on home prices in King and Snohomish counties. The median home price in King County jumped from 1988's $97,500 to $147,000 in 1991. By 1995, the median sale price of a home in King County had jumped to $183,700; Snohomish County homes' median price that year was $141,950.[5] In 1996, for the first time, condominium sales outstripped single-family-detached-home sales in King County. Snohomish County, on the other hand, only had 669 condo sales for the entire year.

As a response to the multifamily housing market heating up, the Association reactivated its Multifamily Housing Council. 1991 President Byron Vadset explained, "We have had many different council changes. We've had multifamily councils, a couple of other councils like that have come and gone depending upon the business climate. Everybody basically, when it comes right down to it, belongs for a reason and it comes down to what's in it for me." One person who got a lot out of the revamped Multifamily Council was Jim Potter, who had specialized in building multifamily units in the Seattle market since the 1980s. He said, "With growth management's passage, I really saw that the market was coming my way. It's going to radically change the business. It's going to change the future. Some

ZAKIR PARPIA

ACHIEVEMENTS:
President, Spokane HBA, *1983*
Washington State Builder of the Year, *1986*
President, BIAW, *1987*
Builder of the Year, *1996*
President, Master Builders, *1997*

Zak Parpia's résumé is starred with numerous presidencies of state associations, several building awards, and extensive community involvement. He owns and manages Himalaya Homes, but don't let the name fool you – Zak is originally from Bombay (Mumbai). Zak started Himalaya Homes in Spokane, then moved to Seattle in 1989. As part of his commitment to measurable customer satisfaction, Himalaya maintains communication after the house they built is sold, and is actively engaged as it becomes a home.

Parpia's company concentrates on providing affordable housing for first-time buyers, explaining that he does not have to compromise on the quality of a less-expensive house. "The quality remains the same, but the features, the buyers' perspectives, are different."

Throughout his career, Parpia has been in the unique position of presiding over several building associations, including the state association and the Seattle Master Builders in 1997. As President, this experience brought great fulfillment to Zak, because of his sincere dedication to the Association. He explains, "I got to motivate people that have no other reason to be involved except for the fact that they love the Association too." Parpia considers the Association an invaluable professional and personal resource. He has recruited about 1,500 members so far and continues to bring in new members. "I'm a believer. I know for a fact that you can't go wrong with an association that works so hard for you, that gives you the kind of benefits that Master Builders Association does." Zak recognizes that any new builder starting her or his own business will make a few mistakes, and he feels that as members, builders can avoid these mistakes by gaining the knowledge of other builder members. There is an extensive network of professional references and contacts at hand.

Zak Parpia sees the Master Builders as central to improving the economy through how the Association promotes and establishes the professional reputations of builders and the building industry as a whole. "We need to bring awareness to the public and the government that builders are a huge value to the community." Parpia sees builders as key to creating jobs and preventing the outsourcing of work. "The only people who actually consistently manufacture and use local labor are homebuilders. If you want to build the economy up by the bootstraps, it will have to be builders who make it happen."

Remodelers, like the ones shown to the right, took the lead on charitable works conducted through the Association. Above is a "Good Neighbor House" in Seattle's Beacon Hill neighborhood, which remodelers volunteered their time and expertise to refurbish and bring up to code.

fourteen miniature masterpiece doll houses that were displayed at Alderwood Mall, in Lynnwood.

The following year, on March 3, 1991, the *Playhouse* auction was repeated. This time, it was held at Southcenter Mall, where eleven custom doll houses were displayed. The $53,848 raised went to benefit the Boys and Girls Clubs of King and Snohomish counties, Childhaven, and Custom Industries. The "Best of Show" and "Best Use of Space" awards went to a dollhouse built by 1991 President Byron Vadset's company Byset Remodeling.

In addition to these fundraising occasions, the Association was able to raise $1.2 million though direct donations for the building of a new facility in Snohomish County for the Boys and Girls Club.

The Association members continued their generosity to the Seattle Master Builders Scholarship Trust. In 1991, scholarship awards totaling $9,000 helped nine students pursuing building-industry careers at University of Washington, Washington State University and Central Washington University. Again in 1996, the Home Owners Warranty Board donated $80,000 to the Scholarship Trust for students in construction programs in those state schools. Two-thirds of the grant money was earmarked

for a skilled-labor program. Then, in an effort to expand the work of the Trust, on June 12, 1998, at the Association's first Education Retreat, a foundation was established to create endowments, seek grant money, and raise funds for educational programs. The foundation would expand the work of the Association's Scholarship Trust.

It was through the leadership and personal commitment of members that the Association was able to achieve so much success in programs that gave back to the community. 1999 President Patrick McCourt reflected, "Support your community, it will support you."

By Vadset said, "Be thankful for what we all have. Somebody else always has something else that we might like or admire, but hey, look at the good side of what you've got and be thankful for that. If you help others, they'll help you. That's really amazing. The act of actually giving is better than receiving."

Member Lennox Scott, the third-generation owner of John L. Scott Real Estate, says, "I don't look at it as giving back; I look at it as experiencing living the life lesson, living life as a contribution. That's what we do with our clients. We get to live our lives as being a professional and expert and being a contribution to them about the possibilities in their lives. That's our higher purpose is

THE FORCE

(back row)
Donna Shirey, Theresa Santerre, Joy Brand
(front row)
Pat Tenhulzen, Shirley Blayden, Sandy McAdams

Women had been active in the Master Builders since at least the 1920s, but had not ever had an official role – that is, not until the 1980s. Through their participation in the Remodelors Council, six women members gravitated toward each other and they became fast friends during the mid-1980s. As they grew closer and found they had more in common, they evolved into a tightly-knit social and business network. Called "The Force," this group was Sandy McAdams, Donna Shirey, Theresa Santerre, Joy Brand, Pat Tenhulzen and Shirley Blayden.

According to Donna, The Force acted as a support network for women in construction that all started when they would meet for lunch once a month. "We were all husband-and-wife teams. We talked, which included some personal talk because sometimes you need some support when you're a woman in construction." A desire to bring about change also guided The Force. Pat recalls, "We were all involved in the Remodelors Council, but our husbands were the main ones involved. We'd be going to these meetings, and I think basically what we were seeing is that the guys were plugging along and doing what they were doing, but there were no changes being made. There was nothing new."

Members of The Force gathered to discuss building-industry topics like marketing strategies, company policy manuals, and state contracting laws such as fighting against contracting without a license. Sandy explains, "We all had ambition and passion for the Association, and we all had lots of ideas and weren't afraid to roll up our sleeves and make things happen and we did. We got dubbed 'The Force' as a result of that. I think that was the beginning of my understanding of what this Association could be for me."

The Force organized events and auctions with themes ranging from fiesta to space age to Mardi Gras. Pat was the first chair of the Remodelors Council, and as members, The Force started the Remodeling Excellence (REX) Awards for excellence in design. Says Sandy, "The Force was pretty much the organizing body of all the things like that that were happening. So many things that the Association as a whole took on happened with us first."

The Force also started a number of charity events that supported their dedication to community involvement. The successful Rampathon program originated in the Remodelors Council. McAdams explains, "I'm a big believer in giving back to the community. I was thrilled when the auction became a charitable event, that we fund our education foundation from the proceeds of the auction." Shirley Blayden's idea to have a toy drive for Hurricane Andrew victims rose during a group meeting and she took the idea to the National Association. As a result, more than 30,000 toys were collected then delivered by the Salvation Army to the children affected by the catastrophe.

Even though they're all very busy, the women of The Force still keep in touch and are involved in each others' lives. Their hope is to inspire the next generation of female builders to "go for it" and achieve success, however they define it.

builders, when they run out of lots here, they'll go to Boise or Portland because they see themselves as single-family guys and that's what they'll do. Builders don't like change very much. They resist it. They think that you should forever be building the same thing just because they once did. And that's not the way the world works."

One way the building industry has always changed is through the "passing on" of family business. In the Seattle Association, many builders are second-generation members. Jack Tenhulzen, 1998 Association President, muses on the fact that so many of his generation of builders are passing their companies onto their children as he did. His son Mike chaired the Remodeled Homes Tour. "He is following well in the footsteps of industry involvement and giving back to the industry."

Builder *magazine and the Seattle Master Builders Association raised $25,000 for the Homeless Challenge in Bellevue.*

Community Giving

Throughout the 1990s, the Affordable Housing Council grew to be one of the largest political action committees in the state. Funding for the program was growing exponentially. In September 1990, Amy Dedoyard of Windermere Real Estate East helped to raise over $105,000 for the council by organizing a fun event to roast the Seattle Master Builders Association's current directors as well as past presidents at the Glendale Golf Club. Chuck Henderson was crowned "King of the Roast," Bud Leamon and the famous Howard Cosell were the Masters of Ceremonies, and though the jokes were terrible, the evening was a great success. The main thrust of the PAC at that time was, of course, challenging Initiative 547.

Not only was money being raised for the Affordable Housing Council, but other charitable contributions made through the Association were at an all-time high. The decade started out with its annual auction on January 20. Its theme, Playhouse '90, raised funds for the Make-a-Wish Foundation. The highlight of the fundraiser was

the possibility of people's lives. The builders we work with, you know, that's what they're doing. They're building a house, but it's bigger than that. It's about the possibilities of those who are going to live within the house, and that's what makes it a home and a great place to live," Scott reflected. "It's one of the strong pillars of our culture and our nation. That's the joy of coming to work."

Over the years, the Remodelors Council took the lead for various fundraising activities such as the auction. When Jack Tenhulzen was the chair of the Remodelors Council, each industry segment had their own checkbook. Each council worked independently and did not answer to the Association. They would raise their own money and decide how to spend it. Under Tenhulzen's 1998 leadership, the councils set up a unified annual budget, detailing every council's anticipated revenue and anticipated expenses. Jack said, "It's worked extremely well since. I think it's been a lot of the backbone of the growth of the Association as a whole is to pull everybody more together instead of these separate factions."

Combining the collective resources of the councils and the committees became the mantra of the Association. At the decade's end, the incredible amount of charitable activity culminated in the creation of the Master Builders

Care Foundation, a 501(c)(3) non-profit. Through the Care Foundation, resources from the home-building community could now be consolidated to benefit the homeless and low-income disabled individuals.

Echelbarger sticks it to Snohomish

On an overcast afternoon in April 1993, Association President Mike Echelbarger was driving between job sites, and happened to find himself in Martha Lake, a town in southern Snohomish County. In the mid-1990s, Martha Lake was undergoing some rapid changes. Echelbarger had been involved in battles to develop some communities in the area which were opposed by a few loudly squeaking wheels. Their opposition had convinced one developer that it would be too hard to develop a business park on the lake, even though the zoning was in place for it, and the land reverted to the county. Snohomish County wasn't interested in a business

SANDY MCADAMS

ACHIEVEMENTS:
Remodeler of the Year, *1999 & 2000*
President, Master Builders, *2002*

Sandy McAdams's experiences, accomplishments, and devotion to the Master Builders are legendary. In an industry that has been traditionally male-dominated, McAdams is a trailblazer who in 2002 became the first woman President of the Association.

McAdams first became involved with Master Builders Association during the early 1980s. She recalls that there weren't many female members at the time, and most were in Remodelors Council or in support businesses. Through her participation in the Council, McAdams met five other women and they became fast friends, called "The Force." Because of this sustaining network, McAdams feels that the most important benefits she has received from the Association are friendship and support. She explains, "Being involved in an Association like this, you develop incredible friendships. I can't even begin to tell you how wonderful that is."

In the late 1990s, McAdams was encouraged to run for President of the Association by fellow members Zak Parpia and Ty Waudé. As she describes, "This Association, at the time I joined, was very much a 'good old boys' Association. There were a lot of men who really didn't see the value of women being involved." Not content to stand by and watch, McAdams knew it was time for a change. "I was very determined. I saw the value of the Association, but I also saw that it was women who got things done. I wanted to become more involved and do more things in the Association

that had always been done by the men, including become President."

During her presidency, Sandy focused on promoting membership and she received the Association's first Life Spike award for recruiting over 350 new members. "We were the second largest homebuilders association in the country. We had over 3,000 members at that point, which was a record for us. Our members were very involved – they weren't just names on a list. They were *involved* members."

In honor of Sandy becoming the first woman President, women in the Association started a charity fundraising group called Women Building Hope. Women Building Hope did literally that – they remodeled a women's shelter and contributed a ramp to the Rampathon. This program, now the Professional Women in Building Council, remains a vital forum for female builders and contractors.

Sandy McAdams believes in the power of mentoring other women in the industry and in remaining positive during tough times. When asked what message she would give to other women in the building industry, Sandy says, "Go for it. Don't be afraid to take a little risk and go for it. Be positive; embrace everyone, not just the women in the Association. I have a real love of this Association and always have." Sandy concludes, "I've given huge amounts of my time and energy to the Association, but I've gotten so much more back."

park, they wanted to create a recreational area on the shores of the lake.

Echelbarger knew that the construction had just begun on the planned park, and he took a detour off 164th Southwest and drove by the site. He wasn't shocked by what he saw – parked heavy equipment and poorly secured fencing. He snuck through the fence to get a closer look,and reflected on the difference between the standards his company was kept to and what the county was doing. Mike returned the next day with a camera at the ready. Snohomish County was building against code. He wrote a memo to the county: this developer must be stopped! They had no filter fabrics to control erosion, they had not filled out a grading permit application and they weren't making erosion improvements. Echelbarger said, "The county might have thrown us in jail if we had done this sloppy of a job."

Echelbarger's whistleblowing alerted the county to the stringency of the requirements they'd enacted. An official from the parks department told the *Everett Herald,* "We required a Cadillac where a Chevy would have worked." Echelbarger responded that the grading violation was understandable, and told the paper, "I think in good conscience, the county probably never realized they had to do this type of thing." He chose to use the park as a way for county officials to walk in the shoes of a developer, and for the county to understand in real-world terms what they asked builders to do.

In response, the Master Builders Association submitted a letter to Snohomish County asking whether fourteen permits, policies and procedures might apply when the county begins developing the park. The list included everything from a wetland mitigation plan to a national effluent discharge permit and an Army Corps of Engineers 404 permit for placing fill in wetland areas. Echelbarger concluded his discussion with the newspaper by saying about regulations, "They have laid layer upon layer upon layer where the sieve is so tight nothing can get through."

Changing of the Guard

As those assuming leadership positions in the organization began discussing strategic planning for growth, it became evident that they would need an Executive Officer who could craft compromises with local jurisdictions regardless of their political leanings and lead the Association into the 21st Century.

Jim Williams had come to the Association as Executive Officer in 1988, and it was time to seek new direction and different skills. Williams left in 1997, and a staff member, Don Davis, stepped in while the board conducted a search for the person to lead the Association and help in meeting its strategic objectives. In the beginning of Davis's career, the Association had 750 member companies. By the late 1990s, there were over 2,500.

Of his role as interim director in 1997, Don recalled, "The role of Executive Officer is tough. Especially when you have so many people who you work for and so many strong personalities; people who own companies." He found himself balancing convergent opinions on policies, and how the Association spent their money as well as doing his own job.

Don served for ten months, while Chuck Crosby, Zak Parpia, Jack Tenhulzen, Ty Waudé and other board members were actively looking for the right Executive Officer. In the beginning, ten candidates, all from other local associations, were brought in to the Association for interviews. Jack remembers, "We went off our first ten, and said; okay, now we are looking outside the industry. Which was very refreshing to me, and I said, okay I want to add women too. That was part of the admission criteria in some of the

interviews. How many women have you placed, and in what kinds of positions. I wanted as broad a scope of candidates that we could possibly look at. The first one outside the industry was Sam Anderson coming from the number two position at the National Ski Areas Association."

Sam Anderson was a lawyer serving as the General Council in Denver, CO, and lobbying in Washington, D.C., for the National Ski Areas Association. "My dad was an Air Force officer, so I traveled a lot. I finally ended up going to grade school in Portland and then high school in Salem. Then I went the University of Oregon for undergraduate school and received a B.A. in Economics. After serving in the Army, I went to law school at the Northwest School of Law, at Lewis and Clark College in Portland. I practiced law for about a year, and then became the Chief of Staff to an Oregon congressman."

Four years later, after the congressman left his elected position, Sam became partner in a law firm representing the largest home-lending savings and loan in Oregon, right at the start of Ronald Reagan's presidency and the era of double-digit inflation, double-digit interest rates and double-digit unemployment. Sam remembers, "That was really ugly." A third of his practice was international law, and that work involved negotiating deals and relationships for clients in China, Korea, Taiwan and the Middle East.

"In 1989, I realized I hated practicing law. I quit the law firm and I went to work as a consultant for Mount Hood Meadows Ski Area and then the other ski areas in the Pacific Northwest working on the spotted owl issue." Soon after, Sam was offered a job by the National Ski Areas Association as Director of Environmental Policy in Denver, Colorado.

When the Seattle Master Builders Association opportunity knocked, it was just what Sam wanted. In addition to the business challenges, he had family living in Portland and two of his children had enrolled at Whitman and at University of Washington Law School. After seeing the job on the internet, Sam contacted the search firm. Sam recalled, "I applied for this job. I didn't know what the Master Builders Association was. I didn't know anything about Seattle particularly. I'd been here a couple of times. I knew nothing about the housing industry. I still don't know how to do much of anything inside a house or outside a house but now I have access to more than 4,000 companies that do that kind of stuff."

When Sam Anderson was being hired, he discovered that the state association had developed a negative reputation; some of their leadership had been branded "the Bully Boys"

of Olympia. And though several Association members had served as Building Industry Association of Washington presidents, over the past decade, the tension between the local and state organizations had grown. To compound the situation, the BIAW had developed a negative reputation with some elected officials important to the Master Builders Association.

Sam worked with his staff to create opportunities to brand the newly-renamed Master Builders Association of King and Snohomish Counties as the good guys. Over the next several years, the Association's name began to carry more clout. Chuck Crosby, 1995 President, described it by saying, "The Association's name packs a lot of weight. People know who you are and they know that you are involved. When we called the county executive's office, the executive answers the phone. Those are some of the benefits you don't even think about when you decide to become involved. It opens a lot of doors for you."

The Master Builders Association of King and Snohomish Counties became the fourth-largest local homebuilders ssociation in the country, out of proportion with the King-Snohomish metro area's homebuilding market, which ranked as thirteenth largest in the country.

Sam Anderson seemed to be just what the board wanted. Jeff Taylor, owner of Valley Supply, thought Sam was the right leader at the right time. "I just think it's amazing what can happen when you create a brain trust of intelligent people, and get them around the table and beginning to contribute things that they have expertise on. I think the Master Builders is a great example of that very thing. It's just about some pretty smart folks getting around the table and figuring stuff out and moving forward with a plan of action. I'm not sure that anyone would have envisioned it even twenty years ago. I mean, wow! It's become way more than I would have thought. It's really grown a lot."

The challenge between the Master Builders Association of King and Snohomish Counties and BIAW was even more interesting because many members with opposing views from conservative and liberal positions were finding it hard to work together to make positive contributions toward a cause everyone could get behind.

Anderson saw the turning point with the media when the Master Builders Association was portrayed as being "good guys" for their partnership with the Cascade Land Conservancy, the largest land conservation, stewardship and community-building organization in Washington State. Moreover, Sam lead the creation of the Master Builders Care Foundation and the Built Green programs. During his tenure in 2005, the Association passed the Greater Atlanta Home Builders Association to

Sam Anderson, right, works with Sandy McAdams on crafting a plan to get the Association into a new, larger building.

become the largest local homebuilders association in the NAHB.

One of the best ways to get good press was the ongoing Seattle Home Show. By February 1995, the 51st annual Seattle Home Show was the oldest and largest show of its kind in the nation. It featured more than 600 exhibitors spread over 300,000-square-feet of exhibition space. Once again, Knoll Lumber donated a three-bedroom model home – a 1,146-square-foot mountain cabin, constructed by union volunteers. At the end of the show, the model home was donated to the Redmond branch of Habitat for Humanity.

The Knoll Lumber and Hardware Company, together with the Seattle-North Puget Sound Council of Carpenters, were presented with a President's Service Award in recognition of the model homes they had built over the last ten years for the annual Seattle Home Show and then donated to charity. The award was one of only eighteen, chosen from more than 3,000 nominees nationwide. President Bill Clinton came to Seattle to personally present the award.

By 1999, the Home Show had more applications for exhibitors than it could fit in one show, so it added a second one. Mike Kalian remembers, "Yes, there were tremendous demands from our existing exhibitors. The majority of our exhibitors get all their work for the year from the show. There was a feeling that if they had something that would kind of kick-start the last quarter – first quarter a little more and that's how the second Home Show came about. It's been a great success."

Challenges on the Horizon

Of the immediate effects that the GMA's passage had on the homebuilding industry, perhaps none was more pernicious than the increasing delays builders faced as they applied for permits for their new projects. Municipalities, faced with enacting the new regulations, were often very slow in passing preliminary approvals of plats. In fact, by 2003, Snohomish County was only able to process 64 percent of applications within four months of their submission. King County continued to be notoriously bad. Several builder members proclaimed the building environment to be the worst in the country for delays and processing.

MASTER · BUILDER

OFFICIAL PUBLICATION OF THE MASTER BUILDERS ASSOCIATION OF KING AND SNOHOMISH COUNTIES

JANUARY 1994

The January 1994 Master Builder *magazine focused on a siding company that specialized in L-P Siding. The article inside said, "Louisiana-Pacific's Inner Seal Lap Siding was introduced to the Puget Sound market by Cedar King in 1987... [these] products soon took over a major portion of the company's business; nearly 90% of all siding work done in the region is of this product... Another benefit from using the L-P products was the elimination of call backs on completed jobs." This would soon seem ironic to the contractors embroiled in the class action lawsuits.*

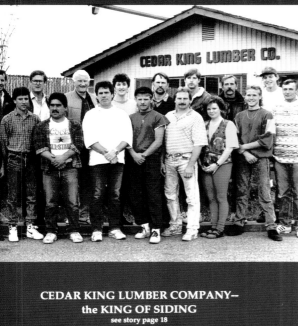

CEDAR KING LUMBER COMPANY--
the KING OF SIDING
see story page 18

One challenge facing builders had nothing to do with the GMA or its offshoots. In 1995, incoming 1996 President John Cochenour recalled a phone call from then-president Chuck Crosby. "He said, 'do you know what your issue is next year?' and I said, 'well, I think I do.' I was wrong. He said, 'your issue will be L-P Siding.'" The lawsuit was a class-action suit filed against Louisiana Pacific Siding of Portland, Oregon, and though some degree of disputes had been going on since 1990, the suit would not be brought to trial until 1996.[6]

Cochenour explained, "Lousiana Pacific was the largest manufacturer of OSB – Oriented Strand Board. They came up with a way to use it as siding, and it was really nice – it had the benefit of being primed, and since it was a manufactured product, there weren't any knot holes in it. It became very, very popular in our marketplace, in a lot of market-places. It probably had an eighty percent market share at its peak." John continued, "The problem with the product was that as water hung on the outside, the drip edge of that board, if it was there long enough it would wick back up into the board. If you put water on that, it swelled, which would split the bottom of the board open, which would, now, let a lot of moisture in the bottom of the board. Then the board started to deteriorate."

The problem with water damage was, at first glance, it didn't appear to be a significant problem. After Cochenour assumed the presidency, he said, "I held a meeting for all the builder members to hear how much of a problem it was, and the truth was, at the very beginning, it didn't appear like there was much of a problem. Everybody went back to their houses, and we found out that, holy cow, there are a lot of failures with the product. It still looked great from the street. It still looked good from five feet away. It really wasn't until you got up at the side of the house and looked up that you'd see these little cracks that had formed on the bottom of the board."

The major problem with the siding, in the builders' minds, was not necessarily that it was faulty, but that they had put up a product in good faith, and wanted the manufacturer to indemnify them from risk. The hearing would take place in Seattle, so the local Association was heavily involved even though they were dealing with a national issue. Locally, Cochenour said, "Once the settlement arrived, we as an industry were able to turn around to go back to our homeowners, and say, 'we are going to come out and inspect your house. If we find any product failure, we will help you submit claims to Louisiana Pacific to get the siding replaced.'"

Some of the suppliers who had acted as middlemen to get products such as the L-P Siding to developers building homes were facing a different kind of challenge. Big-box hardware outlets like Lowe's and Home Depot had expanded to national prominence and were trying to get a piece of the commercial market, as well as catering to do-it-yourself homeowners. As a result, it became more important for members to emphasize their customer service and the importance of doing business with other members who were locally owned. Jeff Taylor of Valley Supply remembered, "It was really the

onslaught of the Home Depot-type store in the market that made me go *I don't know if I want to go up against those guys*. So I started developing relationships with people building homes. I like helping people, I just get enjoyment out of that and so the company has grown with that. We call it our superhero service model. We've had a lot of success in building relationships with builders because we do offer good service." And Taylor is quick to emphasize, his company only does business with members.

As an associate member, Jeff Taylor was sure to point out the other benefits his company gets from being involved in the Association. "The resource that becomes available for your contacts – if you look at the membership directory, either you'll know somebody who will say 'Well these guys did a great job' and you'll call them or you'll have to pick a company from the directory somewhere. The fact that the members of the association do have annual dues is a filter, it legitimizes them. To be able to open up the member directory and see all of those hundreds of names that you could call to say 'Can you help me with that? Who do you know about that? How do you do that?' That's a major resource."

That Master Builders Association members benefit from communication with each other and "learning from each other's mistakes" is undeniable. One new way that they were able to connect was unveiled at the 1996 Seattle Home Show. Billed as "America's Biggest Open House," builder-visitors saw an amazing new tool that would enable members to communicate with builders around the country. They unveiled the first Seattle Master Builders Association website with "links to sites all over the world." The March *Master Builder* magazine boasted, "The information sharing and marketing possibilities are as big as your imagination."

Even as the builders plugged in, increasingly the public was trying to find ways to connect with nature rather than technology. For instance, when Port Blakely Communities broke ground on Issaquah Highlands in 1996, one way that they built consensus even through the challenge of Growth Management Act stipulations was by creating the "Evergreen Building Guide" – a new set of ecological measures all builders in the community had to adhere to. Issaquah Highlands was ahead of the curve on green building standards, but the choices made and the issues discussed were going to have a lasting impact on the discussion surrounding green building in the area. The discussion that started in Issaquah would eventually evolve into the Built Green® program.

Women in Building

Pat Tenhulzen was the chairman for the Remodelors Council in 1992. Her husband Jack had chaired the Council in 1989, and many years before, Omar Brown had served as its chair. Omar was one of the original members of the Council dating back to its beginnings in 1954. A best practice was to provide three years of experience to groom future leaders. As Jack was going off as chair, Pat's name came up to take on the leadership post. Omar was "definitely old school" and didn't believe women belonged in leadership roles in a building association. Jack threw his strong support behind Pat: she was already involved in their company, and he knew her skills well.

The Association, like many others at the time, was still male-driven. Starting in the 1960s, the feminist movement in America had made progress, eliminating both cultural and legal inequalities against women. Now in the 1990s, it became a time to distinguish women for their achievements. Pat started out as the vice chair and in that position was a member

DONNA SHIREY

ACHIEVEMENTS:
President, Master Builders, *2005*
Remodeler of the Year, *2003 & 2005*
Chair-elect, NAHB Remodelers, *2010*

Donna Shirey has been an active member of the Master Builders Association since 1989. She's so enthusiastic about recruiting that's she's brought in over 275 new members. Donna appreciates the network connections, meaningful friendships, and financial expertise she's gained as well as supporting the Built Green and Rampathon programs.

Shirey started in construction in 1971 with a land-development and multi-family construction business on the Eastside. Shirey learned about on-site construction through painting houses, doing concrete work, and performing other types of physical labor shoulder to shoulder with the guys on the jobs. As the "gal on the job" at construction sites, Shirey encountered disbelief that she was actually the contractor and not, say, a secretary or bookkeeper. At the time, the idea of a female construction worker was viewed as extremely unlikely.

Long before "green" became a popular buzzword, Donna Shirey, through her company, demonstrated a deep-seated and passionate pledge to promoting earth-friendly construction practices. Her post-war upbringing and parents' experiences during the Depression instilled in her that the more that could be reused, the better. Back then it wasn't considered recycling; it was survival. As she states, "this is just how we build and finally the rest of the industry is becoming aware." Her company has been active in promoting the use of Structural Insulated Panels (SIPs) since 1987, and they are now included as part of the Washington State energy code.

A project Shirey is actively involved in is the Zero Energy Idea House. This 1,700-square-foot, two-bedroom house is designed to run on the highest level of energy efficiency, with a zero net energy cost. The house showcases a wide variety of energy-saving features such as SIPS, hydronic heating, Energy Star light fixtures and appliances, water conservation features, and even a living retention wall. Donna and her husband Riley Shirey are so professionally and personally invested in the Zero Energy Idea House that they plan to live in it. This will allow the Shireys the opportunity to test out its features themselves: "Nobody knows what's going to work until somebody actually lives there."

In addition to residential construction, Shirey Contracting designs and remodels commercial sites, including the Master Builders Association's Housing Center building in Bellevue, completing the remodel up to the highest standard of Built Green certification.

When Donna Shirey joined the Master Builders Association and the Remodelors Council, she found that the friendliness and social activity level of the council afforded unique opportunities with other husband-and-wife teams who were running construction businesses. Shirey is grateful to be an active member of the Master Builders Association. "Our membership is why we are the company we are today. That's why we're still in business."

of the executive committee which organized the monthly meetings. In the role of vice chair, she was intricately involved in setting up the programs and determining the agenda. She was determined to be a leader who would find opportunities to have more people involved.

In the end, Pat was elected to be the first female chair of the Remodelors Council. Jack remembered, "She did a great job and many more women have followed since."

There were other capable women on the council who had experienced the difficulty of moving up in the industry because of their gender. Donna Shirey started her career in about 1971. She remembered, "There were no other women in construction."

Six very like-minded women were drawn to the Association nevertheless, and they were drawn to each other in the Remodelors Council. All six became a business support system for each other and very good friends.

Through working on successful events sponsored by the Council, Sandy McAdams got involved in the building industry beyond the local Association to work on both the state and national levels. Eventually the glass ceiling was shattered, and McAdams became the first woman President of the Master Builders Association of King and Snohomish Counties in 2002.

Women had assumed a greater leadership role in the organization, as evidenced by this leadership retreat in 1994.

Education

On June 12, 1998, the Association held its first Education Retreat to hold focused discussions on how to encourage young people to get into the building trades. These discussions formulated two visions for the Association: Firstly, how could educational opportunities be created for all kinds of people to attract them into the industry? Secondly, how could the Association meet the needs of continuing education for builders? A committee was formed to find a solution for this secondary need, but action was taken immediately to broaden the scope of the Education Foundation.

The Education Foundation was converted to a separate 501 (c)(3) nonprofit entity of the Master Builders Association. They would work to raise and give out scholarships to students interested in the construction industry by establishing endowments and seeking grant money. The Education Foundation was dedicated to promoting and recruiting for the local residential construction industry by preparing students to enter the workforce. The foundation expanded to include scholarships to community colleges, as well as continuing its current scholarship program to state colleges: the University of Washington, Washington State University and Central Washington University.

Some Education Foundation partnerships were now able to move beyond merely financial support. An educational partnership was undertaken with Seattle Central Community College (SCCC). To address the industry's labor shortage, the College created a new English as a Second Language (ESL) program for carpentry students.

A member facilitates the Education Retreat in 1998.

Millennium Gala

As crowds from around the world gathered in Seattle for anti-globalization protests, the Seattle Center was host to a different sort of gathering. On December 2, 1999, even while hundreds of protesters gathered at the King County Jail, on the opposite end of Fifth Avenue, the Association and local elected officials celebrated the new millennium at Key Arena with Millennium Gala 2000, a black-tie affair attended by 32 past presidents and more than 700 members. After a brief introduction by event chair Amy Dedoyard, Sam Anderson welcomed the group to the party: "I'm pleased and excited that you are all here tonight. This Millennium Gala is an appropriate event to celebrate this unique moment in the Association's history. Think about it: it's the end of the millennium, and we are celebrating ninety years of commitment by all the people in this room to building our communities, because that's what we do. Tonight will be a gathering of old friends, faded memories, and past stories. Make use of it. It's a wonderful way to enter the 21st century. I am extremely proud to be the Executive Officer of the Master Builders at a time when we can recognize the contributions of our many past Presidents. This is the only time in our history that this group of distinguished individuals has been, or will be, gathered in one room, and we need to recognize the legacy that they have created in this Association."

Short speeches by past presidents were shown on a video projector behind the evening's Master of Ceremonies, radio personality Pat Cashman. Cashman joked, "Welcome to the Millennium Gala of the Masters Builders Association of King and Snohomish – but not Pierce – Counties. I am tremendously honored to be a part of this night saluting the long and remarkable line of Master Builders Association presidents of King and Snohomish – but not Pierce – Counties. This is truly being with the best and the brightest, I'll tell you."

1978 President Ed Dean reminisced, "The event during my presidency that was the most fun and enjoyable and memorable was when the state association and the local Association had Ronald Reagan as the guest speaker. As the Master Builders President at that time, I had the privilege of sitting with President Reagan during our lunch meeting and he was a lot of fun. He's just a real comedian. I called him 'Mr. President,' he called me 'Mr. Ed.'"

President Pat McCourt reflected after the party, "Yes, we've come a long way since 1909. The millennium event was a smashing success. We paid tribute to the past presidents in a grand way. We paid tribute to our members. Would the original five members ever have dreamed that this Association would develop into what it is today? Let us learn from this history. There are no boundaries on our horizon, but the boundaries we set for ourselves. I'm proud to have been your President. You showed me you know no boundaries.

"Any organization or group that flourishes does so because of the effort and dedication of individuals. The whole is the sum of its parts, and an association is the sum of its members. Throughout the years, thousands of people have given their time and energy to build this Association into what it is today."

One person who was honored for his contributions of time and energy was Omar Brown – elected "Remodeler of the Millenium." Jack Tenhulzen joked, "When I first joined the Master Builders, my sponsoring member was a past president named Omar Brown. Omar is one of my dear friends and has been a good mentor over the years. My joke on Omar Brown is for the first three meetings that I went to, he introduced himself and I had to remind him that he was the one who sponsored my membership."

More serious business was glossed over in favor of celebrating the achievements of the builders present. Don McDonald, 1963 President, presented the Association as a whole with an award from the BIAW, and Pat McCourt presented the Associate of the Millennium award to Patrick McBride of GMS Architectural group. When it got time for the Builder of the Millennium award, the nominees were announced: Rob Stewart, Ty Waudé, Harry Pryde and Pat McCourt. To no one's surprise, there was a tie. Not only would those men be honored, but all builder-members were told to consider themselves "builders of the millennium."

King County Executive Ron Sims told the audience: "We have one of the best qualities of life of any area in the country. In large part, it is because of you." Governor Gary Locke congratulated members "on an incredible legacy of leadership." The Master Builders were able to close out their first ninety years as the second largest homebuilders association in the country, thanks in large part to the efforts of member spike drives and the energy of Membership Director Larry Chimenti. Chimenti said: "I treated this like a business. Like a sales force. Any successful sales manager becomes successful through the sales people. The way you get success through sales people is get them to do their best for themselves." ♣

CHAPTER 12

Millennial Successes

2000 – 2006

When the new century began, the Master Builders Association of King and Snohomish Counties was going strong. With over 2,800 member companies in 2000, the Association flirted with being the largest in the country, but did not achieve that goal until 2005. Those thousands of member companies were offered an expanded list of benefits as well: from the Return on Industrial Insurance program to health insurance to continuing education, the Association continued to provide for its members. During the early part of the decade, the economy recovered from a brief downturn to become the strongest housing market builders had seen in decades. The Master Builders Association continued to work with local governments on issues of importance and they were able to reach consensus on potentially challenging issues. The 1999 launch of the Built Green program proved to be very successful for member companies, and allowed the Association to lead the charge for environmental responsibility and sustainable construction.

In December 1999, the Master Builders Association welcomed the 21st Century with a gala event honoring the men who had made the Association great. Pictured here are thirty of the Association's past Presidents.

The Association Matures

Puget Sounders woke up on the first Saturday morning of the new year 2000 to discover that computers and microwaves and televisions still worked just as well as they had before. There was a nearly audible sigh of relief from Redmond, when Microsoft employees realized that nothing had happened when the year rolled over to 01/01/00. The members of the Master Builders Association had readied themselves for Y2K and were gearing up for a memorable first year of the new century.

By 2000, the King and Snohomish County Association had ceased to be fighting with the Portland Association about who had more members. Now, the Association was a strong second-largest in the country, with 2,805 member companies that collectively employed over 76,000 workers. They promoted the direct effects of residential construction: according to a press release of 2000, "The construction of 100 single-family homes generates 2,338 full-time jobs in construction and related industries, $79 million in wages, and $42.5 million in combined federal, state and local fees. The construction of 100 multifamily units generates 1,030 full-time jobs in construction and construction-related industries; $33.5 million in wages; and $17.8 million in combined federal, state and local fees." The Master Builders were promoting not only homeownership, but homebuilding, with a tremendous passion.

The members of the Association were also promoting membership with a fervor never before seen. In the late 1990s, the board of directors had instructed Executive Officer Sam Anderson and Membership Director Larry Chimenti to open up membership to all companies that wanted to do business with the building community. The growth was tremendous. From 2000 through 2005, the Association's membership grew by a whopping 150 percent. In 2005, with 4,145 member companies, the Master Builders of King and Snohomish Counties was able to overtake the Greater Atlanta Home Builders Association as the largest local association in the NAHB. Larry Chimenti said, "We go to a NAHB membership training meeting every year, and one year, I remember Atlanta was around 3,500 members. We were at about 1,800. I got up to give my ninety-minute presentation on membership, and

I told them about the importance of setting a goal and keeping it visible. I said, 'For instance, my goal is to bury Atlanta.' Everyone just giggled. But we got closer and closer, and then we zipped by them," Chimenti smiled.

Chimenti and his "Spike Army" accomplished a pretty major feat. Not only did they set a NAHB record for most members gained in a year, but they also grew the Association to a size unimaginable to anyone who didn't know Chimenti and his Spikes. In 2005, Atlanta was number one in the nation for single-family building permits, with 60,950. The Seattle-Tacoma-Bellevue area didn't even make the top ten with its 17,700.[1] Likewise, the area didn't even come close to Atlanta in terms of population. In the 2000 census, the Atlanta Metro area had over four million people,[2] the Seattle Metro area was still just shy of two and a half million.[3]

The demographics of those two and a half million were changing. Bellevue had become the state's fifth largest city, and Seattle residents were moving back to the center of the city. Belltown was home to many of the newly-rich

dot-commers, and exurban areas like Mill Creek and Lake Stevens were enjoying the new revenue from housing being built for families who wanted the best of both worlds: Snohomish school districts were rated among the best in the state, and commute times to downtown Seattle or Bellevue were still within reason.

Pat and Jack Tenhulzen were working in the remodeling industry, and their phone rang often with people looking to expand their homes to match their affluent lifestyles. Jack says, "We started hearing the terms 'nesting' and 'cocooning.' We were putting in a lot of home theaters, home gyms. It got to the point that people didn't have to leave the house for much other than resupply. It fit well with families wanting to keep a watchful eye on their kids and their friends. They would remodel the house so that their kid's friends would want to come over and spend time there."

The Seattle Seahawks were getting a new stadium. But even before the Kingdome had been demolished, the Seattle Home Show had its first year in the newly-designed Seahawks Stadium

Exhibition Center (the name was changed to Qwest Field Stadium Exhibition Center in 2004). Few NFL franchises would ask the director of a home show to aid in their stadium design process. Show Manager Mike Kalian is very proud of the relationship the Seattle Home Show has built with the team's management. "We were on the advisory board for the new Qwest Field when it was built. They asked us to help in the design of the exhibition center to make sure it would work really well for us. That was awesome." Kalian sees the close role as very beneficial, both to the Home Show and the region as a whole: "You have to have a great facility, and we have that. It makes the shows so much better, Seattleites are very proud that everything here is local."

The new Exhibition Center had nearly 300,000-square-feet of exhibition space. In the first year in the new space, more than 122,000 visitors enjoyed exhibits on concrete countertops, the "new generation" of oil heaters, and of course, "Ask the Expert" booths. Quite impressive growth for a sixty-one-year-old homegrown event.

As the Association grew in membership, the staff had to keep up. What had worked before wouldn't cut it any longer; when there are three thousand magazines to mail, a pizza party to affix labels is futile. The staff had grown to the point where they were no longer able to rent out the upper floor of the 112th Avenue NE Association headquarters, and parking was at a premium. Donine Grigsby, who worked on the second floor in accounting, remembered the building best for the experience she had in 2001's Nisqually Earthquake. "The building was wood, and it really rattled and rolled – we were all over the place! But the people downstairs hardly felt it."

By 2003, it was obvious that the Association needed a new office space. A search committee had been formed in 2001, but they couldn't find a building that fit their requirements. Todd Bennett, 2003 President, remembers telling the committee, "OK, guys, here's the future. We can buy this building." The building in question was the former home of Bellevue's branch of City University. "The location was fantastic, it's right on the freeway, and I knew a new off-ramp was coming from the south. I remember thinking that most of the builders are based on the Eastside." Some builders lobbied to find a building on the King-Snohomish border, but there were limited options in the Bothell-Mill Creek area.

The search committee and executive officer knew the building would need some substantial renovation to be ready for use. To head up that remodel, the committee tapped Shirey Contracting. The building would no longer just be offices, it would be the "MBA Housing Center"

Master Builders Association Housing Center

In 2003, Master Builders moved into a new, larger home, 335 116th Street SE in Bellevue. The MBA Housing Center features three stories of offices, classrooms, and conference facilities. The convenient location plus the 33,000-square-feet and 110 parking places allow the Association to better serve members. The facility will accommodate the Association's planned growth in member services for decades to come.

To the right, Sam Anderson, Executive Officer, stands in front of the MBA Housing Center with King County Executive Ron Sims and 2004 Master Builders President Peter Orser.

with three stories of offices, classroom space and conference facilities. The staff worked tirelessly to get ready for the move, and it paid off. Sam Anderson remembered, "The movers told me, 'We've moved hundreds of offices, and none went better or faster than this one.'"

The remodeled Housing Center was top notch: built to the highest green standards of the day. Donna Shirey even went a step further, "We did work on determining the weight of what went out of the building. We looked to recycle everything that we could and keep from putting anything possible into the landfill."

Another change was how leadership of the Master Builders related with one another. Time was, the incoming President and the Executive Officer would sit down in December and map out the strategy for the coming year. With the organization having grown so much, that was no longer a tenable strategic plan. Doug Barnes, 2007 President, said, "We started to, I think, create more continuity of the initiatives that we as an organization were trying to improve upon. We ended up with three- and five-year initiatives and plans rather than having a new president each year with a distinct platform. We tried to really merge those platforms and have a lot of communication between presidents."

Housing Frenzy

After the "dot-com" bubble imploded, many locals who had made their fortune in the rapidly accelerating stock market turned their investment portfolio to real estate. They saw the buildable-lands inventory shrinking, and those who had liquid assets left to invest overwhelmingly chose to tie up their assets in residential real estate. Home prices skyrocketed; based on Multiple Listing Service (MLS) figures, the average home price in King County rose from $150,000 in 1993 to $256,000 in 2003; however, over the next three years, the average sale price jumped to nearly $400,000.

The region's apartment renters, too, jumped onto the homebuying bandwagon. Rental vacancy rates from 2001-2005 were high, and rents were low.[4] However, condominium conversions turned around the trend, also moving available rental inventory to those who wanted to realize the American Dream of homeownership. And homeownership was truly sold as an American Dream come true. Homes, especially those in the "first-time buyer" price range (here, considered to be under $200,000) were frequently the subject of bidding wars, with prospective purchasers agreeing to occasionally ridiculous conditions.

After the terrorist attacks of September 11, 2001, builder and then-president Ty Waudé says, "Everything stopped for us for days, just dead stopped. The market was slow to respond and recover so it was a shock, it was a big shock."

1998 President Jack Tenhulzen thought, "9-11 really shook everybody's confidence. It was one of the biggest turning points for people to start thinking more globally." Builders, then, did become more reflective, but eventually got going again, and quickly achieved fairly impressive levels of activity.

Issaquah Highlands received national attention for its environmentally sensitive attention to stormwater management, as seen here. The community is built to foster environmental awareness and sustainable living.

1999 President and Snohomish County developer Patrick McCourt described the period of 2001 through 2006 as "a helluva ride. It seemed like the sun was always shining. Because the level of activity was very high, there were people scurrying and writing in offers, and you could just feel the momentum gather."

Todd Britsch of New Home Trends says, "After 9-11 came and interest rates dropped, there was a tremendous amount of growth spawned in the North Creek Market area. I would say it produced well over fifty percent of the residents and homes in Snohomish County." Barclays North, Pat McCourt's company, fueled much of that growth. They were developing and platting lots that skirted the edge of the Urban Growth Area, to the chagrin of some neighbors.

In the early part of the 21st century, the effects of the Growth Management Act began to be felt more sharply. Housing starts in GMA-approved locales, like Lake Stevens, accelerated at a frantic pace, and so-called master-planned communities like Issaquah Highlands and Redmond Ridge saw their for-sale signs get "sold" placards attached to them almost as soon as they'd been stuck in the ground. As interest rates continued to drop, more and more people dove into the housing market, which had the unfortunate effect, in some places, of driving up home values too high and too quickly for the market to sustain. There was unchecked inflation on home prices, but the refrain was, "build it, and the buyers will come."

Environmental
I s s u e s

In 1999, King and Snohomish County leaders saw the future of our region with its ever-growing population, and knew it was more than the existing sewage treatment facilities could handle. King County Executive Ron Sims's first job upon taking office in 1997 was a tough one: weigh the sewage treatment options, create a plan that could win a regional consensus, and identify possible locations near the waste that the facility was to treat – and most of that waste would come from South Snohomish county.[5] The battle to site the project was extensive, and expensive. No one wanted a waste-treatment facility in their city, let alone in their backyard. From 95 initial sites, only one emerged as the best location, and it would be costly. King County would be responsible for constructing thirteen miles of pipe to transport treated wastewater to the Puget Sound.

King County encouraged Snohomish County to site the Brightwater Facility on their side of the county line with mitigation money. Sam Anderson described the process by saying, "Santa Claus arrived with a big bag, with a lot of toys." If Sims hadn't pushed Brightwater through, all building in North King County and South Snohomish would have come to a complete halt. Sims told the *Seattle Times*, "A moratorium would shut down the growth of this county and half of Snohomish County... I'm not going to stop the economic growth of this region. I'm not going to be accused of not acting."

At the dedication for the plant's groundbreaking, Anderson praised Sims for being committed enough to take a tough stand. "No one wants a wastewater treatment plant, jail, landfill or other essential public facility in their community, but they are critical to maintaining our economic prosperity and quality of life. Elected officials should emulate the drive of King County Executive Ron Sims who saw the urgency of building this essential public facility, fought for it when the going got rough and compromised to make it happen when he needed to do so."

In 2005, Bob Johns, chair of the King County Builders Council, called the Brightwater Wastewater Treatment Facility the "number-one issue on our Association's governmental affairs agenda," and described its continued stall as "the biggest threat to the building industry in decades." Fortunately, forming coalitions with government offices as well as stakeholders allowed the project to proceed and homebuilding to continue. The Master Builders Association played a key role behind the scenes, with their close associations with both the King and Snohomish county councils. The Association was able to advocate for compromise and keep any disputes between the counties out of the court system, which in the long run helped keep costs down, and helped the project remain on schedule.

Dealing with water was a big issue, whether it was after the house got built or during its construction. Representatives from the Master Builders sat on the Partnership for Water Conservation, as well as the Puget Sound Partnership's Stormwater Work Group. The ongoing debate in that committee was whether new development or the existing built environment was the bigger culprit in polluted runoff, and the Association's presence there allowed that debate to get further than if the work group had been composed solely of a few special interest environmental stakeholders.

Another major issue the Governmental Affairs department addressed was traffic concurrency. The Growth Management Act had mandated that

PATRICK MCCOURT

ACHIEVEMENTS:
President, Master Builders, *1999*
Builder of the Year, *1999*

Patrick McCourt knew from an early age what he wanted to be. He got his real estate license in 1972 at the tender age of 17. In an era when many young men were considering moving to Canada, he chose to go to Alaska. He cut his teeth developing and selling properties in Anchorage during their period of explosive growth following the discovery of oil in Prudhoe Bay. When the market softened in the 1980s, he got his first taste of working closely with the regulators while advocating as a business consultant.

In 1989, seeking greener pastures and bluer skies, he made his way to Washington State. He founded Barclays North and started looking for land to develop in Snohomish County. It didn't take long before he was being recruited to join the Seattle Master Builders Association. He declined at first, but challenged: "If you change the name to the Master Builders Association *of King and Snohomish Counties*, then I'll join." Within two months the name had been changed, and he applied for membership.

Despite his initial reluctance, Pat became a force within the Association. He served on several committees and was a recruiting powerhouse. Using the carrot-and-stick approach, and by stressing the value of the health-care benefits included in membership, he managed to win the Omar Brown Award for recruiting excellence in 1996, 1997, 1999, 2000 and 2001.

In 1999 he served as President of the Association. In addition to his continued push to grow membership, he recalls three highlights of his tenure as President: He met his goal of leaving office with the organization better off financially than when he began. He oversaw the successful planning and implementation of the Millennium Celebration. Lastly, he created the "Big Blue Book." Culled from ninety years of historical data, it was designed as a reference manual to provide organization, structure, policy and procedure, all in one handy volume.

Concurrent with his activities at the Association, Pat would get his second taste of working beside the regulators, getting what he calls his "PhD. in the regulatory arena." He was appointed to the Snohomish County Planning Commission in 1995, and was tasked with developing and codifying the regulations and policies of the Growth Management Act. It involved many, many long nights of public hearings. In fact, the process was so fraught with complications he described it by citing Isaiah 59:10.[*] Finally, the task was completed and builders in the county got to work on its implementation.

After all the action, rough times and successes of the 1990s, Pat thought about retiring in 2000. He decided to give it one more whirl, and using his own words "it certainly was a helluva ride from 2000 to 2007!" Barclays North grew to 180 employees, and either developed or helped to develop over 10,000 lots in six states.

[*] *We grope for the wall like the blind, and we grope as if we had no eyes: we stumble at noon-day as in the night; we are in desolate places as dead men.*

transportation and roads had to meet a certain standard before the population could grow into that area. However, the expense of adding roads and infrastructure in some cases restricted growth. Allison Butcher, Public Policy Director, explains, "Traffic concurrency is part of growth management that says, basically, before a city can grow, their transportation has to be up to par. Roads have to be a certain grade. Ideally, we'd like that to happen, but it doesn't always match up, so it has the ability to halt growth in certain areas. Woodinville, for example, has one urban growth area that's currently zoned one house per acre, and that's not the intent of growth management, but they have worked around it to keep the zoning the way it is. We battle on lots of issues related to how you implement growth management within all these different cities in the two counties."

Built Green

When the Master Builders Association announced their plans for creating a "Built Green" (then still in quotes) program, they had modest expectations. Sam Anderson told the *Seattle Times* that the Association planned to "encourage its 2,600 members to build 5,000 homes during the next decade" that met the standards for green construction. The first home that was showcased as part of the new initiative was built on the Sammamish Plateau by Specialized Homes of Seattle, and it featured formaldehyde-free cabinet finishes, recycled wallboards, glue-free carpets, on-site air- and water-filtration systems, built-in containers for recyclables and "Low E" windows, making it "the new home of the future."[6]

Though at its 2001 launch fewer than thirty Master Builder member companies had signed up to participate in the voluntary certification process, within just five years that number had grown to nearly 300, and the program had certified well over the number of homes Anderson mentioned in the ten-year goal. After just five years, the number of homes that had been certified was rapidly approaching 6,000.[7]

When Sam Anderson began conversations with the board about creating Built Green, he came from a knowledgeable position. He'd worked on salmon and spotted owl legislation in the past, and he knew the importance of creating an industry image the media could support. He reflected on that period by saying, "We have to give people a reason to like us. People read negative headlines in the paper, and even if the remodeling contractor who defrauded the old

If a company offers environmentally friendly products or services, they can enroll in the Master Builders Built Green program. By 2009, membership had reached over 300 builders who certified more than 15,000 homes in King and Snohomish Counties. Members are listed on the Built Green website, and also recognized in the Master Builder *magazine in an effort to promote healthy and safe building practices that protect our environment.*

couple isn't a member, we get painted with the same tar brush. We need to be seen as good corporate citizens, and we have to advertise what we do from an environmental responsibility standpoint."

Despite the fact that they were not the first in the nation, the Master Builders had some of the most pressing reasons to come up with a voluntary certification process. The public was not clamoring for the standards so much as the elected officials of some areas, such as Issaquah, Redmond and Seattle. In the late 1990s, the LEED (Leadership in Energy and Environmental Design) Certification Standards were making headlines in the architecture and building worlds. The standards were developed for commercial buildings and to raise awareness of green building benefits, and they certainly had that immediate effect. After the lines had been drawn for the Urban Growth Boundaries, the county councils began discussing what else was needed to protect the region's natural beauty, and they came again and again to the quality of homes that were being built.

The city of Issaquah was trying to come up with rules for greening homebuilding, inspired by the LEED Certification standards. LEED Certification is a very expensive process, so the city council was not going to require that of their builders. However, they knew they wanted to come up with a set of rules to follow. At the same time, similar discussions were being held in other cities: Redmond, Bellevue and Kent. The Association began talking, builders got concerned, and a committee was formed to respond.

Todd Bennett sat on that committee, called the "Built Green Steering Committee," and he described the environment that created a need for the discussions. "All these different cities were trying to come up with green regulations. And what was happening was they were all a little different, and those of us who build in all those marketplaces were concerned, first of all, about how we would be able to manage that. We were also concerned that the regulations would not be builder-friendly, and that they'd be too excessive, and everybody would have their own rules." Bennett continues, "We have forty-plus jurisdictions where we build, and we might have forty different green rules mandated by each city. We thought, let's get ahead of it."

The Steering Committee was largely made up of people from outside the building industry. Ecological stewards, consultants, stakeholders from across the region, and a few builders sat down and came up with a point system, whereby any builder could choose how to achieve environmental benefits in the way they thought

would be most profitable in the long run. If the builder believed that customers were most concerned about indoor air quality, the builder could earn most of the points in that section. If a builder believed clients cared more about energy efficiency, then the points could be scored with that. Bennett described the scenario the committee faced, "The cities were probably going to address everything. They were going to put $40,000 of cost on a house, which would have really dampened the market because then you couldn't sell it. What we did wasn't all that costly; we just had to learn to make better choices. Toxic paint versus non-toxic paint, the cost is almost the same, so buy the non-toxic one. It was a lot of choices like that."

Once the Built Green Steering Committee had formulated its recommendations, the Association took steps to form a separate board for the program. The builders knew that Built Green was an industry affiliate, but for it to retain a level of objectivity, it had to function as a discrete entity. The Association was responsible for the initial staffing. The checklist that was created may have seemed monumental to the layperson, but it was attainable to an industry insider. To become three-star certified, a single-family home had to meet some basic requirements, mainly dealing with state legislation, attaining a minimum of

180 points in each of four sections: site and water protection, energy efficiency, health and indoor air quality, and materials efficiency. The four-star rating required everything the lower level did, plus gaining an additional seventy points and fulfilling more requirements for indoor air quality. The highest level, five-star certification, required meeting all four-star requirements, plus a fairly exhaustive list of obligatory achievements. To be certified at the four- or five-star level, independent third-party verification that the home was constructed to the claimed standards and point total was required.

Though the checklist was impressive, the fees to become certified were not. The Association knew that they could not impose a stiff financial barrier to the Built Green certification; the builders would not get behind a certification that negatively impacted their bottom line. The fees were essentially $50 per home, whether that was a remodel, or a new home construction, or a multifamily development, but homes being constructed under an affordable housing model could be certified at no charge.

By 2004, seventeen percent of new construction in King County was certified Built Green.

A five-star Built Green home at Suncadia in Roslyn, Washington, was the showcase of green building and practices. The home was the first "resort-level" home in the region to demonstrate that a custom home could use green building techniques for the same costs as traditional building practices. The National Green Building Awards ceremony in 2006 awarded the home at Suncadia the Best Green Marketing Project. A second Association member, Mithun Architects, also won a multifamily award for their work at West Seattle's Highpoint.

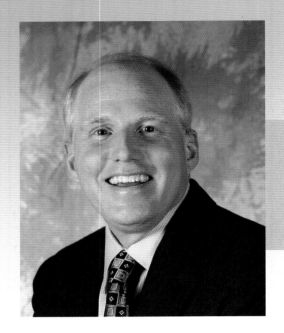

DOUG BARNES

ACHIEVEMENTS:
President, Master Builders, 2007
Builder of the Year, 2005 & 2007

Doug Barnes started working with the building industry in the early 1980s. He came to the field from an accounting background, but soon discovered his niche. Throughout his career, first with partnerships building multifamily homes, then with IntraWest building townhomes and single-family homes, through his most recent position as Executive Vice President of the Northwest Region for Centex homes, Doug has brought his passion and commitment to detail to housing the region's families.

In the Northwest, where national companies have failed to find a significant foothold, Barnes helped Centex Homes create a considerable presence through his work. "Before I got involved, they actually had a very small presence here and were only doing about a hundred homes a year. I thought that there was tremendous potential to really grow that business with Centex; and we were able to do so."

Barnes, in his position with IntraWest (later IntraCorp), developed skills working with King County, doing the platting and entitlement processes for Talus, a master-planned development on the edge of the "Issaquah Alps" highlands. "We were able to get input from the Mountains-to-Sound Greenway group, and Save Lake Sammamish. I think Talus was able to take real advantage of doing a large development; a planning process."

After that experience led him to Centex, Barnes ramped up his involvement with the Master Builders Association. He made "a full commitment that not only am I going to be involved, but our company's going to be involved and other personnel are going to be involved." As he took the presidency in 2007, both the real estate market and membership numbers were peaking; "you could start to see that the market was going to change on us. How do we take this huge organization that we have and how do we take it to the next level? What is the next thing we've got to do? We started asking ourselves some of those questions." The answers that the executive committee came up with led back to the members. Improve member services, create public support and focus on the benefits of being a member.

"It's a great organization with great people and the biggest benefit you get is to network and be involved with a great pool of people. To me that's the number-one benefit; the amount of resources and people that are here. It's great to do business with a member and there are some great members out here. I didn't take advantage of that as well I should have through the 1990s. Once I jumped in, it's like anything, what you've put in, you get back. We're going to go through a very difficult period for the next year or two and I really think that the landscape is going to change how we do business. I think one constant, one thing that can help us get through it, is the Master Builders Association."

That percentage was quite high, and it was only possible because of the coalition of the industry and the stakeholders. Large production builders like Quadrant Homes and Centex chose to seek Built Green certification rather than coming up with unique brands, because they knew the program watched out for their best interests and served the interests of the homebuying public.

Aaron Adelstein, who became Built Green Director in 2006, emphasized the importance of marketing green building to environmentalists and builders alike. "We think that the program is stronger as a market-based, voluntary approach than if it's written into code. If it becomes code, then people aren't striving for better, it's something to settle for. Builders are continually trying to out-compete each other to get better, and that has a more long-term merit. We can react faster as new innovations come out."

Expanded Services

As the membership numbers continued to grow, Sam Anderson and his staff began to look at ways to increase benefits to the members. The political and public-relations arenas were powerful assets to all members, and the ROII program and the Health Insurance Trust provided tangible benefits to members' bottom line. To inspire companies to join the Association, it had to start thinking as a service-based organization, a resource to the larger community of builders and those who engage in business with them.

In 2005, they started brainstorming how the Master Builders could provide more affiliated benefits. No idea was dismissed out of hand; the staff and leadership were just looking for things that all members needed. Sam Anderson felt that if members could purchase as a group, even the smallest company could see significant savings through volume discounts. The Association found Amerinet, a Virginia Mason subsidiary, which had a volume discount program for hospitals and fire departments. The Home

Networking helps builders find best practices, the best employees and make new friends. Golf and auctions are only two of the ways to get to know colleagues outside of business meetings.

Doug Barnes, 2007 Master Builders President says, "I enjoy the golf events. You're out having too much fun to actually improve your game, so I can't say that. But it does improve my disposition."

At the "2001: A Space Odyssey" auction, money was raised for the Omar Brown Scholarship Programs, which were created that year to honor Brown's devotion to recruiting members for the Association and industry education. During Omar's 46 years with the Association he served on every committee and held every major leadership position, serving as Association president in 1974. He also served as President of the BIAW in 1977 and became a Life Director. Brown helped organize the BIAW Remodelors Council and other remodelers councils around the state. He was also a member of the NAHB Membership Hall of Fame and the NAHB Remodeling Hall of Fame.

Builders Purchasing Program was formed to take advantage of Amerinet's experience and program for Association members. Among the products and services the Home Builders Purchasing Program promotes are Verizon Wireless service, Staples office products and FedEx shipping.

The other item that came out of a brainstorming session was the need for expanded networking opportunities. The days of a few builders meeting each other over gin and golf to work out their strategic plans were over. Networking now happened in more structured environments via the Associates Council Referral Network, but continued the more casual events like the Annual Member Picnic, golf tournaments or the Crab Feed. The Association began to roll out programs designed to formalize networking and expand the menu of sponsorship and advertising opportunities, which were a separate way for companies to market within the Association.

Career Connection

The Master Builders had been involved in inspiring the next generation of housing professionals for decades; in fact, one can trace the impetus back to the initial objectives spelled out in 1914. For the homebuilding industry to advance, there must always be an upcoming group of builders who are skilled and committed to continuing the tradition of quality workmanship. However, in the later part of the twentieth century, the skilled trades had fallen out of fashion for youth graduating from high school. Vocational classes were out of favor in school districts pushed to meet testing standards that had nothing to do with whether a student could operate a miter saw, and community college programs had a hard time keeping up with the industry's changing standards.

The Master Builders Association saw a gap that needed to be filled, and created the Master Builders Education Foundation, a 501(c)3 non-profit organization that would grant scholarships for students to attend the University of Washington and Central Washington University to study construction. However, a study was undertaken in the early 2000s of those students who had received scholarships, and found out that most of them were not pursuing careers in the residential market. "We found out that we were essentially funding everyone to go into the commercial market," says Cathy Feole. Feole was hired to re-tool the Education Foundation, and she quickly found out that the name itself was the source of confusion. As the Master Builders Education Foundation, many members confused the foundation with MBA University (the Association's education program), rather than an outreach program. So the name was changed to Master Builders Career Connection, and Feole got to work updating the curriculum.

"We want to bring anyone who's interested in the industry, not just kids. We want to bring in skilled workers and get them the hands-on training they need to become good employees," she says. To do that, they started several new programs. One that Cathy is very proud of is called Charlie's House, named after philanthropist and former member Milo Charleston. In groups of sixteen or twenty, students work together to build a nine-foot by eleven-foot house. They break into three teams, and select team leaders who must explain the process of how the house will be built. The floor is laid first, then the walls, then the cabling, then the roof. It takes about an hour and a half to assemble, and the students then participate in presentations about what they've done.

Through the process, the high schoolers not only learn teamwork, but also learn green-building techniques: they install solar panels on the roof and complete pre-prepared wiring, water and finishing modules. "They can even plug in their iPods when they're done," beams Feole. She continues, "You have to cultivate your next generation. The pipeline of people hasn't kept up with demand."

A secondary thrust of the program is retraining for adults who have been excluded in some way from the job market. Career Connection offered a course in siding installation. Adult students came to six weeks of night classes, then were given a two-week internship to get hands-on experience. Thus, they have some experience and are more attractive job candidates for companies.

In 2003, MBA University was created as a consolidated program to provide continuing education to members. Todd Bennett, 2003 President, undertook a massive structural reformation of the education program. He explains, "We as an industry were struggling with how to educate our workforce. As I went through the chairs at the Master Builders, I saw

Todd Bennett, MBA University Board Vice Chair (left), and Jack Tenhulzen, MBA University Board Vice Chair (right), cut the ceremonial ribbon opening MBA University on September 9, 2003. MBA University Board of Governors included Sandy McAdams, Curriculum Committee Chair; Shirley Blayden, Marketing Committee Chair; and Cathy Waidelich, Staff Liaison.

Department chairs were instrumental in launching MBA University and included: Donna Shirey, CGR, CAPS, Built Green Department Chair; Janice Bristol, CPA, Business Management Department Chair; Sherman Colson, Computer and Internet Department Chair; Michael Tenhulzen, CGR, CAPS, Consumer Education Department Chair; Lisa Kennan-Meyer, AIA, Design and Architecture Department Chair; John Bratton, CGR, CAPS, Government Affairs Department Chair; Juli Bacon, Human Resources Department Chair; Robert Thorpe, AICP, Land Development Department Chair; Darylene Dennon, Leadership Development Department Chair; Diane Glenn, Project Management, Codes and Regulations Department Chair; Traci Tenhulzen, Safety Department Chair; and Bill Kreager, AIA, MIRM, Sales and Marketing Department Chair.

a lot of councils and committees offered training of some type, but there was no consistency, and there was no quality control. We hatched this idea, saying, let's have a central group that can manage the curriculum and the teachers. Let's make sure the instructors are trained. Let's make sure the curriculum is correct. Make sure the proper classes are taught."

Bennett saw an opportunity to build in classroom space in the former City University building the Master Builders had just purchased. He began by polling those who had taken classes from the Association in the past, and he was disheartened. "Nobody had ever done this. Nobody had ever asked the participants of all these classes over these many years whether they liked the class or not, was the information good or bad, or did they like the instructor. We found out that some teachers had been teaching crummy classes for twenty years."

In a press release, Sam Anderson talked about the launch of MBA University and the value of education. "This initiative is the future of our industry in an information-based and globally competitive economy. Every industry must work smarter; ours is no exception."

One thing which Bennett and others involved in planning the MBA University saw was that homebuilders were increasingly called on to structure complex financial deals. It hadn't been that long since the procedure to get a construction loan was as simple as picking up the phone to call your friend at the bank and explaining the project to him. However, as financial instruments got more and more complex, builders almost needed an accounting background to make sense of them. Some builders, like Todd Bennett and Doug Barnes, did have degrees in accounting, but the rest of the industry needed education to get up to speed. The continuing education classes offered by the Association helped builder, remodeler and associate members cope with a rapidly changing industry.

Caring for the Community

The homebuilding industry is arguably the best suited to tackle the issues concerning homelessness – but individual companies are often too small or too busy to implement large or complex charitable projects. The Master Builders Care Foundation speaks directly to one of the stated missions of the Seattle Master Builders dating back to 1936: the promotion of charitable life and the civic welfare of the community. In 1998, President Jack Tenhulzen and Executive Officer Sam Anderson came up with an innovative way to accomplish that – make a foundation, so that employees' contributions could be tax deductible, and all the donations could be pooled.

The Master Builders Care Foundation had not done much since its inception until one board meeting in April 2000 when Mike Lennon, president of HomeAid America, came to speak. He made a presentation to the board, and recently seated member John Day remembered thinking to himself, "We've got to try this." Day

Vision House is a nonprofit agency, providing transitional housing and support services for families overcoming homelessness who are dedicated to turning their lives around. On February 7, 2007, four new apartment units were dedicated. Scott Camerer, one of the founders of Vision House, proudly announced, "The units will be home to women and children in need of shelter, providing safety, security and a place to begin rebuilding their lives."

The Master Builders in 2003 reached out to the Fremont Public Association with a gift of basketballs and hoops.

volunteered to head up the organization and got to work. At the time, HomeAid provided transitional housing for women and children by partnering with local homebuilders associations. HomeAid didn't directly construct the shelters, nor did they create infrastructure for finding the people who needed their services. Rather, they looked to the Association to make connections and assist in facilitating solutions.

A staff member, Lynda Hester, knew Susan Camerer, who had been running a transitional facility for the homeless called Vision House. Day knew that would be a perfect fit for the HomeAid project. He explains, "We have been

very successful at it, and in fact it has been an amazing experience. We can really contribute to solving this problem because we are the ones who provide housing in this region, and our members have been extremely generous. On average, we are able to build these facilities for fifty cents on the dollar." As the philanthropic arm of the Association, the Foundation is able to focus the goodwill of the member companies, and truly make the community appreciate members' expertise.

In addition to the work with Vision House, the Care Foundation sponsors Rampathon and Painting a Better Tomorrow. Rampathon is a one-day event where member companies construct free access ramps for needy individuals who are disabled and can't leave home without assistance. Rampathon applicants are screened rigorously. First and foremost, there must be a need. Few applicants would be denied based on that. The applicants fall into two broad groups: the elderly, striving for independence and the ability to age in place, and parents of disabled children. Once need has been established, a screening committee goes to the potential recipient's home. Because ramps must be constructed to ADA standards, the remodeler has to make sure there will be enough room for the proper slope and rise, and the property will allow for the width needed. "There's an intense amount of work that goes into each ramp," says Donna Shirey. "We do designs specific to each house."

John Cunningham, whose home got a ramp in 2006, was effusive in his thanks. "The Master Builders Association and Shirey Contracting displayed great kindness and charity in this effort. This ramp will make things so much easier." His daughter, Crystal, has multiple disabilities. "It had gotten so difficult to carry Crystal."

Rampathon volunteers often take on more than just constructing the ramp itself. In 2004, White Center resident David Huff found that out when he struck up a conversation with the builders from Vanderspek Remodel and Build. Huff suffers from cerebral palsy and gets around on a motorized scooter. The only battery powerful enough to charge the scooter was his car's, so Huff would have to sit inside his car for up to six hours at a time, leaving it running and the scooter plugged in, because he worried that someone would steal one or both of the vehicles. Vanderspek team members took it upon themselves to solve his problem, and constructed a secure shed and wired it for electricity for recharging the scooter.

A ramp that nearly didn't get built because of design challenges has given the Hribernick boys of Edmonds the freedom to go outside and play. Twins Cole and Ryan Hribernick share David Huff's disease, but their father's home was situated on his property in such a way as to make a ramp nearly impossible to build. Their dad, John, was making four trips to get the boys and their wheelchairs up and down seven steps

Association members divide up into teams for Painting a Better Tomorrow. A fresh coat of paint and minor repairs help out local shelters and nonprofit agencies — another commitment to helping neighbors in need!

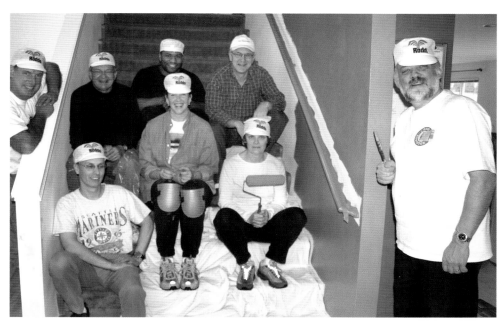

anytime they wanted to leave the house. The wheelchairs are about forty pounds apiece, and the boys weighed in at seventy pounds when John heard about Rampathon.

"They didn't think it was anything anybody would be able to take on," Chuck Russell said. Russell is the owner of Woodinville-based Westhill, a general contractor who organized the team of 32 to build the Hribernick's ramp. "We went out and took a look at it. And once we met [the Hribernicks] and saw how much the father was struggling – how much it meant to them and how the kids couldn't get outside – we just couldn't say no." Russell estimated the cost of the ramp at $18,000, and said it took the team about six hours to complete it.

"I am constantly inspired how Rampathon has the ability to improve the lives of ramp recipients, and also changes the lives of volunteers," said 2005 Co-Chair Joe Schwab. Indeed, there are more than 200 families in the Seattle metro area whose lives have gained independence because of the work of volunteers. One of those families is Joe Martineau's.

Martineau, the Executive Officer of the Association for eighteen years, is now in his eighties. He and his wife, Annabel, live with their daughter, in a split-level home in Kirkland. Annabel Martineau is a petite, bubbly woman in her mid-eighties, and Joe began having a hard time keeping up with her. Though not confined to a wheelchair, it started to become very difficult for him to get out of the house without assistance, and Annabel wasn't always there to help. Joe remembers, "I called up and asked about the Rampathon, I wanted to get involved in it. I don't own this fancy house, and I haven't got the money, so they said they'd put it up. I expected maybe a wooden slat with some two-by-fours, but it looks really classy." Tenhulzen remodelers showed up at the Martineaus' house with concrete, and they built the ramp in an afternoon.

Annabel laughs, "I went out and got coffee and rolls, but they brought everything, it was like a big party." The party notwithstanding, the team did a tremendous job. When Joe gives directions to his house, he says "look for the ramp," but it is so well designed that it fits seamlessly with the neighborhood's construction. ♣

Inset below, former Executive Officer Joe Martineau thanks Jack Tenhulzen for captaining the construction (right) of his new wheelchair ramp. Below, Jackson Remodeling puts the finishing touch on their 2007 ramp.

Rampathon

presented by

HomeStreet Bank

May 19, 2007

Captain:
Jackson Remodeling, LLC

MASTER BUILDERS Care Foundation

PETER ORSER

ACHIEVEMENTS:
President, Master Builders, *2004*
Builder of the Year, *2004*

Peter Orser has made impressive waves in the construction industry, especially for someone without a formal background in building. With a graduate degree in Urban Planning at the University of Washington, he got involved in a project for Quadrant Homes in 1987. He credits his achievements to an approach that works toward mutual success, a commitment to providing quality affordable housing, and Master Builders Association membership.

At Quadrant Homes, Orser started a new division to develop multifamily housing. He now runs the company. "Over the last ten years we've been working on a homebuilding operation and trying to reengineer ourselves to be leaner, more focused, and offer more house for less money. In that process we grew to become the largest homebuilder in the region." Even amidst growth, Peter remains committed to customer service. "I've been dedicated to service for the first time homebuyer. I have always been very engaged as a Master Builders member. It is about building great communities, making not so much the sticks of the house go together, but the fabric of the community come together."

Peter's innovative approach to home design led to an amazing accomplishment: houses that could be entirely built in 54 days. The streamlined building process developed a program that manufactures panels off-site. The quality improved since these panels were constructed in a dry warehouse. "I was more about the process, and the outcome of affordability, and community, and not so much about the hammers and nails."

Orser joined the Master Builders Association in the late 1990s. "I've always been involved in a lot of political issues around entitlements, and the Master Builders Association has always played a big role in helping us with that. They've also had some really positive marketing initiatives." Orser is an active advocate of the Built Green program and works to help engage members in the program. Quadrant Homes' clients from can customize their new homes and add environmentally responsible features such as rain barrels and energy-efficient furnaces.

During Orser's presidency in 2004, the Master Builders Association was rapidly gaining on its rival to be the largest homebuilders association in the country. Using a hands-on approach, Peter recruited new members by calling them himself. He continues to be a proud member. "I think sometimes we take for granted the role the Association plays for us when all of these things just kind of happen on automatic pilot. Truth be told, each of us as individual builders would not be as effective without the synergy that gets created in the Association."

CHAPTER 13

Calm in the Eye of the Storm

2006 – 2008

By the fall of 2006, area homebuilders discovered that they were no longer at the peak of a market which had been on an upward trend for five years. They reacted, but not quickly enough to stop the construction prior to the downturn. The Association reacted to the economic crisis by offering expanded educational services and being proactive about media coverage. Govermental relations assumed a role of increasing magnitude as builders had difficulties with tax bills on properties they couldn't develop, and plats which expired before builders could build on them. The downturn reached its lowest point by the end of 2008, and builders have recognized a new paradigm in how they run their businesses. Many reduced staff and began to operate leaner companies. Despite a dismal economy, builders continued to volunteer their time and efforts to the programs of the Master Builders Care Foundation.

At the Annual Membership Day in 2008, members enjoyed hot dogs and watermelon while they waited to pick up their Return on Industrial Insurance checks.

The Bubble Bursts

In the summer of 2006, homebuilders around our region were looking at reports of the collapsing industry from elsewhere around the country. By and large, they thought, *It can't happen HERE! We're different from the rest of the nation.* Local editorialists agreed – people were fleeing California's rapidly collapsing economy just to strengthen the great Pacific Northwest. Housing prices were continuing to escalate, and trendwatchers predicted continued growth and only mild challenge ahead.

However, builders who paid close attention to the national picture saw signs of the trials to come. Todd Bennett, CEO of Bennett Homes, pinpointed the date the market crashed at August 3, 2007. Other builders put the shift significantly earlier. To Todd Britsch of New Homes Trends, the progression was analogous to a marathon. A marathon runner cannot come to a complete stop just because their left foot has crossed the finish line, likewise, builders couldn't put the brakes on their projects all at once. Some builders saw that finish line as early as summer 2006, but the

momentum they had carried them through 2007 at rates of construction and permitting that were essentially untenable. The industry had achieved a velocity it could neither sustain nor control.

By late 2008, according to the Mortgage Bankers Association, 7.88 percent of all mortgages were thirty days or more overdue, and 3.3 percent were somewhere in the process of foreclosure. These numbers were the highest

Members, such as Tracy Cromwell (right), participate in the annual auction to raise money for Master Builders Care Foundation projects. Even in tough economic times, giving back to the community is a priority, and members reach deep to fund these community service endeavors.

recorded over the survey's nearly four decades. In past recessions, foreclosures were generally not seen at rates above one percent and didn't rise above two percent until late 2007.[1]

The causes leading to the slowdown and eventual collapse of housing markets around the country were many, but the main culprit was a mortgage market with loosened standards for credit and lack of oversight. Builders were constructing homes at a record pace. There were qualified buyers with financing in hand lining up to purchase them. What few people realized was that a significant percentage of those "qualified" buyers had not been scrutinized or were counting on rapidly appreciating home values to resell their house in a few months.. Buyers were qualified on so called "NINA" loans, or No Income, No Asset.[2] Some buyers shouldn't have purchased a home, some lenders shouldn't have made the loan and some builders knew better than to sell and keep on building. But all were convinced that real estate was a safe investment; and they'd continue to do better for their families in the long run. The homebuilders weren't the guys out there making incredibly risky decisions. They saw a simple economic paradigm: there is demand for our product, so we'll make more supply.

The causes of the housing slump, the weakening of the stock market and the ensuing economic recession will be analyzed and discussed in painstaking detail for years to come. But a simple fact remains: the wrong businesses got into the mortgage industry for the wrong reason. Mortgages ceased to be primarily a vehicle for the American family to purchase a home, paying a bank back over thirty years; on the secondary market, they became a bundled, securitized and traded commodity. Once that happened, lenders faced tremendous pressure from the secondary market to continue providing this now valuable commodity. Some banks never intended to keep the mortgages on their balance sheets, so there was no reason to consider the actual assets backing up the loans, nor the people who would be responsible for payback. The banks sold the mortgages to a firm further away from the actual house, and thus got more money to make more loans. And so, for the first time, the housing industry and the financial traders who created these new mortgage-backed securities started what became a global recession.

The prospect of considerable profits fueled speculations far beyond what we saw in our region, where there remains a limited supply of land on which to build houses. The first signs of real trouble came in the so-called "Sand States" – Nevada, Florida, California and Arizona. Despite these states holding only twenty percent of the

The presentation by Dr. Bernie Markstein at the Northwest Builders Show (above) on December 12, 2007, reported that NAHB forecasted a modest rebound in residential construction activity by third quarter 2008.

nation's mortgages, they have accounted for over forty percent of foreclosures.[3]

"Hindsight is always twenty-twenty, but land prices in our area should have ceased escalating in the second quarter of 2006." So states New Home Trends' Britsch. "In August of 2006, the Southwest region stopped and you could feel it here. It was as if somebody kicked the real estate market in the gut, but we had 30,000 or 40,000 buyers waiting on the sidelines."

The recession of 2006-2008 felt different to builders who had undergone recessions in the 1970s, 1980s and 1990s. "The difference is fear," says Membership Director Larry Chimenti. His background is in commercial sales within the homebuilding industry, and he recalled one customer telling him in the 1980s, *"Please God, give me one more building boom and I promise not to waste it this time.* There are folks out there now feeling the same way."

Other members have slightly different perspectives. Chuck Crosby, who now splits his time between the hard-hit Phoenix area and southern Snohomish County, says that "The bad loans that were out there, we have never had to deal with that. In the 1980s, you couldn't sell a house. Unemployment was very high, and the interest rates were through the roof, but you didn't have the foreclosures." Crosby was optimistic that 2008 saw the deepest the recession would get, "Once the inventory stabilizes, the prices stabilize. Once the prices stabilize we will start

TODD BENNETT

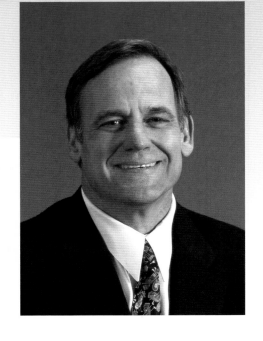

ACHIEVEMENTS:
President, Master Builders, *2003*
Builder of the Year, *2003 & 2005*
Built Green Hammer Award, *2006*
Built Green Pioneer Award, *2007*

Todd Bennett's financial expertise, sharp eye for industry and market trends, and commitment to building excellence have helped propel Bennett Homes to a position as one of the top construction companies in the Seattle region. Home-grown in Bellevue and a graduate of the University of Washington, Todd is a certified professional accountant who specialized in construction clients. He formed his own company, Bennett Homes, in 1984; it is devoted to providing "superior quality and craftsmanship." Bennett explains that as the building industry grew in the 1980s, it became necessary to have a solid knowledge of finance. "We could talk to banks and it was more important to be a business manager than a homebuilder."

A long-time Master Builders Association member, Todd's accounting background has contributed to making him a valuable member of the Association. "Early on we had gotten involved in some committees and pretty quickly decided to come on to the board. I served on the board of directors of Master Builders for many years and then at some point decided to go through the chairs and become President."

As President in 2003, Todd noticed a need to better educate the building workforce, and the MBA University was born. He collaborated with other members to renovate the courses that were currently taught through the Association and make it something better. Using guidance from the NAHB, Bennett asked builders what classes they would like to take and revamped the entire curriculum. During his presidency, Bennett was instrumental in acquiring the Association's current building in Bellevue. He says, "When I was President we bought, remodeled, and got the new building. It was all part of my tenure. I am pretty proud about that."

Bennett Homes is an avid supporter of the Master Builders' Built Green program. "We always wanted to have the most homes certified at the highest level and be the most creative in doing that." In this case, it's not about the bottom line. "We are okay if it cost a little more, we feel better about it. That is the benefit we get. We are being better custodians of the planet."

Todd values his Master Builders membership, especially how being a member puts him in touch with his professional competitors and the knowledge gained about new trends and innovations in building. He explains, "Master Builders involvement allowed me to meet the owners and key executives of probably the top twenty homebuilders in a positive manner. That is a very good contact base. We are all pretty good friends even though we are competitors." Bennett Homes remains active in the Master Builders Association, and even though he has experience with other associations, Bennett reflects, "This is a great organization. It's a powerful, helpful, useful organization. That is where my focus will always be."

seeing the return of the value coming back to properties. And there's not that much land to build on here."

Public perception had shifted over the boom years. Many people became convinced that home prices were going to continue to rise indefinitely, and the definition of "affordable" changed for many. So, as housing costs outpaced personal income, many families reassessed what was "affordable" for them. Some families became used to spending half (or more) of their monthly income on their mortgage, and were convinced that homes should continue to appreciate in value and sales price.

The local housing market downturn, which began in the fourth quarter of 2006, gained momentum throughout 2007, and got extra fuel from the August crash of the sub-prime loan market. Dozens of builders attended a series of summit meetings held by the Association and asked for help to motivate consumers and combat a rising tide of negative and misleading media coverage.

In response to those builder-summits, the Association conducted focus groups in 2008 of self-identified first-time and "move-up" buyers to gauge attitudes toward the market and level of understanding regarding recent changes in the mortgage market.

What they found was that consumers were interested but unsure where the market was headed. Uncertainty and fear of making a "bad" decision (not waiting until the bottom of the market, buying a home and having its value decrease, locking in a mortgage rate and then having the rate drop, etc.) led to inaction by consumers. They realized it was a buyers' market and also felt it was a bad time to be selling a home. They saw 2008 as both the best and worst of times to be in the market. Focus-group participants also had a basic understanding of the options for financing a home purchase but were unfamiliar with recent changes to loan limits under FHA, Fannie Mae and Freddie Mac.

The rapid changes to mortgage financing options as well as the varying experiences of different markets across the country were confusing to not only consumers, but the media as well. It became apparent that local news media fueled this sort of uncertainty by not differentiating between local and national conditions. The Association responded by ramping up consumer outreach, education and advertising efforts in what was an increasingly confusing time.

Immediately, the focus of advertising shifted to educating consumers about changes to the marketplace. The new ads focused on driving consumers to the Association's website as a source of trusted professionals. Communications department staff established advertisements such as the Master Builder Minute on local radio stations and a new column in the *Seattle Times' New Homes Saturday* section called "Dwell On This" in order to provide market-specific advice. All channels encouraged consumers not to wait to buy a home.

Communications and Public Affairs staff, along with an outside public-relations firm, worked with local media to highlight the differences between local and national real estate markets; point out positive, local real estate news; and identify experts for local news stories. A follow-up survey at the end of 2008 revealed that half of those surveyed reported seeing positive news coverage and felt that now was a good time to be looking for a new home.

Association research also revealed consumers used a variety of websites for information but would be interested in a website that provided not only local information but a wide variety of information on buying, selling and financing. The Association, along with other real estate organizations, created RightTimeToBuy.org and a Spanish language version, CompraHoy.org, to educate the local public and act as an honest broker of accurate homebuying information In 2009, the website was retooled and renamed NWHomeFacts.com. Information about local neighborhoods, mortgage rates and educational classes was added.

The Cost of Regulation

Builders have been lamenting the increasing cost of regulations since the first fees were put into place. In the 1970s, builders complained that the fees they endured would make housing too expensive when the total fees to build a home were $630. However, as the Master Builders Association looked at the factors keeping housing from being truly affordable in the area, the cost of regulation was repeatedly a major culprit. Housing in the area not only must meet (and pay for) local regulations, there are also state-mandated Growth Management Act issues. As state and federal budgets faced shortfalls in the recession, local jurisdictions tried to compensate for that by imposing additional fees on builders. The Government Affairs department lobbied to keep builders' costs down, but was not always successful.

Remodeling Excellence Awards (REX) help to get people involved while honoring the best. These social events promote the professional camaraderie that enable members to get to know each other, so that during tough times members find the support they need.

Though member companies had been complaining to anyone who would listen about the costly regulatory environment they had to contend with, the public at large tended to think that it was a case of empty bellyaching. John Cochenour of Bellevue's Lexington Fine Homes sees a clear relationship between the impact fees and the lack of affordable housing in the area. "I used to pay $19,000 to get a lot and get it ready to develop. We got worried when they got to $25,000. By the time I saw prices go up to $50,000, I realized it wasn't as important what the land price was as long as I could resell the house. If I have paid $150,000 for a piece of ground, I will have to sell that house for $525,000. So the

question is not, why did I pay the $150,000 for a piece of property, it's can I sell it?"

With land selling for six figures, of course housing prices escalated rapidly. Builder Chuck Crosby said, "The general public doesn't understand that the regulations slow us down, but in the end, they don't really affect us at all. We take whatever costs we incur and pass them on to the consumer. These costs are not being absorbed by the builders." The Master Builders Association had always been supportive of more affordable housing in the area, but how was more affordable housing going to get built by market-rate builders if just buying dirt cost so much money, to say nothing of the fees associated with doing something with that dirt?

The Master Builders set out to examine exactly what costs the builders were passing on to consumers. Finding a clear analysis of costs for regulation proved difficult, so they were nearly ready to undertake their own detailed study, until University of Washington Economics Professor Theo Eicher beat them to the punch. His study of 250 major cities found that the Seattle area was consistently near the top of the list in terms of expense; in fact, in Seattle proper, the cost of regulations totaled $203,000 per dwelling. He examined further, and found that in all three of the major cities in King and Snohomish

At the 2007 Crab Feed, members enjoy talking about what makes them successful while they eat Dungeness Crab.

counties studied (Seattle, Everett and Kent), fees associated with regulation account for 45 percent of a home's price.[5] Nationally, the NAHB calculated the cost of regulation, and pegged it between ten and twenty percent of the cost to build a home.[6]

A breakdown of prices that King County builders face is simply staggering. Snohomish County builders don't have it much better. The Master Builders' Public Policy department undertook a massive campaign to address what they viewed as the most striking problem in the permitting process – the delays in the short plat process. Basically, the platting process must be undertaken prior to developing land, and for each "simple" plat, a builder will invest upwards of $10,000. The county will review the actual land to be built on, and they will determine how many lots that land can hold. The builder works with an engineer to determine where the roads will be, where the stormwater drains will be, and then submits that plan to the county for review, prior to even getting a preliminary approval.

What began happening as builders reacted to the downturn was that the permit deadlines began to run out. Builders had paid the counties for preliminary plat approval, but had become unsure whether or when they would actually be constructing houses on those plats. Public Affairs Director Allison Butcher explains a piece of the challenge: "Right now, plats expire in about two years. With the economy in a recession, we asked the counties to essentially extend the permissions they'd already given. In addition, we are trying to make it easier to go through the tax reevaluation process. If a member has a piece of property that's been platted, they are paying property tax on it that may be very out of line with what the current market value is, and that can be very costly."

Members Helping Each Other

"It's always important to support each other. We do business with as many members as we can," says 2005 President Donna Shirey. Especially in an economic downturn, members help each other out by making sure all their business is done with other member companies. Jeff Taylor knows firsthand how important the business connections are. "I wanted to do some business with Charlie Conner, this was back in 1989, and he called me back. 'Well, your prices look good; I've heard your service is good. But there's one other thing, we only do business with members of our Association.'" Taylor laughs, "I said, 'where do I sign?' You can't question the value of those relationships."

Remodeler John Bratton picks up the story. "You establish your network, your support group, people you can call and ask questions that non-members wouldn't answer for you. Members will openly share anything because we all have been through the same experiences; we're suffering the same consequences. The people outside of this organization are really suffering, because they have no mentors, they are just stuck. Rather than sitting behind the computer trying to figure out how to run a business, you actually have people you can talk to and have a cup of coffee and compare notes." By sharing information, members can be strong enough to weather the storm.

The Associates Council created a structured referral network. Started in January 2007, the referral network gave members a sixty-minute networking session where they could share what business they needed, what business they had, and make new connections.

The demand for classes, at first to hone members' skills and then to cope with the changing market, caused MBA University to grow significantly during this period. In 2006, the University only offered eighty classes to a thousand students. By 2008, the number of students had more than doubled to 2,268, who enrolled in 119 classes. The University had been undergoing a major retooling; Todd Bennett had started the education overhaul in 2003 and launched MBA University in 2004. "2003 through 2006 were a hard three years. We had to get together everything that was being taught, and really go over it from soup to nuts. We came up with a whole new curriculum, and started asking for builder feedback," says Bennett.

The builder feedback led to a varied and responsive curriculum. Classes were offered in 2008 on recession survival skills, like working with lenders in a credit crunch, and strategic planning for economic recovery. Courses were still being offered in more traditional career development areas, though. Builder members could earn their Certified Master Builder certification; remodelers could become "Certified Aging-in-Place Specialists" or Certified Graduate Remodelers, and there continued to be a whole slew of courses in green building techniques.

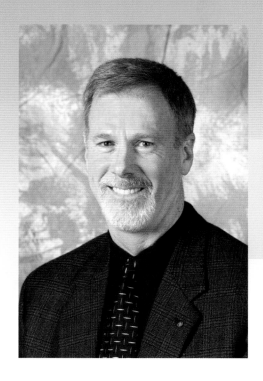

JIM POTTER

ACHIEVEMENTS:
President, Master Builders, 2006

Association member Jim Potter is not your typical builder: in addition to his many real estate properties, he owns and invests in several businesses ranging from bowling alleys to roller rinks. Jim's restless creativity and interest in trying new things has led him to pursue various successful building opportunities, including running over 25 properties from Olympia to Burlington, purchasing forestland, and working to improve the state of multifamily building. A member since 1986, he has used his entrepreneurial spirit to further the Association's goals through active roles in the Board of Directors, the Master Builders' Multifamily Council, the Housing Policy Committee, and eventually the presidency in 2006.

Potter came to construction from a varied background. His goal is to provide housing to people who fall outside the mainstream. "I want to deliver housing without any government subsidy, and deliver to people who are trying to get into their first house, or their first condo, or their first apartment. I have always had a passion for delivering that product. That's always been what I like doing."

Jim's unique building background and interests make him an "odd duck," as well as a voice representing diverse interests within the Association. While the majority of Association members focus on single-family homes, Potter's businesses build mostly multifamily units. Potter's extensive knowledge of Seattle's building codes and zoning regulations inform his involvement in Seattle's city council meetings, where he helps create new policies. He has shown himself to be a versatile builder during unpredictable markets, and credits the Growth Management Act for "making a difference" by recognizing the value of building on multi-family lots. Jim explains, "Once Growth Management happened, I knew the world was coming my way. I tried to get people to understand what that's going to take. It's going to radically change the business and the future."

Jim Potter appreciates the benefits of his involvement with the Master Builders. "The Master Builders is an organization that has clout. It has gotten stronger, better, and bigger in my time with them." The sheer size ensures that builders' voices are heard. Jim praises its "political muscle" in local and state legislatures to push for laws that benefit and protect builders.

Through his leadership, involvement with external associations has expanded. As a result of these efforts, the Master Builders Association has "grown incredibly." The medical benefits alone are worth becoming a member, and Jim praises the ROII program. Potter reflects, "It's like you join our organization and you actually get paid to join our organization for people that have employees. Pay your 500 bucks and join a group that's going to write you a check back. That's a pretty good deal."

Programs for Prosperity

By 2007, the Master Builders Association had grown to a staff of 45, many of them focused on serving as a conduit for information between local governments and member companies. The legislative activity affecting builders going on at any moment is dizzying. Fortunately, the staff at the Association can translate the laws into terms anyone can understand.

In 2007, stormwater was the hot-button issue. The Washington State Department of Ecology required that every construction project go through a stormwater permitting process, which mandated buffer zones, sediment controls and flow rates. Snohomish County needed to create and implement revisions to its stormwater codes, and the Master Builders public policy and government affairs departments were very active in making sure the builders' perspective was heard.

Allison Butcher explains, "We send out once-a-week updates. With technology, we've been able to maintain better communication with the builders. Then, with the downturn, our local lobbyists became very focused on economic stimulus, and the rest of us also focused on outreach. We sit on several regional groups that play a role in land use and the environment, including the Puget Sound Partnership, the Puget Sound Salmon Recovery Council, the Stormwater Work Group. To the extent that we can be there, be involved, and relay that back to our members, that's a good thing. Our members' time is focused on a lot of other things right now," Butcher smiles. Involvement in the Puget

Sound Partnership helped ensure that the 2020 Action Agenda, which is the working blueprint for protection and restoration of the Puget Sound, did not create any new regulatory burdens on the homebuilding industry or business as a whole.

The working relationships that were created out of the Association's active participation in environmental forums have allowed the Association to be viewed as a moderate voice in the contentious landscape of policy discussions. Government Affairs Director Don Davis echoed the sentiment, "You need to work with the political environment as it is. I think to be in business, you have got to understand where the other side is coming from. If your approach is just to say no, you won't get very far in our region. Moderation is the key to success."

Concerned citizens needed to look no further than the Built Green program to realize the Master Builders' care for the environment was real. 2006 was a record year for Built Green, with over seventy percent membership growth. Aaron Adelstein, Built Green Director, says, "Built Green is a partnership between the Association, King County and Snohomish County. We have people from both counties on our executive committee. Our cities and counties understand green building and have it as a priority, but it has been tremendously advantageous to be a part of the building association as well. We're approached with an implicit level of trust from both sides."

There has always been a degree of skepticism on builders' parts about whether Built Green certification had any measureable return on the bottom line. In 2007 and 2008, Adelstein and his staff set out to answer that question. Using a database of certified Built Green homes they had been compiling since 2001, they were able to analyze actual sales data on the homes. "We cross-referenced address data with MLS data and assessor's data, and what we found is that Built Green homes are selling for more than non-certified homes. We also found that you can't just rely on a green certification if it's a big upcharge. You have the old real estate standbys of location and design aesthetic that have to meet buyers' needs, but it those things are in place, people will pay more for green properties. The properties are also selling faster than non-certified properties."

Custom-homebuilder Grey Lundberg used to be one of the skeptics. He says, "Like a lot of builders, I used to reject the 'green building' movement out of hand, thinking that it was environmentalists trying to force their fringe agenda on my business practices. Until I had a good client of mine ask me to build a home for them that would be a 'green' demonstration project." That demonstration project was the Built Green

Profile

DAVE MAIN

ACHIEVEMENTS:
Builder of the Year, *2006 & 2008*
President-Elect, Master Builders, *2010*

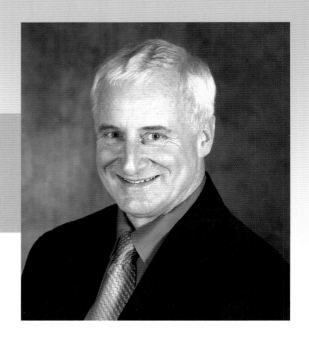

Dave Main has worked in the building industry since he was fourteen years old, but his educational background boasts diverse interests. Dave received an English degree from Washington State University and studied liberal arts. "I think the biggest thing anybody gets from a college education is the ability to learn how to learn. Once you master that skill, the world's wide open."

Main has been a member since 1977, though he didn't start Main Street Builders until 1980. Family owned and operated, Main Street Builders constructs and remodels custom homes, working closely with buyers during every step of the process. "If I had a big pile of everything that went into a home and one helper I could build the house. So I understand the mechanics of everything from start to finish, and can actually even do the work. That's why I love custom-homebuilding so much. Because I get to take a client and actually work shoulder to shoulder through the process of building their home and make it fun for them."

Dave is proud of the diversity he sees in the Master Builders. "The increase of the number of women that participate both as builders, remodelers, suppliers, and the number of people of color that we see in the group now, it's a much more vast cross-section of the community that we live in and work for. I like that perspective, I like where we've gone." Main describes how programs such as the Master Builders Care Foundation enrich the lives of builders and the communities. "Offering learning opportunities to young people who wanted to enter into the homebuilding business, just that outreach is fantastic. The bigger builders have obviously stepped up and shared some of our homemade projects." Main is also involved in the Rampathon program. He is especially inspired by the story of a young man with cerebral palsy who lives in Kent, and just wants a "normal" life. The Kent area is meaningful to Dave. "It's an area of the county that I know very, very well, and I built quite a few homes down there, and it's just a nice opportunity to give something back to that community. Specifically to these people that need it."

Looking ahead to his presidency in 2010, Dave is excited about "kicking off the next 100 years." In considering what lies ahead, Dave looks back to the Association's roots 100 years ago. "It was created out of a need to craft a healthier industry. That's kind of where we are now today." Dave wants to continue to help the Association become "a more diverse and cooperative organization" and continue to expand programs like the Care Foundation and Career Connection. "As an industry we've got a lot of work to do, but we've got great minds, great people. Building quality products and participating now in giving back to the community. As a whole, I'm pretty proud of our industry."

Home at Suncadia resort, in Roslyn, Washington. The home would be the first "resort-level" home in the region to showcase green-building practices and components, and was constructed to "demonstrate that a custom home could use green-building techniques for the same costs as traditional building practices," said developer Brenda Nunes.

When she called Lundberg, he began researching how green building worked. "I found out that green building was aligned very much with my building philosophy – building a house that will last for generations, one that is extremely energy efficient, is very healthy for our clients to live in, and most importantly being an excellent steward of our business practices. Green building fit perfectly for us," Lundberg smiles. "It was a very good decision for our business." The home won accolades from the NAHB for best green-marketing project of the year.

If builders in Redmond or Kirkland constructed a certified Built Green home, they became eligible for expedited permitting. Throughout King County, building a five-star project allows the county to assign a single project manager to become an internal advocate within the permitting department. "We've also worked with Seattle and King County to offer a cash incentive to members who step up to the four- or five-star levels,"

2008 Built Green Conference
Picured here are (from left) City of Kirkland Green Building team members Stacy Clauson, Tom Jensen, David Barnes and Scott Guter. Accepting the award for the City was Kirkland's Mayor, James Lauinger.

beams Adelstein. He's cautious of programs that mandate green-building standards, though. "I've always said that a thousand homes that are built moderately green have a much greater impact than three homes that are perfect and completely sustainable, because you don't get the economy of scale." Built Green has clearly achieved such scale – in early 2009, they certified the 14,000th Built Green home.

Caring for the Community During Difficult Times

As the Association rode the crest of the boom times into the trough of the housing downturn, their commitment to the community was unwavering.

The Master Builders Care Foundation and the homebuilding industry had two record-breaking ramp-building years for the 2007 and 2008 Rampathons. A significant achievement was reached in 2007, with the construction of the 200th free ramp. During the 2008 Rampathon, more than 400 volunteers built thirty ramps. Every participant on the remodeler and builder teams felt extremely fortunate to be able to use their knowledge and skills to help someone in need.

The Care Foundation also recruited builders Shea Homes, CamWest Development and Centex Homes, who in turn enlisted more than 300 subcontractors and suppliers, to complete three new multifamily facilities for homeless transitioning toward self-sufficiency. The Master Builders Care Foundation has built ten facilities that have added a cumulative 57,000 annual bed nights at local agencies supporting homeless and those in need of temporary housing.

Andrea, a client at one of the projects recalled how she'd gathered her children, removed them from an abusive situation and started a new life at one of the projects that couldn't have been completed without the help of the Master Builders Care Foundation. Now she's on a mission to be a good parent and graduate from nursing school.

Other homeless services agencies around the two-county area also benefited from the Care Foundation's Painting A Better Tomorrow program; a day-long facility maintenance and painting spree. Over 200 member volunteers worked with agency staff and homeless individuals to repair and brighten their living facilities.

The history of Association giving and the current efforts of the Master Builders Care Foundation has been, and continues to be possible, because of the resources, unique skills and generosity of the Association's members. ♣

CHAPTER 14

Moving into the Second Century

2009

As the Master Builders Association looked forward to its second century, members and staff alike were filled with optimism for the building industry. The public is strongly behind the Built Green program, and many others are grateful recipients of work done through the Master Builders Care Foundation. When members reflect on the accomplishments of the first century of their Association, they are filled with pride. To honor the commitment to creating the communities we all call home, the Association embarks on an ambitious "100 for 100" community service campaign, wherein member companies will donate time and materials to complete 100 charitable projects in 2009. Executive Officer Sam Anderson says, "We've survived a century which was like 500 years to the home building industry. And we'll be around another century, serving our members and providing value to them."

Bennett Homes is proud to be one of the only builders in Washington state to construct homes that are certified by the American Lung Association as "Health Houses," like these in the West Highlands neighborhood at Issaquah Highlands.

A Strong Start for the Next 100 Years

Seattle-area residents awoke on Thursday, January 1, 2009 to yet another gray day in a string of gray days. The winter had been rough so far, with more snow falling than had been seen in decades. To some, the bleak weather was pretty reflective of the economic climate: no sunny news there either.

But there was hope – when 2010 President-elect Dave Main looked at the landscape, he saw signs of a recovery. "I don't think we climbed as high or fell as far, but we're suffering some of the business hangover," Main reflects. "As we embark on our second hundred years, we've got some problems to fix, but we have some good things happening out there too. We're seeing marked increases in sales; we're seeing decreases in inventory available out there. I think that the Pacific Northwest will recover a lot quicker than most other market areas in the country."

Economic indicators seem to back up Main's prediction. King and Snohomish county foreclosure rates have stabilized, and home prices in more affluent Snohomish County have settled around $350,000 – down approximately seventeen percent from their high of $426,000.[1] In January, a report was released saying that the Seattle-Bellevue-Everett metro area was third in the nation for job growth, behind Washington, D.C.'s influx of government-related jobs, and trailing the much larger Dallas metro area.[2] In July of 2009, mortgage applications were up 7.2% from a year earlier[3] and home sales in King County were at their highest level since 2007.[4]

As the old saying goes, the three most important things in real estate are "location, location, location," and the Seattle-Bellevue-Everett metro area has it. *Forbes* ranked the area as one of the ten most likely to recover from the downturn, with the caveat that "homes are still expensive, which could slow a housing recovery."[5] But housing must remain one of the most important industries in any region. As one builder put it, "you're never going to be able to outsource home construction."

For years leading up to the downturn, Master Builder members were focused on the lack of affordable homes in our area. The supply of land is strictly limited by geographic and topographic considerations; add to that the growth management boundaries, and environmental and wetlands impact restrictions, and it's easy to see how finite the housing supply in King and Snohomish counties truly is.

People will continue to migrate into the Puget Sound region, drawn by our enviable natural beauty, quality of life and strong job base. When they do, they will need someplace to live. Todd Britsch, who makes his living forecasting housing trends, has this to say. "I do predict that by 2013, we will have a critical lot shortage inside the Puget Sound. Currently, our planning process from application to final recording is a four- to five-year term." That process is going to begin to take longer, he says, not only because of the limited supply of land, but also because jurisdictions have laid off qualified employees. The new hires won't have the experience necessary to "rush" through applications.

As other local home builders associations around the country are losing members, the Association has found that the services they offer have become more and more necessary. The Return on Industrial Insurance continues to be a powerful draw for companies considering membership, but the Association's continuing education classes are an additional boon to companies trying to navigate a new landscape. Education classes are able to react to the current market conditions quickly: a recent survey of

MBA University offerings included courses on selling homes to buyers with lower-than-perfect credit scores and how sell to buyers demanding contingency agreements.

Another way the Association has responded to members' needs is by strengthening relations with the local media. "Reporters are surprised," says Dan Klusman, Communications Director. "When we talk about everything our members do – from charitable good works, education, and workforce development to green building, quality home building and remodeling – we've got a great story to tell. By building value in the Association, the public perception of membership becomes increasingly valuable."

Members have opportunities to network with each other, and share advice of how they have prospered in downturns, the most recent included. Past President Zak Parpia shared his experiences, "I can pick up the phone and call ten of my builder friends. Or the banks can call their banker friends. Now we're not calling each other on cold-calls, we know each other personally; the Association has given us, then, a certain level of acquaintanceship or trust. Our job as members is to continue learning from each other."

Membership director Larry Chimenti smiles and picks up the story. "The thing that will make this a successful organization for the next one

Rampathon 2009 was a record-breaking year for the Master Builders. Builder-captains oversaw construction of 32 ramps by more than 460 volunteers making it happen. The total number of ramps constructed by Association members through the annual Rampathon is well over 200. 2009 ramp recipient Lois Elliot said, Rampathon volunteers "are the most wonderful people I've ever met in my life. You can come back to my house anytime."

hundred years is the very same thing that got us through the first hundred years, and that is relationships. Business relationships between members." Members can meet each other over a Cosmopolitan or a brown bag lunch, and build the connections which will further their business success.

"If I didn't have the Master Builders Association, I'd know about four people in my life," laughs 2009 President John Day. "Over many years now I have just developed a lot of great friendships and had the opportunity to meet just so many more people than I would have imagined. Early on, I did not hold much regard for the social and networking aspect, but I now find it to have been a real benefit."

On January 15, 2009, Master Builders members gathered in Renton to dedicate the first of the "100 for 100" Community Service Projects. The group of builders and press stood shivering in the gray damp, but they were standing filled with pride at the good work they'd accomplished. They were, once again, at Vision House, which provides transitional housing for homeless women and families, and which has been the recipient of goodwill and hard work by the Master Builders through the Care Foundation for ten years. Fitting, then, that the first of the Centennial Community Service projects would be construction of a new building (Building B) at the Vision House Children's Village. After all, who better than homebuilders to address the problems of homelessness?

Builder-captain Centex Homes coordinated donations as well as scheduling construction. On the day of the dedication, Centex Division President Doug Barnes beamed with pride at being involved. Construction of Children's Village alone would allow fifty children and their mothers to have a safe, warm place to stay as they transitioned back to self-sufficiency. Barnes, the 2007 Association President, said he "made a full commitment – not only am I going to be involved, but our company's going to be involved, whether it's Rampathon or Vision House." He smiled, "Centex is proud to give back to the community by providing housing to those in need. The help of our subcontractors has been amazing and we appreciate all that they have contributed to make this building a reality for Vision House."

JOHN DAY

ACHIEVEMENTS:
Care Foundation Founder, *1999*
Builder of the Year, *2002*
President, Master Builders, *2009*

"Let them think you're a genius." This is the slogan of John Day Homes, started in 1987 as Middlefork Development Corporation. John Day Homes constructs single-family, custom homes from Mercer Island to North Bend. Founder John Day joined the Master Builders Association in 1993. Starting on the board, his work with Master Builders spans across several areas, from nonprofit program leadership to committee chairing to the presidency in 2009.

John Day's fire for nonprofit building work was sparked by an organization called HomeAid, the nonprofit arm of homebuilding associations that builds transitional housing for women and children. John explains, "They gave us a presentation and afterwards I said, 'We have got to do this, and I will volunteer to be the chair of their organization.' I served as president of the Master Builders Care Foundation for five years until I basically had agreed to become a chair officer for this organization, which leads up to being president."

John founded the Care Foundation, the Master Builders' nonprofit group, and worked extensively on HomeAid projects. Master Builders captains oversee the construction for the transitional housing, Vendors "get excited about [Home Aid], and they want to give us the best thing they have. Instead of having laminate countertops, we end up with granite countertops because the vendor wants to make that much of a contribution. The quality of these projects has been really amazing. Not only are we building these houses for fifty cents on the dollar, in the end we are

building a much higher quality product because of the pride that our members have in the work that they are doing. They look at this problem and go, 'Wow, this is something we can really contribute to because what we are doing is providing housing for homeless women and kids.'"

John also appreciates how the Care Foundation provides an outlet for members to contribute through their expertise. "That is one of the other really great things about the Care Foundation and HomeAid and Rampathon as well. They give our members an opportunity to give back to the community that they otherwise would not have."

As president, Day is very devoted to promoting housing and builders' rights in the state. "First and foremost, we are advocates for housing. Our efforts in controlling government regulations are the single most important thing we can do to make sure we have a thriving housing market. We can't control or influence the market in any way, shape, or form. It is not a place for our association, but we can take steps to limit the amount that the government can impose unnecessary regulations on us." John sees the Master Builders as integral in this process.

John Day's appreciation for the Master Builders Association echoes a common theme that its members consistently bring up, he remarks, "You know, one of the greatest benefits that really has surprised me is that over many years now I have just developed a lot of great friendships and had the opportunity to meet just so many more people than I would have imagined."

Students enjoy playing in the mud while they learn about ecosystems and nature in this wilderness preserve in the heart of Bellevue. The adults celebrate the Master Builders Association's commitment to community service at the groundbreaking for the Mercer Slough Environmental Education Center Wet Lab II, in July 2009. From left are: Kim Person, of Grey Lundberg, Inc,; Conrad Lee, Bellevue City Councilman; Dave Main, Main Street Builders; Sam Anderson, Master Builders Association; Jim Ellis; Patrick Floran, Bellevue Parks Department; Martha Rose, Martha Rose Construction; Mark Johnson, Jones & Jones Architects; Grant Degginer, Bellevue Mayor; Jerry Henry; Bryce Seidl, Pacific Science Center..

feel alone... I know deep inside that I would have never made it without the help and support of Vision House. They are giving me a chance at life I couldn't get anywhere else."[6]

Children's Village Building B was just the inaugural dedication for the "100 for 100" commitment the Master Builders made to the communities of the region. Jay Schupack, director of the Care Foundation, remembers discussions surrounding how to celebrate the centennial year in the community, "at one time, we talked about doing a hundred ramps. That wasn't realistically going to happen, but we knew we wanted to celebrate by giving back to the community. It's amazing how generous this industry is. Even during this time where there is a downturn, we see a growth in the number of volunteers who want to do this."

In April of 2009, the Master Builders embarked on a different type of volunteer project. Part of the Centennial Celebration was the construction of Wet Lab II at the Mercer Slough Environmental Education Center. The lab, considered by the Association as a gift to the community, will allow

Vision House residents aren't there because of drug dependencies, or mental health issues. Women come there from all walks of life with a single commonality: they've run out of options for a safe place to raise their children. Especially in a time of economic downturn, the sacrifices mothers will make for their children are significant; the Children's Village allows those sacrifices to be a little easier.

While there is a continuing challenge helping homeless families get off the street, places like the Vision House are a welcoming transitional step. Bright and open, rooms are decorated with kid-friendly colors and toys, and others can be sanctuaries for moms rediscovering self-esteem. As one mother who found herself as part of the working homeless put it, "The people at Vision House give you your confidence back. They are there for you no matter what. I never

students to understand how their actions affect the natural world, and will foster an appreciation of how buildings and the environment can interactively relate. Once the center's expansion is complete, it will accommodate visits by more than 40,000 children, teachers and families each year.

Looking Towards the Future

The Association remains focused on improving the regulatory environment for homebuilding. A slew of issues face builders, especially those working in what has been repeatedly called "the toughest regulatory climate in the country." However, the Government Affairs department works on behalf of all builders, members and non-members alike, to ensure that the industry continues to have a voice.

One issue on which the Association prevailed was the short plat extension process. This was the first priority of the Housing Stimulus Package, advanced in late 2008. The proposed legislation extends the validity of preliminary approvals for plats and short plats to seven years from the current five year period, and grants the option for a third extension for building permits where substantial work has not begun. The extension applies to any plat that received preliminary approval on or after December 1, 2003.[7] Allison Butcher, Public Affairs director, said, "The extension would give builders a longer amount of time they have to build. And it's nice – there should be no cost to local government."

Builders in Snohomish County won a victory in February, when the county council voted to pass the Rural Cluster Ordinance along the lines

CHARLIE'S HOUSE

PRESENTED BY

Career Connection

In honor of Mylo Charlston and his contributions to the Master Builders Career Connection

Developing Tomorrow's Workforce

that the Association's members had lobbied for. Another Snohomish County victory came in July, when the controversial Sprinkler and Fire Mitigation Fee Ordinance came up for a vote. Association staff argued so successfully against the draft ordinance that it was not even "seconded."

As Association members spoke about the future, about the second hundred years, a lot of different topics came up, but a single recurring thread was the increasing impact of environmental legislation. One idea of how the natural world and the building industry would relate in the future concerned carbon emission fees, which might mean a higher level of sensitivity to the number of truck trips taken to each site. Another suggestion was that the types of landscaping able to be used might become more regulated, with mandates for native plant species being enacted. It's impossible to predict just how the environmental regulations are going to change, but it's certain that they will, and they will get more stringent.

Executive Officer Sam Anderson is on the front lines of the policy discussions. "The challenge is going to be that there's more and more pressure to build in the context of environmental consequence. On the one hand, you're trying to protect the environment, and that's not cheap. On the other hand, you have 1.5 million people who are going to show up here in the next twenty years wanting to buy a house, and it may not be affordable. Somehow you've got to figure out how to balance those two needs."

It's a complex issue, and there are no simple solutions. The Master Builders Association is in a powerful position to form an alliance between disparate groups: planners and environmentalists and builders and business developers. It will take a whole-systems approach to really develop a true response to the dual needs of affordable housing and environmental sensitivity.

Todd Britsch has analyzed the situation dispassionately. "We're definitely going to see a climb in lot values in King and Snohomish County close to $200,000 in the next five years. The upturn didn't last forever; the downturn will not last forever. We recovered from the 1970s. We recovered from the 1980s. We recovered from the 1990s, and we'll recover from this one as well. Financing options will become available again, but it's going to take a while to clean up this mess."

He explains that typically, housing recoveries start from the population centers, in this case Seattle, Bellevue and Everett. But because the outlying areas felt the recession earlier, this time, recovery is also being driven from the outside

The Master Builders Career Connection brings "Charlie's House" to local schools so students can get a taste of what construction is like. The house was made possible by a donation from longtime member Mylo Charleston.

in. Prices in Pierce and Kitsap Counties dropped further, and were more affordable to the first-time buyer. And, as more first-time buyers come into the market, the better the market as a whole is able to recover. Third-generation-Realtor® Lennox Scott clarifies it. "We're already seeing the market reactivate itself in the more affordable price ranges, but we need more sales. You create a base of first-time buyers, and then you get the chain reaction up to higher price points. By reactivating itself, the psychology of the market is back. Sellers are putting their homes on the market and moving up."

A Lasting Legacy

King and Snohomish county builders continue to have a lot of reasons to be proud of their membership in the Master Builders. Donna Shirey, who will be the NAHB Remodelers Council Chair in 2010, reflected on her role, and the calling card that her membership has given her. "Nationally, the Master Builders Association is very well respected. People know that this Association has great ideas and how to gain and to keep members. They also love to hear the

Spikes were elegible for membership in the "Century Club" after they recruited at least three new members in 2009.
The plaque in the center recognizes these members for recruiting members and laying the foundation for the Association's second century.

things we do because we have a great Association. We do lots of innovative things."

Bill Sherman, who has been a member since the 1970s, considered, "Housing is one the most important things in life. The Master Builders are able to help bring together all of the things that are necessary for housing to be of quality construction, and for homebuilding to remain a good industry. It's not going to be too long from now that this region is going to experience more growth, and we need to stay poised to provide the necessary housing for all people."

It's evident this Association has something more ephemeral that is lacking in other professional associations. Peter Orser, head of Quadrant Homes, described it, "I think sometimes we take for granted the role the Association plays for us, when all of these things just happen on automatic pilot. Truth be told, each of us as individual builders would not be as effective without the synergy that gets created in the Association. Every industry has its association to try and take advantage of that, but this one has been truly extraordinary. You have these associates, and you have these builders, and they work together for the betterment of housing. It's kind of an amazing story." Orser leans back and reflects, "There is a chemistry in the organization that has really been valuable. The elected officials understand that too, they understand that we are a force to be reckoned with. We have thoughtful insight, and you shouldn't be making a political move without talking to the building industry."

Innovation is just part of the daily routine for most members. Bonnie Miller Waudé, who has been involved with the Master Builders in roles from associate member to board member, says, "It's amazing because the industry is evolving. We're trying to make it affordable, we're trying to make it green, I believe that the industry is really making just a superior effort to conform to how the world is changing." Her husband, Ty, picks up her thought. "If you want to feel you're part of a group or you want to be part of the process, join the Master Builders and understand that we are fighting this, these challenges and inequities on your behalf."

When asked what Master Builders membership meant to him, former Centex president Doug Barnes said, "That's an easy one - it's a great organization with great people. The biggest benefit you get is to network and be involved with a great pool of people. It's great to do business with a member and there are some great members out here. I think if you'll join and you'll actually get in and you'll meet the network of people here, the benefits are unlimited; just absolutely unlimited."

at some of the successes that we've had. I always said, 'the most important word in the term Master Builders Association is *association.*' My own experience of having the greatest benefit began to occur when I actually started associating with other members. It's been a really neat deal."

Speaking about the network of business connections, "It's the epicenter of the epicenter," says Life Spike Kevin Kartak. "The chance to network with the four-thousand-some businesses at all these different events, it's become more than business. It's just a lot of fun. certain events that happen every year and you think, '*Boy, I can't wait for that one again.*'" Associate members often come to rely on connections made through the Master Builders for their business.

Jeff Taylor explains, "I was a member for seven years before I showed up. Once I did, I just said, 'Wow.' You have access to an amazing amount of information; all sorts of resources are available to you." Taylor, who owns Valley Supply Company, credits his involvement with the Association for bringing him all of his biggest clients. "The Association is made up of people in the construction business and the trades that are associated with that. It should be no surprise

Past President Sandy McAdams admonishes, "If you join Master Builders and you don't get anything out of it, you have no one to blame but yourself. Because everybody here is so open and so sharing and so giving and so willing to help. If you get involved and people get to know you and trust you, you really gain a lot from being a member. But if you don't get involved, if you just join, write your check and show up once in awhile for a dinner meeting or something you won't get anything out of it."

And the sense of involvement, in true commitment to the communities we call home, is the evolution of the idea that those original five builders had – to elevate the homebuilding industry, to strengthen the ties between builders, and to provide quality housing for our region. ❖

MASTER BUILDERS
A S S O C I A T I O N
of King and Snohomish Counties

1909-2009

100 Years of Building Community

Acknowledgements

Though there is one name on the cover, no book is possible without many creators. This is no exception.
-Beth Yockey Jones, October 2009

Sam Anderson
Thomas Brown and the staff of HistoryLink.org
Allison Butcher
Lynn Eshleman
Alex Gouirand
Susan Hagy
Dan Klusman
Carolyn Marr of MOHAI
Bill Pease
Shelley Price
Rob Stewart
Cathy Waidelich
Jo Ann Yockey

The research on this book was aided in large part by the Seattle Master Builders'
An 80-Year Journey Through History, *written by David J. Vergobbi in 1989.*

Thank you to all those who agreed to be interviewed for this book:

Aaron Adelstein	Mike Echelbarger	Jim Potter
Sam Anderson	Cathy Feole	Ann Pryde
Doug Barnes	Donine Grigsby	Marc Pryde
Todd Bennett	Mike Kalian	Dick Rokes
John Bratton	Kevin Kartak	Jay Schupack
Todd Britsch	Dave Main	J. Lennox Scott
Fred Burnstead	Joe & Annabel	Bill Sherman
Allison Butcher	Martineau	Donna Shirey
Rick Chaffey	Sandy McAdams	Rob Stewart
Larry Chimenti	Patrick McCourt	Larry Sundquist
John Cochenour	Don McDonald	Jeff Taylor
Bill Conner	Maxine Narodick	Jack & Pat Tenhulzen
Chuck Crosby	John Nord	Byron Vadset
Don Davis	Peter Orser	Ty & Bonnie Waudé
John Day	Zak Parpia	

Master Builders Association
Hall of Fame

(by year inducted)

2006

Fred Burnstead

Bill Conner

Mike Kalian

Don McDonald

Zak Parpia

Harry Pryde

Dick Rokes

Bill Sherman

Rob Stewart

Larry Sundquist

2007

Omar Brown

John Nord

Brien Stafford

2008

Bill Finkbeiner

Joe Martineau

2009

Sam Andersen

E. J. Groseclose

F. R. "Dick" McAbee

Office Locations of the Association

From	Through	Location
1909	?	Central Building
1914	1915	Boston Block
1916	1922	4190 Arcade Building
1923	1935	unknown
1936	1939	1910 1/2 Fourth
1940	1942	1908-1910 Fourth Avenue
1943	1947	1908 Fourth Avenue
1948	1956	1930 Sixth Avenue *(During this time, the Seattle Builders & Contractors built their headquarters at 170 Mercer Street; when the groups re-merged, both moved in to that building.)*
1956	1983	170 Mercer Street
1984	2003	2155 112th Avenue NE, Bellevue
2003	present	335 116th SE, Bellevue

Executive Officers/Secretaries of the Association

From	Through				
1939	1942	J. Ray Taylor			
1943	1947	Irene W. Jones	*Executive Officers of the Seattle Builders & Contractors*		
1948	1954	Vyvyan C. Dent	1949	1954	Lee N. Canon
1955	1956	John C. Reuter	1955	1956	Kenneth E. Mauck
1956	1975	Joseph Martineau			
1976	1982	William Winn			
1983	1985	Falk Kelm			
1986	1988	Donald Chance			
1988	1997	James Williams			
1997	1997	Don Davis *(interim director)*			
1998	present	Sam Anderson			

Presidents of the Association

Year	Name	Year	Name	Year	Name
1914	John J. Frantz	1951	SMB: Ross Hebb	1979	Pete Hansell
1916	C.C. Cawsey		SB&C: Hans Floethe	1980	Paul Nolan
1916	Neil M. McDonald	1952	SMB: A. C. Goodwin	1981	James Summers
1917	Edgar S. Booker		SB&C: Herbert Dahl	1982	Rob Stewart*
1919	Charles W. Carkeek	1953	SMB: A. C. Goodwin	1983	Dean Chausee
1921	J. E. Shoemaker		SB&C: Axel Thornberg	1984	Fred Burnstead
1922	H. B. Warrack	1954	SMB: Dan Narodick	1985	Don Dally
1923	(none - the Association was part of the AGC)		SB&C: Don Kielbauch	1986	John E. "Bud" Tynes*
1924	Edward L. Merritt	1955	SMB: Al LaPierre	1987	Dick Rokes*
1926	Stanley Long		SB&C: E. E. Roman	1988	Larry Sundquist
1927	Gardner J. Gwinn	1956	Sid H. Brase	1989	William A. Sherman
1928	J. L. Grandey	1957	C. Fred Dally*	1990	Charles L. Henderson
1929	Roy Lipscomb	1958	E. L. "Buzz" Flowers	1991	Byron J. Vadset
1930	A. J. Allen	1959	H. K. Schroeder	1992	Colin Quinn
1931	Capt. C.S. Sapp	1960	E. B. "Tug" Vaughters	1993	Mike Echelbarger
1933	Sam Andersen*	1962	Archie Iverson	1994	Rick Lennon
1936	E. J. Groseclose	1963	Don McDonald*	1995	Chuck Crosby
1940	E. M. Bucholz	1964	Gregg Wilson	1996	John Cochenour
1941	Bernard Dahl	1965	Harry Pryde*†	1997	Zakir Parpia*
1942	Thomas Conrand	1966	Cecil Powell	1998	Jack Tenhulzen
1943	H.E. Forsman	1967	Al Mullally	1999	Patrick McCourt
1944	F.R. "Dick" McAbee	1968	Don Wick	2000	Charlie Conner
1946	Cliff Mortenson	1969	Vern Gambriell*	2001	Ty Waudé
1947	Lew Hykes	1970	John Nord	2002	Sandy McAdams
1948	V. O. "Bud" Stringfellow	1971	Jim Burns	2003	Todd Bennett
1949	(The Association split)	1973	Harry Thornberg	2004	Peter Orser
	SMB: V. O. Stringfellow	1974	Omar Brown*	2005	Donna Shirey
	SB&C: Bernard Dahl	1975	Bill Conner*	2006	Jim Potter
1950	SMB: Harold Larsen	1976	Dave Dujardin	2007	Doug Barnes
	SB&C: A. N. Walker	1977	Leiv Vikingstad	2008	Joe Schwab
		1978	Ed Dean	2009	John Day

An asterisk (*) indicates the person has also been president of BIAW.
A cross (†) indicates the person has also been president of NAHB

Master Builders Association
Builder, Remodeler and Associate of the Year

1973
Builder: Dave DuJardin
Associate: *(not listed)*

1974
Builder: Larry Hillis
Associate: Jim Bender

1975
Builder: Brien Stafford / Pete Hansell
Associate: Pat Reiten

1976
Builder: Bill Conner
Associate: Bill Robinson

1977
Builder: Omar Brown
Associate: Bud Converse

1978
Builder: Norm Davis
Associate: Hugh Goldsmith / Doug Webb

1979
Builder: Pete Hansell
Associate: Hank Radke

1980
Builder: Paul Norman
Associate: Roger Shaeffer

1981
Builder: Bill Conner
Associate: Tom Murphy

1982
Builder: Fred Burnstead / James Summers
Associate: Fred May

1983
Builder: Rob Stewart
Associate: Chuck Richmond

1984
Builder: John Nord / Dean Chausee
Associate: Chuck Steward

1985
Builder: Larry Sundquist
Associate: Bill Hurme

1986
Builder: Chuck Moriarty
Associate: Jim Betzler

1987
Builder: Sheldon Blue / Bud Tines
Associate: Bill Valela

1988
Builder: Dick Rokes
Associate: Deborah Gohrke

1989
Builder: Chuck Crosby
Associate: Bill Kreager

1990
Builder: Chuck Henderson
Associate: Paul Bogel

1991
Builder: William Sherman
Associate: Diane Pospisil

1992
Builder: Colin Quinn / Zakir Parpia
Associate: Pat McBride

1993
Builder: Chuck Crosby
Associate: Suzanne Britsch

1994
Builder: Patrick O. Lennon
Associate: Ed Barker / Greg Tisdel / Kim Ward

MASTER BUILDERS ASSOCIATION
BUILDER, REMODELER AND ASSOCIATE OF THE YEAR

1995
Builder: Nik Halladay
Associate: Pam Barker

1996
Builder: John Cochenhour
Associate: Paul Bogel / Pat McBride

1997
Builder: Zak Parpia
Associate: Mariann Danard

1998
Builder: Ty Waudé
Remodeler: Jack Tenhulzen
Associate: Bob Johns

1999
Builder: Patrick McCourt
Remodeler: Sandy McAdams
Associate: J. J. Johnston

2000
Builder: Charlie Conner
Remodeler: Sandy McAdams
Associate: Charlie Brown

2001
Builder: Stafford Homes
Remodeler: Gordon Gregg
Associate: Jeff Taylor

2002
Builder: John Day
Remodeler: Sherry Schwab
Associate: Shelli Lucus-Kennedy

2003
Builder: Todd Bennett
Remodeler: Donna & Riley Shirey
Sherry & Joe Schwab
Associate: Darylene Dennon

2004
Builder: Peter Orser
Remodeler: John Bratton
Associate: Jeff Taylor

2005
Builder: Doug Barnes / Todd Bennett
Remodeler: Joe Schwab / Donna Shirey
Associate: Diane Glenn

2006
Builder: Dave Main
Remodeler: Denny Conner
Associate: Juli Bacon

2007
Builder: Doug Barnes
Remodeler: John Bratton
Associate: Myra Williams

2008
Builder: Dave Main
Remodeler: Joe Schwab
Associate: Myra Williams

2009 Chair Officers

President	**John Day**	*John Day Homes Inc.*
First Vice President	**Dave Main**	*Main Street Builders LLC*
Second Vice President	**Lynn Eshleman**	*Pacific Ridge Homes*
Secretary	**Shelli Lucus-Kennedy**	*American Insurance Associates*
Immediate Past President	**Joe Schwab**	*H C S Construction Services*

2009 Board of Directors

Affordable Housing Council	Jim Potter	*Kauri Investments*
Associates Council	Cathy Waidelich	*Prudential Northwest Realty, Inc.*
Built Green®	Grey Lundberg	*Grey Lundberg Inc.*
King County Builders Council	Bob Johns	*Johns Monroe Mitsunaga PLLC*
Master Builders Care Foundation	Tracy Cromwell	*Cromwell Consulting*
Master Builders Career Connection	Gary Turner	*Puget Sound Energy*
MBA University	Duana Koloušková	*Johns Monroe Mitsunaga*
Membership Council	Juli Bacon	*J B Consulting Systems*
Past Presidents Council	Ty Waudé	*Waudé Building & Land Inc*
Remodelors™ Council	Wayne Apostolik	*Northwest Homecrafters*
Sales and Marketing Council	Bill Russell	*Keller Williams Realty*
Sales and Marketing Council	Kristi Sundquist	*Sundquist Homes*
Seattle Builders Council	Brittani Ard	*Ard Consulting LLC*
Snohomish County Builders Council	Brian Holtzclaw	*The McNaughton Group LLC*
Professional Women in Building	Wendy Albee	*Albee Interior Design*
Professional Women in Building	Jamie Hsu	*Lakeville Homes*
Board Member	Doug Barnes	*DJB & Associates Northwest*
Board Member	Paul Bogel	*Lexington Fine Homes*
Board Member	John Bratton	*J W Bratton Design/Build LLC*
Board Member	Janice Bristol	*Bristol Financial Management Group*
Board Member	Eric Campbell	*CamWest Development*
Board Member	Kevin Kartak	*AAA Kartak Glass & Closet*
Board Member	Steve Kirk	*US Bank*
Board Member	Bob Murphy	*Murphy Building Company*
Board Member	Ken Paauw	*Washington Trust Bank*
Board Member	Chris Raftery	*CareCyte LLC*
Board Member	Sherry Schwab	*H C S Construction Services*
Board Member	Gary Upper	*Conner Homes*

ASSOCIATION STAFF

(as of October 2009)

Executive Officer Sam Anderson

Chief Operating Officer	Rick Miller
Director of Administration	Lynda Hester
Director of First Impressions	Jasmina Kahrimanovic
Built Green Director	Aaron Adelstein
Built Green Coordinator	Emma Palley
Care Foundation Executive Director	Jay Schupack
Care Foundation Manager	April Wetmore
Career Connection Executive Director	Cathy Feole
Career Connection Manager	Gabriel Blanco
MBA U Education Coordinator	Kristin Parker
Communications Director	Dan Klusman
Communications Manager	Melanie Workhoven
Communications Manager	Ryan Brett
Graphic Designer	Anne Gray
Events Director	James Cadungug
Events Coordinator	Alexis Welch
Events Coordinator	Rachel Collins
Controller	Jeff Danks
Accounts Receivable Manager	Donine Grigsby
Accounts Payable Coordinator	Ha Tran
Government Affairs Director	Don Davis
South King and Seattle Manager	Garrett Huffman
King County Manager	David Hoffman
North Snohomish County Manager	Mike Pattison
South Snohomish County Manager	Jennifer Jerabek
Information Systems Director	Janna Parry
Information Systems Specialist	Patrick Mamaril
Business Development and Marketing Director	George Capestany
Sales and Marketing Manager	Julie Applegate
Marketing Manager	Laura Groth
Sales and Marketing Coordinator	Andrea Morrison
Membership Director	Larry Chimenti
Membership Coordinator	Vicki Hobbs
Membership Coordinator	Loretta Moran
Public Affairs Director	Allison Butcher
Public Policy Director	Scott Hildebrand
Public Policy Coordinator	Daniel Arbolante

ENDNOTES FOR CHAPTER 1

1. Harrell, Debera Carlton. "Seattle teenager gives voice to the Great Fire of 1889." *Seattle Post-Intelligencer*. June 5, 2007.
2. HistoryLink.org Essay 1923
   "Seattle Public Library housed in Yesler mansion burns down on January 1, 1901."
   http://www.historyink.org/index.cfm?DisplayPage=output.cfm&file_id=1923
3. HistoryLink.org Essay 692
   "Alaska-Yukon-Pacific Exposition groundbreaking ceremonies take place on June 1, 1907"
   http://www.historyink.org/index.cfm?DisplayPage=output.cfm&file_id=692
4. The word bungalow derives from the Gujarati word *banglo* and means "Bengali," used to communicate "house in the Bengal style." Such houses were traditionally small, thatched and had a wide veranda.
   See http://dictionary.reference.com/browse/bungalow

ENDNOTES FOR CHAPTER 2

1. Friedheim, Robert L. *The Seattle General Strike*. Ithaca (NY): Cornell, 1965.
2. Chasan, Daniel Jack. *The Water Link: A History of Puget Sound as a Resource*. Seattle: Puget Sound Books, 1981.
3. AGC Website. www.agc.org/cs/about_agc

ENDNOTES FOR CHAPTER 3

1. Hall, Thomas E. and Ferguson, J. David. *The Great Depression: An International Disaster of Perverse Economic Policies*. Ann Arbor: University of Michigan Press, 1988.

ENDNOTES FOR CHAPTER 4

1. http://en.wikipedia.org/wiki/Yesler_Terrace,_Seattle,_Washington
2. HistoryLink.org Essay 3462
   "Seattle Neighborhoods: Wedgwood–Thumbnail History"
   http://www.historylink.org/index.cfm?DisplayPage=pf_output.cfm&file_id=3462

ENDNOTES FOR CHAPTER 5

1. McNerthney, Casey. "Memorable Moments from Memorial Stadium." *Seattle Post-Intelligencer,* February 26, 2008.
   http://blog.seattlepi.com/thebigblog/archives/132781.asp?source=rss
2. 1967 compendium of League of Women Voters archival information. Retrieved from
   http://www.uic.edu/depts/lib/specialcoll/services/rjd/findingaids/LWVchicago.pdf
3. Boswell, Sharon and McConaghy, Lorraine. "The Booming of the 'Burbs." *Seattle Times,* August 18, 1996.
   http://seattletimes.nwsource.com/special/centennial/august/burbs.html
4. HistoryLink.org Essay 313
   "Bellevue–Thumbnail History"
   http://www.historylink.org/index.cfm?DisplayPage=output.cfm&file_id=313
5. "Builders Hit High Down Payments" *Seattle Times*, Sept. 5, 1952
6. Ibid.
7. *Seattle Times*, October 14, 1955.

ENDNOTES FOR CHAPTER 6

1. Frantilla, Anne. "The Seattle Open Housing Campaign, 1959-1968–Detailed Narrative: Housing Segregation and Open Housing Legislation." Seattle Municipal Archives.
    http://www.seattle.gov/cityarchives/Exhibits/Openhous/narrative.htm
2. http://en.wikipedia.org/wiki/Fair_housing
3. Timeline of the Seattle Open Housing Campaign, retrieved from
    http://www.seattle.gov/cityarchives/Exhibits/Openhous/timeline.htm
4. HistoryLink.org Essay 63
    "Sam Smith (1922-1995)"
    http://www.historylink.org/index.cfm?DisplayPage=output.cfm&File_Id=63

(no endnotes for Chapter 7)

ENDNOTES FOR CHAPTER 8

1. Fuller, Mike. "The Seattle Pilots Baseball Team." http://www.brandx.net/pilots/
2. Metropolitan King County Countywide Planning Policies Benchmark Program
    Affordable Housing Indicators, retrieved from http://www.metrokc.gov/budget/benchmrk/bench02/02bench_ch3B.pdf
3. Lacitis, Erik. "Iconic 'will the last person' Seattle billboard bubbles up again." *Seattle Times,* February 2, 2009.
    http://seattletimes.nwsource.com/html/localnews/2008696819_lightsout02m.html
4. HistoryLink.org Essay 1993
    "1970 Census: Population of Seattle dwindles to 530,000, less than half of total King County population of 1,150,000, in 1970."
    http://www.historylink.org/index.cfm?DisplayPage=output.cfm&File_Id=1993

ENDNOTES FOR CHAPTER 9

1. Anderson, Bendix. "How Hills Tamed HUD." *Affordable Housing Finance*, November 2008.
    http://www.housingfinance.com/ahf/articles/2008/nov/1108-special-manager.htm
2. Royer, Charles. "Seattle's housing squeeze." *Seattle Times,* November 11, 2007.
    http://seattletimes.nwsource.com/html/opinion/2004005761_sundayroyer11.html
3. Sommerfeld, Julia. "Our Social Dis-ease: Beyond the smiles, the Seattle Freeze is on." *Pacific Northwest–The Seattle Times Magazine*, February 13, 2005. http://seattletimes.nwsource.com/pacificnw/2005/0213/cover.html
4. Reagan, President Ronald. "Remarks at a Meeting of the National Association of Home Builders." May 16, 1983.
    http://www.reagan.utexas.edu/archives/speeches/1983/51683a.htm

ENDNOTES FOR CHAPTER 10

1. Note: this information comes from an August 10, 1988 press release from Larry Sundquist's office. There is no citation therein of the study it summarizes.

Endnotes for Chapter 11

1. HistoryLink.org Essay 7759
   "Washington Legislature enacts Growth Management Act on April 1, 1990."
   http://historylink.org/index.cfm?DisplayPage=output.cfm&file_id=7759
2. (RCW 36.70A.010), text retrieved from Washington State Department of Community, Trade and Economic Development,
   www.cted.wa.gov/growth
3. Ibid.
4. Ballot initiative measure 547 to the people: "Shall state growth and environmental protection goals be implemented by measures including local comprehensive land use planning and development fees?"
   http://www.secstate.wa.gov/legacyproject/pdf/OH854.pdf
5. Rhodes, Elizabeth. "Home prices' long rise: Is the end near?" *Seattle Times*, September 3, 2006.
   http://seattletimes.nwsource.com/html/businesstechnology/2003241541_appreciation03.html
6. History of Louisiana Pacific Corporation from
   http://www.fundinguniverse.com/company-histories/LouisianaPacific-Corporation-Company-History.html

Endnotes for Chapter 12

1. Permit data from *Nations Building News*. Retrieved from:
   http://www.nbnnews.com/NBN/new/downloads/2005_Permits_Usage.xls
2. Data from Metro Atlanta Chamber of Commerce. Retrieved from:
   http://www.metroatlantachamber.com/macoc/business/img/MSAGrowthStatsReport2006.pdf
3. http://www.city-data.com/us-cities/The-West/Seattle-Population-Profile.html
4. From the O'Connor Consulting Group "The Seattle Apartment Market Report," October 2007:
   "Seattle's apartment market languished post dotcom bust through early 2005. In 2006, everything changed and we saw record rent increases. The Seattle and Snohomish markets experienced rent increases of 15%, while rents increased 13% in the Eastside and a more modest 7% in the Southend. The major driver of this huge turnaround in apartment rents was due to a rapidly declining supply of apartments - everyone was building condominiums, or converting apartments into condominiums. The supply of existing and new apartment stock rapidly dwindled causing vacancy rates to plummet and rents to rise. Retrieved from www.ocgp.com/about/news/2007_02.pdf
5. Ervin, Keith. "How Brightwater soared to $1.8 billion, and why you're paying more," *Seattle Times*, March 31, 2008.
   http://seattletimes.nwsource.com/html/localnews/2004316832_brightwaternew31m.html
6. Ko, Michael, "Builders Launch Program for environmental housing." *Seattle Times*, October 3, 2000.
   http://community.seattletimes.nwsource.com/archive/?date=20001004&slug=4046070
7. As of December, 2005, 5,691 homes had been certified since 2000.
   http://www.builtgreen.net/news/news_dec05.html

Endnotes for Chapter 13

1. Lewis, Marilyn. "Tax credit lifts housing market." *MSN Money,* May 29, 2009
   http://articles.moneycentral.msn.com/Banking/HomebuyingGuide/HomePriceReport.aspx
2. The summation in this section is heavily drawn on that of Alex Blumberg and Adam Davidson, from a program titled "Giant Pool of Money," originally aired May 9, 2008.
   http://www.thisamericanlife.org/extras/radio/355_transcript.pdf
3. Olesiuk, Shayna and Kalser, Kathy. "The 2009 Economic Landscape: The Sand States: Anatomy of A Perfect Housing Market Storm." *FDIC Quarterly,* April 27, 2009. Retrieved from:
   http://www.fdic.gov/bank/analytical/quarterly/2009_vol3_1/AnatomyPerfectHousing.html
4. Evans School of Public Affairs and KCTS9. "What Can We Do About Housing Costs In King County?"
   www.macneil-lehrer.com/btp/local%20backgrounder%20FINAL.pdf
5. Eicher, Theo S. "Housing Prices and Land Use Regulations: A Study of 250 Major US Cities." Seattle: University of Washington Press, 2008. *Note: Eicher laments the lack of Bellevue-specific data, but includes it in "Seattle" data.* Retrieved from:
   http://depts.washington.edu/teclass/landuse/Housing051608.pdf
6. *The Truth About Regulatory Barriers to Housing Affordability.* NAHB publication.

ENDNOTES FOR CHAPTER 14

1. Lyda, Jess and Julie. June 16, 2009
    http://snohomishcountymarketstatistics.blogspot.com/2009/06/snohomish-county-average-home-prices.html
2. "Seattle area job growth near nation's top, says federal report." *Puget Sound Business Journal*, January 7, 2009
    http://www.bizjournals.com/seattle/stories/2009/01/05/daily19.html
3. Mortgage Bankers Association Press Release, July 8, 2009. Retrieved from:
    http://www.mortgagebankers.org/NewsandMedia/PressCenter/69534.htm
4. Pryne, Eric. "Home sales climb in June in King County; median price drops from year ago to $395,000." *Seattle Times,* July 6, 2009. http://seattletimes.nwsource.com/html/realestate/2009424140_webhomesales06.html
5. Zumbrun, Joshua. "The Best And Worst Cities For Recession Recovery." *Forbes.com* June 10, 2009.
    http://www.forbes.com/2009/06/09/recession-economy-cities-business-beltway-recovery-cities.html
6. http://www.vision-house.org/vh_residents.htm
7. http://www.mba-ks.com/library/issues/GA_Issue_Tracker.pdf

INDEX

BOLD NUMBERS INDICATE A PHOTO. RED NUMBERS INDICATE A BUILDER PROFILE.